THE BRITISH SYSTEM OF GOVERNMENT
AND ITS HISTORICAL DEVELOPMENT

The British System of Government and Its Historical Development

CHRISTOPHER EDWARD TAUCAR

McGill-Queen's University Press
Montreal & Kingston · London · Ithaca

© McGill-Queen's University Press 2014

ISBN 978-0-7735-4428-4 (cloth)
ISBN 978-0-7735-4429-1 (paper)
ISBN 978-0-7735-9655-9 (ePDF)
ISBN 978-0-7735-9656-6 (ePUB)

Legal deposit fourth quarter 2014
Bibliothèque nationale du Québec

Printed in Canada on acid-free paper that is 100% ancient forest free
(100% post-consumer recycled), processed chlorine free

The author acknowledges a research funding award from Wilfrid
Laurier University.

McGill-Queen's University Press acknowledges the support of the
Canada Council for the Arts for our publishing program. We also
acknowledge the financial support of the Government of Canada
through the Canada Book Fund for our publishing activities.

Library and Archives Canada Cataloguing in Publication

Taucar, Christopher Edward, 1968– author
  The British system of government and its historical development /
Christopher Edward Taucar.

Includes bibliographical references and index.
Issued in print and electronic formats.
ISBN 978-0-7735-4428-4 (bound). – ISBN 978-0-7735-4429-1 (pbk.). –
ISBN 978-0-7735-9655-9 (ePDF). – ISBN 978-0-7735-9656-6 (ePUB)

  1. Great Britain – Politics and government. I. Title.

JN175.T39 2014   320.441   C2014-904875-0
                                     C2014-904876-9

Typeset by Jay Tee Graphics Ltd. in 10.5/13.5 Sabon

In the style of seventeenth-century writers, I dedicate this book to God, to Country, to You

Contents

Introduction   3

PART ONE   THE BASIS OF GOVERNMENT, DIFFERENTIATION WITHIN GOVERNMENT, AND THE COMMON LAW COURTS

1 Overview, Pre-Conquest, and the Conquest of 1066   17

2 Constitutional Settlements: Differentiation within Government, Magna Carta, and the Common Law Courts   58

PART TWO   PARLIAMENT

3 Parliament's Development through the Reformation and Its Relation to Courts   91

4 The Great Rebellion and Revolution of 1688   109

5 Parliamentary Sovereignty (and Its Doubters)   138

PART THREE   THE EXECUTIVE, AND FURTHER PUBLIC LAW DEVELOPMENTS

6 The Executive and Parliament's Relation to It   179

7 Public Law in the Eighteenth and Nineteenth Centuries   202

Conclusion   236

Appendix: Table of Kings and Queens   249

Notes   251

Bibliography   291

Index   301

THE BRITISH SYSTEM OF GOVERNMENT
AND ITS HISTORICAL DEVELOPMENT

Introduction

The British system of government has not only served the British well throughout their history, but it has also had a positive and significant influence on much of the world, including in establishing and spreading democracy. Over the span of many centuries, Britain developed parliamentary government, as well as fundamentally important concepts, such as the Rule of Law and the liberty of the individual, and helped to influence many parts of the world in these respects. These important developments and contributions make the study of the British system of government valuable in its own right.

Furthermore this system, in its most basic features, forms the background to the establishment and development of sovereign states that achieved self-government and full independence from Britain, and that accepted the parliamentary model of government. Accordingly, it is a necessary component and starting point to understanding the system of government in these later established states. The legacies of the British system of government that became part of the law of these states include: the nature of government, particularly Parliament and law-making; the laws actually incorporated; and the nature of courts and their jurisdiction. From the basis of these legacies, one can begin to fully and accurately explain the system of government in the newer countries, including any modifications that were made to the British system of government that these former colonies established. For example, modifications that arose included establishing a pre-eminent law in the form of a written Constitution, and further developments such as federalism, as in the cases of Canada and Australia. This study can also serve as useful background to the American system of government, although the changes made there were more dramatic. Nevertheless many background principles remained, such as the common law system, and the ideas of checks and balances and separation of powers, which were given greater institutional definition.

The purpose of this book is to outline the foundational elements and to trace the main building blocks in the development of the British system of government. It does not go further to detail the influences of this system of government upon other countries. A separate study is necessary for each country. The main ideas discussed in this book are straightforward, generally known, and understood. Identifying the main features of one's system of government, the inter-relationship among its components, the rules deducible from that system, and its implications for state institutions are generally not difficult tasks. Surprisingly, these tasks are not commonly done.

From this description of the British system of government, various incontrovertible rules are evident or immediately deducible, which can only be changed by legal means as set out in the law of the constitution. These basic rules of the system of government can be employed as a measure against the actions or decisions of the legislature, the executive, and the courts. Many will be astonished to learn how often they can demonstrate that these actions or decisions are consistent or inconsistent with these basic rules.

Accordingly, understanding a system of government is useful as basic knowledge, which all citizens should possess. Understanding the system's basic rules also allows ordinary citizens to judge the actions or decisions of government officials, including courts, and in many and important cases to determine them to be correct or incorrect, or to be outside of the institution's jurisdiction based on the authoritative and objective standard of the system of government and its rules. The reason for this ability is that every system of government is knowable and is based on law, and state power holders may only act according to law and within the bounds of their jurisdiction. The system of government rooted in sovereignty and law is the authoritative basis under which its state power holders may be held to account. This statement is no less true of a country such as Britain which lacks a formal, pre-eminent written constitution.

For example, one issue of recent interest, including in Britain, is whether judges can strike down or override legislation by referring to unwritten principles. The answer is clearly not within a system of government based on a parliamentary supremacy model and with a court exercising delegated jurisdiction. Nevertheless, courts have in some countries usurped this power, while citizens have been completely unaware. Understanding the British system of government, its basic rules, and the basic jurisdiction of its Parliament and courts will reveal such practices within that system to be incorrect or unauthorized.

If one desires to actually judge the legality of the actions or decisions of state power holders, the system of government and the basic rules coming from that system provide the necessary legal framework to do so. In the case of Britain and the states that obtained independence from it, the two important components are Parliament as supreme law-maker and the nature and jurisdiction of courts.

The knowledge of citizens and the power that this knowledge itself can have in keeping governments to honest and prudent paths should not be underestimated. This knowledge and a strong 'supremacy of law' mentality, which were common in medieval times, are important factors in upholding liberty, rights, and the rule of law, and are obstacles to oppressive government or to governing bodies and officials, including judges, acting outside of their authority or otherwise abusing power.

Another important aspect of knowing the system of government is understanding a country's history. The danger of losing this knowledge, or having it rewritten by those holding other or incompatible political ideologies, is that a country's future can be more easily rewritten in ways that undermine the underlying philosophies, structures, values, and ideas which not only sustained the system of government, but brought it to prosperity and liberty. All of this can be done without most people being aware of what is occurring and what is actually being lost. Accordingly, knowledge of our history can be a powerful antidote to attempts, such as those in the last half-century particularly, to change our government and cultural values, and to put them on a new basis.

Ideas have life. They animate the development and workings of laws and state institutions. When such ideas are discarded and replaced with others, the very basis and benefits of the system of government can be in jeopardy. For example, William Holdsworth and others have noted the important effect of ideas when German thinkers went further back into and romanticized the history of the earlier Germanic tribes, including as a root of democracy, while ignoring the Christian roots of Western civilization. Indeed, they attempted to destroy its spiritual foundations. The result was the loss of values upon which Western civilization was based, and the replacement of those values by National Socialism in the twentieth century, leading to destructiveness on a scale previously unknown.[1] A similar challenge to our century-old traditional values or ideals is occurring today.

Once the animating spirit or overarching basis of the system of government has declined or been overtaken, it must necessarily be replaced with something else. Every state is guided by an overarching grand principle, to which all other laws and policies in the state will seek to conform.

Changes in a system of government, in the ideas of the people about government, or in cultural values can have tremendous and even imperceptible influences on that government. Parliamentary government, the rule of law, and a tradition of liberty have led to freedom and prosperity. Parliamentary sovereignty without these values can lead to a most tyrannical exercise of power.

These sorts of revolutions can occur by force or fraud, either consciously and openly, or imperceptibly. They can occur due to any of a number of state and non-state actors, such as academics, judges, the media, teachers, foreign influences, and so on. If such changes are to occur, they should at least be made openly and subjected to rigorous scrutiny and debate.

Losing our history can also make us forget what it took to obtain our system of government, and the effort and awareness necessary on the part of all to maintain it.

In every country in the world today, a system of government exists and can be described (though theoretically and in very exceptional circumstances there can be territories over which no sovereign government exists).[2] A system of government is a legally based system which is rooted in sovereignty and provides the pre-eminent legal rules for a state, including the jurisdictions of that state's main institutions. It is much better to speak of a system of government, which is rooted in sovereignty, as opposed to relying on the concept of sovereignty itself. It naturally incorporates the benefits of sovereignty theory without its difficulties. This book will not be able to

Introduction

trace the history and spread of sovereignty theory;[3] however, some brief observations may be made. Although this is not a problem in the British case, in some states it is difficult to locate the sovereign, be it a person or body. The system of government, on the other hand, comprises the totality of sovereign powers which may be legally exercised within a country. Sovereignty is a legal concept understood to be indivisible. Indeed, that indivisibility posed significant theoretical problems for countries that established federalism. Our political experiences over the centuries reveal that sovereign states may not have an actual sovereign, or at least not one readily locatable, exercising unlimited power. States might legally possess only partial powers which are either granted or limited through a written Constitution, or pre-eminent law. The sovereign system of government signifies the legally humanly unlimited power of government over a particular geographical territory, which is sovereignty. At the same time, it provides the content for the incidents and exercise of sovereign power, which may be dispersed among one or more legal persons or bodies who together exercise the totality of sovereign powers; or, the sovereign system of government may legally limit powers making void any action outside that jurisdiction.

Sovereignty underlying the existence of a state or system of government can only be ultimately grounded on certain bases. Not only is it possible to imagine that either divine law or natural law, often synonymous with perfect reason, is capable of acting as such, but in fact divine and natural law ideas were widely held in countries such as England, particularly during medieval times but also during the crucial times and events which firmly established the nature of British government and even thereafter.[4] Today, the most commonly recognized grounding of sovereignty is an established political organization – a system of government – exercising exclusive formal authority over a given geographical territory. Any other views are partialistic, be they artificial, philosophical, or social constructions of society, class, or corporatist views based on gender, class, or whatever. In any event, these partialistic views are nowhere in existence in the world as the sovereign basis of a state. It is, of course, possible for a state's animating spirit to be guided by such values, but that is different from sovereignty itself. Additionally, perhaps, there may be historical justification for adopting the Lockean view of the state as social contract, at least for England.[5]

It is not necessary to solve the question of whether divine or natural law forms the real basis of government or sovereignty. The reason is that, as a practical matter, a satisfactory answer can be found in the fact that the basis of sovereignty in Britain is readily determinable by its historical development, resulting in parliamentary sovereignty. This system of government created its own reconciliation of state sovereignty and government with divine law or natural law.

The term 'system of government' is used instead of 'constitution' as the latter term is usually used in various countries, such as Canada or the United States, to mean the written Constitution.[6] The actual legal authority and composition of legally created bodies are also sometimes termed 'constitution,' and their jurisdiction can be established and determined by various sources of law, which may or may not include the provisions of a written Constitution. Accordingly, the term 'system of government' is clearer than the term 'constitution.' Also, the former term focuses the reader's attention on exactly what is being examined: the most foundational elements of the system and its main institutions. The concept of the system of government is broader than that of the constitution (understood as the written Constitution). It deals with the powers of the main state institutions and their jurisdiction, which may be set by various sources, including legislation and prerogative, and need not be necessarily created by a pre-eminent sovereign body or by a written Constitution. It also deals with the legal status of the elements involved in the system of government and their legal relation to each other more precisely.

The goal of this book is to describe the British system of government as it is established today, its main building blocks and development, and the jurisdiction of its main institutions and their legal status and relation. The necessary approach is to examine history, politics, and law, together with a suitable analytic jurisprudence, particularly in relation to sovereignty and the system of government.

The approach is different from the work of the historian, although it shares some similarities. This book draws on the works of historians, particularly legal historians, which detail the historical events, intellectual influences, and legal developments that establish the main building blocks. The approach is not a full-scale inquiry into every period of British history, but an extraction of only the relevant elements and events which make up the foundations of the system of government, particularly with respect to the exercise of sovereign power. For students of English legal and constitutional history, the endnotes provide some additional details, sources, considerations, and points of interest.

This book does not assume that the powers exercised by any institution are or were within its jurisdiction. It pays careful attention to questions of jurisdiction, and not merely the exercise of state power, which may be greater or less at a particular point in time.

This work also differs from that of others who, while taking a similar approach to examining the legal significance of historical events, are limited to supporting the proposition that parliamentary supremacy was established in Britain. Such studies do not aim to explain the nature and essential features of the British system of government, to outline its development, and to describe the relationship of the elements that make up that system, particularly the relationship between Parliament and the courts.

This book fills a gap in the literature, not only allowing readers to understand the basics of government, and to understand the framework within which state power holders act, but also providing a useful measuring stick by which to judge the actions or decisions of state actors. Once a system of government is understood and described in its relevant features, including the jurisdiction of various state actors, then conclusions of correct or incorrect practices or decisions made within the system are at least sometimes possible, and the imperatives of the system themselves can provide meaningful guidance. Accordingly, the approach is a unique one. It is not readily situated within the literature of contemporary scholarship.

The two key elements in understanding the British system of government are Parliament and the courts, together with their respective natures and jurisdictions within that system. The British system is characterized by parliamentary sovereignty, in which Parliament may legislate anything except that which is impossible, and, aside from debates about the manner and form of legislating, one parliament may not bind a future parliament. These limitations are legal limitations; Parliament is not limited by other means, be they moral rights, unwritten principles, or common law principles. In turn, courts have no legal authority to invalidate statutes thought to be contrary to fundamental legal or moral principles.

Courts are state institutions created by, and which can only operate according to, applicable law, with judges as their officers. They exercise a legally delegated jurisdiction, primarily by legislation, and originally by prerogative. There is a narrow jurisdiction of inherent powers based on necessity. Court jurisdiction can be changed or even abolished by parliamentary legislation, and their decisions can be declared to be incorrect, overridden, or modified.

One further foundational element is that the only limitation to parliamentary supremacy is based in natural law or divine law, giving rise to a right to disobey a law, or in more extreme circumstances of oppression or tyranny, a right to rebellion. This species of higher law is not a law or legal right that can legally limit Parliament's jurisdiction within the British sovereign state's system of government, unless such principles have been incorporated into its domestic law and not later overridden. Nor does it confer any legal jurisdiction within a state, including upon judges, although natural law is often appropriately used by judges as an aid to interpretation. In effect, natural law within the British system of government constitutes morally existing higher rights.

Understanding the foundational elements of the British system of government requires examining foundational points in its development. This book is divided into three parts. Part I deals with the basis of government, the differentiation that occurred within the government, and the common law courts. Part II focuses on Parliament and the establishment of parliamentary sovereignty. Part III examines the executive and public law developments of the eighteenth and nineteenth centuries.

Chapter 1 focuses on the pre-Conquest period and the Conquest of 1066 A.D., primarily the fifth to eleventh centuries. Chapter 2 examines important early constitutional settlements, including differentiation within government, and Magna Carta. It also examines in detail the nature of courts and their jurisdiction. Legislative and executive government, including courts, overlap in the first stages, until there is greater definition and separation with respect to these branches or functions of government, beginning in the twelfth century. This process is largely complete with respect to all common law courts by the end of the fourteenth century. During this time, courts can increasingly be examined and described to a great extent separately. From this point, it is most accurate to focus on the develop-

Introduction

ment of Parliament and its sovereignty largely separately from courts. In the course of this institutional development and exposition, the relationship between the courts and Parliament within the British system of government will become evident.

An examination commencing with the pre-Conquest period establishes the importance of divine law and natural law as pillars within the British system of government and law. Considering this period is important in order to begin to understand the nature of courts and their jurisdiction. It is also useful in tracing the development of parliamentary sovereignty, including parliamentary powers and Parliament's relationship to other state actors.

The post-Conquest era establishes the supremacy of legislative power, including over the common law and courts, and the inability of the common law or courts to void or strike down legislation. As distinction within government grew, including between Parliament (the legislature) and Council (the executive), discretionary crown powers ceased to be exercised though common law courts. Court jurisdiction became substantially limited in comparison to the time it was part of Council because it no longer shared in the power of the Council when it became separate from it. This limitation of court jurisdiction is not only determinative, but is confirmed through an examination from other perspectives, such as: the source or basis of court power; the *Quo Warranto* episode; the existence of various common law courts and their actual jurisdiction, as well as their substantively and procedurally bounded jurisdiction; and the simultaneous existence of other courts which exercised rival and inconsistent jurisdictions. Not only were common law courts, such as King's Bench and Common Pleas, inferior to Parliament, but they were at times inferior to other courts, such as the Court of Exchequer Chamber, Council, and even Star Chamber. Court power is by nature delegated. Courts did not automatically or inherently have all such jurisdiction as may have been necessary or desirable to enable them to deal with all disputes arising between parties. Furthermore, it is also telling in terms of the respective status of legislature and courts that the courts' jurisdiction can be added to or taken away by legislation.

Chapters 3 and 4 examine other foundational constitutional settlements, focusing on Parliament and the establishment of parliamentary supremacy. This development involves considerations of how Parliament became a true legislative assembly, particularly from the thirteenth century onwards; the sixteenth-century Reformation; parliamentary control over court decisions; the Great Rebellion; and the Revolution of 1688. Some relevant debates about parliamentary supremacy are examined.

Generally speaking, in the British case and for other states that have adopted parliamentary government, it is not necessary to consider the executive branch of government in order to understand the ultimate rules of the system of government and the jurisdictions established in terms of the exercise of sovereign powers. However, further details are provided to explain the actual way in which the system operates in its most fundamental or sovereign aspects, and to clarify the executive's link with the legislature. This aspect is also important for understanding the governments of other states that use the British model. Chapter 6 examines the executive branch and Parliament's relation to it, covering the period of the Conquest to the seventeenth century. Chapter 7 examines further public law developments as well as court reform in the eighteenth and nineteenth centuries, ending with a discussion of inherent court powers. An important focus is on the various events or means by which, over a very long period of time, the House of Commons was able to put a check on the influences that the king or Council exercised on its activities in legislating, as well as how the Commons obtained ultimate control over the executive.

Outside of the system of government, which is the ultimate legally based system in the state, constitutional conventions exist. These conventions constitute the actions and understandings of the relevant political actors involving the way in which the constitution actually functions in practice. These conventions are not legal, and governments acting or making decisions contrary to them cannot be adjudged by courts to have behaved unconstitutionally or illegally. Nevertheless, these conventions are treated as very important, sometimes more important than some rules of constitutional law.

British constitutional conventions also formed part of the background to the creation of the newer colonies, their progression towards self-government, and their histories thereafter. These conventions, in some cases, continued to be unwritten, or they might be made part of a written Constitution; or, as in the case of Canada, some were made part of the Constitution, but most were left as unwritten conventions. Accordingly, British conventions, particularly based around responsible government, will be examined. Conventions should not be confused with the system of government, which is a system created and established in law.

Some will object because this book concludes there can be right and wrong answers, authoritatively and objectively determined, on a whole range of political and legal questions. Incidentally, the outright rejection of the objectively demonstrable or of truth, and the denigration of reason, is itself part of the movement attempting to undermine and change the values upon which our systems of government rest.

On the contrary, the approach is not immodest at all. It is objective and relatively simple to apply. Another strength of this analysis is that it does not depend on the author's or any political or ideological preference, but is independently, authoritatively, and objectively verifiable. By analogy, even if it is possible to disagree with the concept of mathematics, one cannot disagree that $2 + 3 = 5$, whether based on one's feelings, perspective, or otherwise. Accurately describing the system of government is accomplished through examining that system from several angles (or non-ideological perspectives), and if the answer(s) are consistent, there must be a true or accurate description. Even on complicated, hard, or unclear matters, the system of government can provide correct answers, and at least eliminate wrong answers, if not point to the best answer.

On the other hand, the objection of immodesty can be redirected to those who, for example, encourage judges to change the constitution or interpret it according to the judge's political agenda, as long as it agrees with their own, or who encourage judges to interpret the constitution according to what the judge believes will bring about the best results. If anything, such positions are themselves arrogant, as they entail substituting one's own personal and political opinion for the system of government and rule of law. Immodesty also includes activist judges thinking they posess, or cloaking themselves with, the authority and the practical ability to change legislation, and even more immodestly the Constitution, to produce what they see to be the best outcome.

The findings of this study question the assumption in an influential stream of contemporary scholarship that there can be no correct answers to legal questions, which is a relativistic philosophy or assumption. If the conclusions in this study are robust, then this strong version of relativism must be rethought.

The approach seeks to debate the issues raised rationally and in scholarly fashion, in which the merits of the ideas, the quality of reasoning, and the strength of the evidence are the criteria for validity. The approach is conducted in the belief that true respect for people can only occur through the tolerance of ideas in the form of free discussion and the free expression of ideas, and not through forced acceptance of any assumption, idea, or ideology. The reader is invited to engage in discussion upon this basis. The reader is also invited to enter into a good faith understanding whereby if my description of the British system of government together with the deductions or inferences are accurate, then my conclusions must be accepted as valid. If, on the other hand, there are descriptions or conclusions expressed that contain some inaccuracies, then as an objective scholar, without any agenda or ideology to forward, I welcome such correction as may be based on reason and evidence.

Not all, or even most, cases need necessarily engage the most fundamental rules of the system of government. This book, therefore, does not state that there will always be one uniquely correct legal answer for every case. However, court or other state actors ignore these foundational elements at their peril, in which their decisions may be incorrect as being outside of the system of government or their jurisdiction. Also, they may lose the benefits of considering the imperatives of the system which would otherwise provide real guidance for their decision-making.

From the basis of the book, further study can be undertaken in applying the system of government to measure against the actions or decisions of state institutions in particular circumstances. Further study might also address fully questions about whether or not there is one or a best legal interpretive style; interpretation when statute may appear ostensibly unclear; whether or not courts may ever properly consider extra-textual considerations, such as principle or conventions; whether or not jurisprudence may properly change over time; and so on.

PART ONE

The Basis of Government, Differentiation within Government, and the Common Law Courts

1

Overview, Pre-Conquest, and the Conquest of 1066

The foundational elements and main building blocks in the development of the British system of government are outlined in this book. These foundational elements establish the nature and jurisdiction of important institutions, particularly of Parliament, courts, and judges.

PRE-CONQUEST: THE NATURE OF THE SYSTEM OF GOVERNMENT AT THIS TIME

General Influences

The general influences between the fifth and eleventh centuries provide necessary background to understanding the foundations of law, as well as underpinning concepts relevant to the legal system, such as the supremacy of law. Holdsworth observes: "the foundations of the systems of law of Western European states were laid in a world governed partly by remnants of Roman law, but chiefly by [tribal] custom tempered by Christian theology, and by those political and legal ideas of Roman lawyers which the Church perpetuated."[1] Furthermore, the Church introduced ideas of political organization, as well as higher notions of law and morality, to the tribes, though the tribes were unable to make full use of these more advanced political and legal ideas.[2] Yet, in time, the Christian ideas that the Church brought revolutionized English law, as Harold J. Berman (in a two-volume study) and others have shown.[3] While this book cannot comprehensively examine all of these influences, some discussion of them is appropriate in order to provide for an understanding of the system of government arrived at in Britain by outlining its main influences.

The Church was the one body which exercised universal jurisdiction, and which could act as a bond of union between the divergent forces. The unity achieved had lasting results upon law and society. Le Bras states:

> The ideas of good faith and equity which underlay the canonist theory of contracts still influence the legislators of to-day, and those shrewd conceptions of the just price and a just wage are more vital than any system that has been practically applied, because they express our permanent ideal. Thus the present is linked to the distant centuries of Innocent III and Gregory VII; and indeed even to those more distant, for many of the ideas which bore fruit in the classic age were the heritage of past civilizations. The care of the poor and the oppressed which was characteristic of Judaism, the Roman love of order and authority, the Greek conceptions of political economy and formal logic, the enthusiasm and scrupulousness of the Celts, which were shown more particularly in their penitential system, – all these conquests of the human mind, which seemed to her in accordance with her fundamental principles, – went to the enrichment of the Church's law, and were assimilated to her own doctrine after such modification and correction as was required to bring them into harmony with her own point of view. It is indeed the highest moral tradition of the West and of the Mediterranean peoples which has been gathered up and handed down to us in the classic law of the Church.[4]

While the organization of the Roman Empire was slowly breaking down, that of the Church was growing. The Empire ruled from Rome was being replaced for many purposes by Christendom ruled by the Pope.[5]

Roman lawyers accepted the universal rule of the all-powerful emperor, but it was founded on the consent of the people. The aim of the state was the promotion of justice, and law was the instrument. The universe the emperor ruled was governed by law, and all were expected to obey it, including the emperor.[6] There were two types of law. *Jus naturale* is defined by some as the law common to all living creatures, but most referred to it as the ideal body of right and reasonable principles common to all human beings. For example, humans are free and equal. *Jus gentium* is the law common to all people. It falls short of the ideal *jus naturale* in its failure to attain the ideals of freedom and equality, but the two tended to become confused. A third type of law is the law of the particular state. The idea that the state could make and change its law is a characteristic of an advanced state of political development.

The Christian Fathers adopted these ideas, but gave to them a theological colour, thus somewhat modifying them. The aim of the state was the promotion of justice and the law of God. All men were equal before God. The state identified natural law with the law of God. This conception strengthened the idea that the universe was ruled by law. Both the emperor and the Church had their respective laws, and the head of the Church could change Church law.[7] The state was a divinely appointed remedy for sin. Resistance to the ruler was a sin and crime. On the other hand, rulers were bound by the laws of God, and Church teachings constantly placed before them the ideals of justice and equity and obedience to law. Later, the teaching stated that all rulers were subject to the law of the Church.[8] In the Middle Ages, there was no separation between the Church and State. The Church was the State and the State, or civil authority, was merely the police department of the Church. It was generally agreed that both the Church and State had spheres of authority, and there was harmony between them. Only later did conflict erupt.

Most of the tribes were governed by a chief and some sort of national assembly. The law was unwritten customary law declared in their assembly. When the king was influenced by the political ideas of the older civilization, he began to make written codes of customary law, and even new law was promulgated by the counsel and consent of these assemblies. This process tended to make people think that they were bound by divine law or natural law, and that these were the law of the state.

Theodore Plucknett also observes that the existing tribal organization was weak and inefficient.[9] One of the influences of Church teachings was the enhanced value placed upon monarchy, and the resulting tendency towards larger national units. A few large kingdoms emerged, ruled and administered by kings who observed European methods and learned Roman taxation. The clergy were important and influential. An early link between English law and Continental law was Lanfranc, who became William the Conqueror's chief advisor and the Archbishop of Canterbury. There are even greater influences of Roman and canon law with Henry II.[10] Laws were made and written down in the Roman style, such as in the *Domesday Book*. Roman influence on Anglo-Saxon laws can be seen in the Charters, which used forms and expressions definitely traceable to the Continent and Christianity.[11]

The Church also had important influence on the substance and procedure of the laws themselves, and helped to fill in the gaps that arose with political developments. Its influences included the sanctity of the king and through the king the authority of the state, which made for law and order. The importance of the individual and of moral right and wrong led to stress laid on motive and intention, which tended to modify the archaic notions of legal liability for wrongdoing in Anglo-Saxon codes. The law was in a primitive state in which society was organized largely on the basis of kindred, but would be replaced with feudalism after the Conquest. Law based on kindred determined who avenged and who paid or was paid *wergeld* in order to avoid the blood feud. Liability was based on the logical outcome of such a system, which focused the attention on the feelings of the injured person or kin, not the conduct or intention of the wrongdoer. Thus, any act causing physical damage had to be paid for, even if it was an accident or necessary for self-defence. The amount to be paid also reflected the status of the individuals involved. The Church's influence was to have these principles re-examined. Church laws looked primarily to the state of mind of the individual sinner. The sense of individualism in Christianity was opposed to the solidarity and joint responsibility of the kindred,[12] and also reflected the exhortation or duty of doing justice and loving mercy.

In terms of criminal law, physical force was the method of redressing wrongs, which often led to blood feuds. The influence of Christianity and the growing organization of the state increased the number of offences which were thought not to be compensable by money and should be dealt with by the king, until finally the groundings of criminal liability rested on different principles. The assize, or indictment procedure by the jury of inquest (and, later, through the growth of their powers, by the justices of the peace), superseded all local jurisdiction, both in the manner of trial and in the consideration of profits derived from exercising such jurisdiction. In earlier times, the king could not prevent the injured or his kin from prosecuting an appeal for war based on old tribal principles. Furthermore, canon law's influence gave greater precision to the law. For example, asking what guilt was morally imputable in a case led to refined distinctions about the degree of guilt to be attached, such as the distinction between murder and manslaughter. This influence also helped to overthrow the older system. This new terminology and the use of moral distinctions also gave a rough test to distinguish crime from tort.

In terms of criminal procedure, much formalism would be abandoned and much left to the discretion of the judge in the examining of witnesses and the weighing of evidence. Canon law also influenced important aspects of trial by jury involving challenging jurors for cause, as derived from canon law rules disqualifying witnesses on the ground of relationship, interest, and so on.

Medieval punishments were frequently cruel, and in many cases capital. The Church introduced the idea of imprisonment in an endeavour to bring the offender to repentance.

The Church introduced the conception of the last Will of a deceased, opposed feudal notions which excluded women from the inheritance of land, and influenced the law of intestate succession. The Church introduced the custom of conveying land by written documents, which led to the use of the instrument of Land Charters and, with ecclesiastical sanctions, made for freer alienation of land and individualism.[13] The principle of the assize of *novel disseisin* was deliberately borrowed from canon law, which it developed from Roman models.[14] While the theory of possession and ownership was wholly unknown to English law, the canonical idea was easily adapted and disseisin was protected by Henry II's Assize in the same way as a recent dispossession in canon law. The theory of possession also modified the Roman law of prescription by insisting good faith was necessary. There were other influences of the Church, for instance with respect to movable property. Church influence also brought contract law into being. Contracts of sorts existed already, for such practices as marriage, the payment of *wergeld*, and, after the Conquest, the action of debt. However, the Church's ideas of good faith allowed for the much needed development of contract law in other areas, such as insurance and the assignability and negotiability of debts, as well as the enforceability of a simple promise, which contradicted Roman law and the custom and practice of most of the other systems of secular law. Additionally, the Church influenced the very important area of family law. Marriage laws were based on canon law even after the Reformation.

The Church was at the forefront in attempting to stop and to mitigate slavery, which was recognized in Anglo-Saxon laws and practiced.

Later, the theories of the Middle Ages were used in the religious and political conflicts of the Reformation, and were applied to the needs of the modern state, including using such principles to adapt the common law to modern circumstances. Even after the Reformation, canon law influence was still powerful, and so the Reception was often as much a reception of canon as of civil law.[15] Indeed, the ideas of good faith and equity which underlay the canonist theory of contracts still influence the legislators of today.

Thus, during the Middle Ages, the powers of all human rulers, including the Pope, emperor, and king, were regarded as derived from and limited by higher divine and natural laws. Loyalty was not to man but to a system of law, and order believed to be a reflection of the law and order of the universe.[16] However, those limits were rarely, if ever, thought to be legally enforceable by any other human agency.[17] It was said, for example, by Thomas Aquinas that the Prince is only morally obliged to obey the law as there is none competent to pass sentence on him.[18] Therefore, while the concept of sovereignty is not stated in Bodin's terms, as we will see, its essential features were evident in this period.

In this way, the concepts of natural or divine law emerged and had influence. The influences of Christianity on the development of the British system of government and law were profound. Kings, statesmen, judges, and lawyers were Christians, and influenced by Christian ideas throughout English history, as we will continue to see. We may pause to cite two further examples. Charters and oaths of the king made reference to and venerated God, such as a certain person being king by the grace of God. For example, a Charter made by Edgar stated, "By the great clemency of Almighty God, who is King of kings, and lord of lords, I, Edgar, king of the English and of everything, emperor and lord of all the islands of the ocean which surround Britain, and of whatever nations they enclose ..."[19] Magna Carta's preamble states, "We unto the honour of Almighty God, and for the salvation of the souls of our progenitors and successor kings, to the advance ment of Holy Church and amendment of our Realm, of our meer and free will ..." Coke, a leading lawyer, judge, and statesman of the seventeenth century who perhaps did most to modernize the common law, began the prefaces to several of his Reports with "To God, to the country, to you," and in part three of the *Reports* states, "[s]o without question, [law arose by the divine will (trans.)], and this admirable unitie and consent in such diversity of things proceed from God the fountaine and founder of all good Lawes and constitutions."[20]

Feudal systems were formed because of the lack of central government, and order could not be kept, resulting in the rise of local customs of small districts ruled by feudal chiefs. However, during the tenth century, the Restoration of Empire and reform of the Roman Catholic Church and the office of the Pope gave rise to the revival and development of these political and religious ideals, which in the following period led to political and legal developments and theories that permanently influenced the political and legal thought of modern Europe.[21]

The Nature of the System of Governance at This Time

Prior to the Conquest of 1066, there was no central court regularly administering a law common to the country. England had a hodgepodge of customary laws, the three main bodies of which corresponded to the main political divisions of the country (West Saxon, Mercian, and Dane), and within these districts the customs of different localities varied. Such differences were accentuated by the institutional structure. The system of communal courts, including the county and hundreds, administering this customary law, represented a national system of jurisdiction and government. These courts existed alongside various franchise courts, and other private jurisdictions belonging to larger landowners, lay and ecclesiastical, representing feudal ideas. Thus, competing courts and conflicting jurisdictions had their roots in various principles, and in various rights: rights of the king, the Church, feudal lords, and ancient communities.[22] The greatest part of judicial and administrative work was done in these local courts.

The influence of the older civilization through the Church gave rise to the growth of governmental machinery and law. But feudalism,

24   Basis of Government and Common Law Courts

with its growth of private jurisdictions, rendered the nascent organ-ization of government ineffective, and prevented the growth of a national law.[23]

Another Church influence was the growth of the practice of cit-ing historical precedents in debates on legal, constitutional, or pol-itical topics.

Romanists maintained a scientific attitude towards law. The prac-tice of applying a scientific approach to bodies of non-Roman law in court cases was usually due to the example of Roman law. Leading English writers such as Glanvill and Bracton[24] are examples. Glanvill was also influenced by canon law rules.[25]

Sources of English law included the Anglo-Saxon Codes, first pub-lished in the sixth century; another source was later Norman compil-ations, including those of Saxon custom, before they were rendered obsolete by the reforms of the Norman and Angevin kings. These laws represented a primitive state of society. As stated, that soci-ety was organized on the principle of kindred, especially illustrated by payments to kin of a slain man to avoid a blood feud (*wergeld*), or for other injuries. When later codes were written, society was becoming more organized, but was also feudalized. Land Charters were important in feudal times, involving the conveyance of land or privileges over land. Many of these grants were royal. There were also other more direct ecclesiastical influences on English law, par-ticularly given the tendency to use the rules of a more advanced body of law to address the gaps that developments disclosed. Later codes were direct sources of Anglo-Saxon law, supplemented by custom, and by other codes of custom, particularly dealing with technical forms of procedure which had to be observed in legal proceedings or the case would be lost. The proceeding was not a search for truth. At any time, a duel could be demanded. While the law was of little avail when passions were aroused, it did provide a rule for peace-ful settlement of disputes in ordinary cases. In the later period, the most important authority was the Norman Domesday survey, which described the condition of the country for Edward the Confessor.

William Blackstone notes that the origin of Parliament is lost, as is much of its progression.[26] Nevertheless, the broad lines of that origin and development are evident. From the ninth century, with unification under Egbert, England began to emerge out of the war-ring groups that had remained after the Romans left. Kingship

Overview, Pre-Conquest, and 1066   25

began to exist from the seventh century, when the dignity of the chief progressed from a leadership position to a superior power, and coincidentally the office of judge, keeper of the peace, and protector of the Church. Such superiority was seen as the continuing privilege of some family renowned in war.[27]

Built around the notion and institution of kinship, periodic assemblies of the whole people (that is, freemen or free tenants) occurred. During the tenth century, the king and Witan (see below) were recognized as having authority over all England. It may be that the Anglo-Saxon assemblies which were frequently associated with legislation were modelled upon ecclesiastical councils, and the two sorts of bodies were sometimes impossible to distinguish.[28] Over time, because factors such as geography, effective working of assemblies, and cost made it inconvenient for the people to attend, these general assemblies were replaced by those based on representation, with a further narrowing of the duty to attend to those most prominent in areas such as military service, courts, and the Church. Still, free men never abandoned the right to take part in general resolution, and there was no law setting a decided limit on attendance.[29] The king fixed the time and place of the assembly. The personal summonses were made according to traditional usage, and cooperation was required. The most important matters deliberated were in relation to war, courts, and the Church.

This body made changes to the customary principles of law. It made appointments to the court, brought an action, protected individual right, and ensured the enforcement of punishment. Legislation was enacted in the time of Egbert, who had visited the court of Charles the Great. There he learned about the imperial idea of the power to legislate. However, the first known Anglo-Saxon law was made two hundred years earlier. This legislation made provision for a completely new class of society, the clergy, which had not existed in law, including custom, before that date.[30] The only imperial influence for legislation must have been from the Church rather than the Empire, and it is certain that early Christian missionaries to England deliberately adopted the policy of magnifying the office of the king. As Plucknett notes, whatever its ultimate origin, there is a fairly constant stream of legislation from the beginning of Anglo-Saxon legal history, about the year 600. During some periods, this legislation was more important than in others, but when radical legislation became necessary, the power and the machinery to pass it and give it effect existed.[31] There was never any doubt that in England royal statutes were binding throughout the land. Legislative methods, however, changed over time.

Customary law growing out of social life was regarded as the inborn right of free man, and not subject to change without his assent.[32] In this way, in the Middle Ages, bodies of custom developed and adapted themselves to changing conditions, because these customs proceeded from the people, expressed their legal thought, and regulated their civil, commercial, and family life; this continued until the decline of feudalism and society's rapid development required a greater reliance on legislation.[33] The idea of right, from which the conception of law developed, operated with the formation of medieval courts of law. These rights were thought not to be under the control of any superior authority, but only determined by the court of the people according to their best judgment. If new laws were desired, the people had to be persuaded to adopt them. In this way, limits were interposed on (superior) authority. No change in the fundamental principles in the framing of law was introduceable or effective without the decision of the popular assembly. It was considered equivalent to the general assembly of the people. The close connection between the court of law and the assembly deliberating on law remained throughout the Middle Ages.

The mixing of court of law proceedings and resolutions about law continued in the Witan. The Witan was the people's court, which came to be composed of the most prominent people, such as the largest landowners, the highest church functionaries, and the king. Election of the king by the Witan, normally from the royal family, was the rule in Anglo-Saxon days.[34] Just as in the Middle Ages, the courts of law could only be conceived of as being under the formal control of a superior authority, comprising also the men of law endowed with a power to assent. Also, the shaping of new legal maxims could only be effected with the concurrence of the king and the joint resolution and assent of the Witan. Furthermore, resolutions of Anglo-Saxon popular assemblies tend to show that customary laws, coming down from the ancestors, could not be altered by the king alone, but required also the consent of the people, or the Witan in the name of the people. For example, ordinances often stated they were selected and fixed upon with the consent of advisors, or the consent of the Witan.[35]

Regulations concerning the external administration of justice and containing no modification of national law could be accomplished by the king alone. If such regulations were meant to establish a lasting ordinance with important consequences, however, it was advisable to ask for the Witan's concurrence. Similarly, a king could issue injunctions for peace and the maintenance of civil order on the basis of prerogative derivable from his position as lord of war and of justice. For the actual preservation of peace, the warrant of the Witan was advisable, and to give such injunctions a lasting character, such as with respect to regulating land, many important regulations were made with the concurrence of the Witan.[36]

In terms of the composition of the Witan, the summonses were addressed to those whose presence the king might require and from whose counsel and cooperation a certain authority and influence might be expected. For example, general regulations and changes in popular law necessarily had to be deliberated by those with customary control of courts, such as ealdormen appointed by the king, more distinguished shire-gerefas, and also great thanes as lords in their own courts and over their own vassals.[37] In practice, a recognized expert in law in judicial assemblies would draw up the formula.

The hundreds was a division of the shires, or later counties, for the purposes of taxation, military matters, maintenance of peace, and settlement of local pleas, which were carried out in the assembly or court of each hundred. The origin of the hundreds court has been difficult to track. It was a territorial division of a court, and also performed other government functions. In hundreds court, matters of interest to the smaller free community were indirectly determined, including civil matters and petty crime, and its powers allowed a larger scope for the people to take part. The sentencing power was exercised by a narrower circle of experienced men of good reputation, who by their cooperation became the interpreters of the customary law. The others were bystanders who ratified the sentence. If there was dissent, an early appeal form involved the appointment of other sentence-'triers.'

The collection of fines and amercements as penalties for offences and defaults was a major part of the sheriff's duties. It constituted an important source for finances. Some hundreds were under royal officials, while others were in private hands. Sheriffs were the important channel of communication between the king (as well as the post-Conquest central government) and the private hundred, except for the most privileged. After the Conquest, the hundred became liable for various offences.

The framework for administration and government process was the same. The writs were the king's writs, and bailiffs were the king's and answerable to the sheriff for all that concerned the king's business.

The shire courts comprised a wider circle geographically. Before and long after the Norman Conquest, the shire or county court was the most important court of general jurisdiction. A small group of large landowners, local officials, and free men of the district were specially summoned. Bystanders might be present in the shire courts, but had few powers. Chrimes notes that in every county, some persons by name were required to render suit, and some units, such as the vills, were required to be represented at least on some occasions, and a mixed body of knights, freeholders, and villeins together with the sheriff made up the personnel of the court.[38] The sheriff was the most important of all local officials until the rise of a centralized judicial system. His court was the county court. Except for certain post-Conquest writs, he was not a judge, but spoke for the court and acted as the chairman. The decisions were reached by the suitors, and the sheriff merely announced them.[39]

The jurisdiction of the shire court was varied and extensive. The civil jurisdiction was considerable, including resolving disputes under certain set amounts, settling disputes among inhabitants of various hundreds, and determining questions of law among more influential parties; the shire court also had some ancient jurisdiction involving trial by duel and seisin. The procedure was the same as in the past. There was some tendency to reduce formalities; for example, ordeal by fire or water was in time no longer needed, and the use of the jury and lawyers grew. This court dealt with minor criminal offences, and similar matters in which there was a failure of the manorial courts to do justice.

The Witan was composed of the king as well as the largest landowners and the highest church functionaries specially summoned. In the Witan, bystanders were wholly passive.

Conclusion

Nothing in pre-Conquest times gave judges deciding cases the right to change the law or principles of law. Customary law, which was seen as an inborn right, had to be applied. The law or its principles could only be created or changed by the representative assemblies. There was no ability for judges deciding disputes to invent unwritten constitutional principles or other legal principles.

In addition to the basic system of government, including royal power, the broad outlines of the effective origins of parliamentary government can be traced back to this period.

PREROGATIVE FROM PRE- TO POST-CONQUEST TIMES

The different incidental crown prerogatives come from different periods in English history and are based on different ideas. For example, some can be traced to the feudal conception of king as lord of his tenants; some came from Roman law, such as the idea of the treasure trove; some prerogatives were deductions from the fact that the courts were the king's courts; others arose from the need for maintaining the king's dignity and securing his freedom of action; and still others came from the king's position as head and representative of the state. These ideas became the starting points for the development of technical rules. These rules were continuously developed from an early date as the king was a constant litigant in his courts in many capacities. This development led to the elaboration and accentuation of the incidental prerogatives. The judges did not forget they were the king's servants, and they favoured the king. As the political idea of the supremacy of law became dominant, judges began to think crown prerogatives should be subject to law, and so a number of limitations also grew up.[40]

Direct prerogatives included foreign affairs, powers in relation to national defence, and arbitrating commerce. Some matters of national defence were closely connected with powers over commerce. In terms of powers related to national defence, the king was first in military command. The Norman kings successfully asserted the principle that all military service was due from the tenant to the lord, and that this service was owed to the king. One implication

THE CONQUEST

Perhaps one of the most hotly debated points in English constitutional history is whether William I took the throne of England by conquest or as heir in 1066, and perhaps no more so than during the 1600s. What was at stake in this debate was nothing short of the perceived ultimate question of whether sovereignty lay in the king alone or in the king and Parliament. If the common law was immemorial, including the existence of Parliament, as the parliamentarians and common lawyers often argued, then it existed before any king, and the king could not change it. On the other hand, the royalists such as Filmer argued that the laws and liberties of England had come into being at the will of a sovereign king; consequently, they could all be revoked or modified at his pleasure, including the capacity in which Parliament was called, if at all.[41] Other royalists, perhaps even as late as the Revolution, used the concept of the immemorial constitution to support the doctrine of immemorial prerogative. Many parliamentarians feared that to deny the antiquity of the Commons was to deny them a share in legislative power, leaving them with only the authority named in their writs of summons that the king and his council enacted.

This aspect, and by no means the whole, of the debate over sovereignty in its theoretical dimensions, had its corresponding historical debate. An important question for the royalists was whether William changed the entire basis of the law with the Norman Conquest by instituting a highly developed form of feudalism, representing its final or most developed stages, including land being hereditary and alienable, as Spelman and Brady maintained had occurred. Thus, it was argued by these royalists that even though William stated that he retained the laws of Edward the Confessor, this claim is overshadowed by the new basis upon which he put that law and changed it. For them, William's statement could not directly determine the rights and liberties of Englishmen who no longer lived under such a system. On the basis that all land was henceforth held under feudalism, or the *feudum*, they asserted that it determined all land law and hence public law.

In terms of this historical debate, it was common for parliamentarians and common lawyers during the seventeenth century, such as Selden, Petyt, Atwood, and Coke, to assert an immemorial quality of the common law and of Parliament. For example, Coke traces the common law back to the ancient Britons, and the connection between British and French Druids. He refers to books of English law written in times Before Christ (B.C.), and books of law After Christ (A.D.) written by Kings Alfred and Edward.[42] Some other writers held that these liberties were derived from the Goths (early Germans). On the other hand, the 'discovery' of the Germanic element in early English history encouraged the spread of myths rather than checking them.

There is evidence that contradicts the royalist generalization that all lands were incorporated into the *feudum*, and there are contradictions or inconsistencies with that view as contained in the *Domesday Book*. Petyt argued that William did not confiscate the land of the whole kingdom, but confirmed much of it in the hands of those who held it before the Conquest, and that William revered existing law and rights, including those of the nonfeudal freemen, including through representation in Parliament.[43] These authors pointed to the origins of Parliament in a time out of memory. Coke attempted to trace Parliament back to King Arthur. Lambard and Harrington pointed to the existence of totally deserted and decayed boroughs still returning representatives to Parliament as proving the pre-Conquest antiquity of this right. In 1689, during the Lords' debate over the Commons' resolution that James had broken the original contract between king and people, Petyt argued that the contract existed. He argued that the original concept of government came from Germany, that kings should be elected, that there were laws made by what was later called 'parliament,' and that all kings acted and transacted by 'parliament.'[44]

These parliamentarians stressed that William and his successors confirmed the laws of Edward the Confessor, though with changes they made, and that the kings swore the coronation oath before they became kings and before any did homage. In this way, writers such as Pym and Mason maintained that William and his successors bound themselves by compact to observe the laws. Also, Selden and others established that Anglo-Saxons also had some kind of feudal tenure, which was used to minimize somewhat the extent of the (nonetheless important) Norman changes actually incorporated into England; they thus attempted to establish that such changes could only have occurred by the authority of custom and statute.

Another problem with the feudalism argument is that while it attempts to mount an argument against the 'ancient constitution,' it focuses more on process. It does not address the system of government existing at the time and its legal conception, the jurisdiction of the state and its institutions, the hierarchy of laws within the particular system of government, or how the system of its laws could be changed. Again, the necessity of understanding the system of government, and the perils of not doing so, are evident. The assumptions of humanist feudal historians detract from the real question, as is evident from their statement that there should have been a growing realization that the affairs of the eleventh to thirteenth centuries were the affairs of a remote period with a social structure all its own, and could be understood only by constant reference to the main principles of that structure, which did not corresponded to sixteenth-century Stuart England.[45] However, the question is not about social structure and the changes occurring within it, but about the system of government, and the changes occurring within it at both a 'constitutional' level (with respect to the jurisdiction of state institutions exercising sovereign power, or the most fundamental rules of the system), and with respect to particular laws under examination.

Another illustration of the humanist historians' approach leading to difficulties is their statement that even if the authority of the monarch had once been primarily that of a feudal lord over his vassals, then this too was no longer the case, and the prime duty of the historian is therefore to discover how the monarchy survived and on what foundations its authority now rests. It is clear that this approach cannot lead to a full and accurate understanding of a system of government. Rather than looking at the authority of the king, and of other state power holders exercising sovereign powers, these historians examine a particular way in which laws existed at a certain time or in a certain society. Did the monarch lose this authority, and, if so, how? This sort of humanist only states that the social conditions, and even particular laws, changed. However, that does not explain the ultimate power of the king or Parliament to change those laws. The question is important. If the political institution lost its authority, was it done legally, by laws limiting that authority, and can it be gotten back? In this way, the humanist portrays history in a narrow or parochial way, and ignores the relevant legal continuities over time,[46] for example in or through the system of government, or even in the basic values or principles that animated that system or laws, and fails to trace those influences to new circumstances being dealt with by the system or laws.

Humanist scholarship is interesting from a particular perspective and offers some benefits over some previous approaches, including the insistence that particular periods of time should be studied on their own terms and according to what people of that day actually thought; but, that is another question. At least some versions of the approach as discussed do not beneficially assist in our task, which is to identify and describe a system of government and to assess the legality of actions or decisions within that system, or the legality of changes made within particular areas of law or to the system as a whole. Adopting the humanist approach for our purposes would lead to the fallacy of conflating a particular set of laws at a particular point in time with the system of government itself. That approach would also promote the error of assuming that when circumstances change, the past's laws or its influences become irrelevant to the present.

In terms of the sixteenth-century debates, it also seems to be a false choice to insist that if a king exists before laws, then he is sovereign, but if not, then custom is. For example, suppose that the people gathered in some kind of neo-Gothic assembly to create a king. They may have only delegated to him a certain amount of authority as prerogative. However, that assembly may have reserved the rest of the sovereign powers to the Witan, in which the general populace never gave up a right to be represented. At that time, there may have existed a custom which grew up simultaneously with the creation or existence of the king, and of custom which could only be changed in the Witan, as appears to be the case, at least for the latter. As it is, the exact origin and full details of the government in England may now be lost.

The challenging nature of the question was put in an interesting way by Hobbes:

Then let us consider next the commentaries of Sir Edward Coke upon Magna Charta and other statutes. For the understanding of Magna Charta it will be very necessary to run up into ancient times, as far as history will give us leave, and consider not only the customs of our ancestors the Saxons, but also the law of nature, the most ancient of all laws, concerning the original of government and the acquisition of property, and concerning courts of judicature. And first, it is evident that dominion, government and laws are far more ancient than history or any other writing, and that the beginning of all dominion amongst men was in families.[47]

What is required is that one must go back to the origin of government and law, and consider what relationships give rise to government and law. A state is composed of various units, from the lowest natural ones, such as the individual; to the family as the basis for the reproduction of the species and for the replenishment of citizens inhabiting a particular geographical area, and in which children are reared; to larger and indeed created institutions, such as the state, which is the largest juridical unit. Mere power or dominion, such as the power of parents over children, or an armed robber demanding that others obey his will by handing over money, does not entail law. This sort of comprehensive inquiry into the past is beyond the scope of this book, save to say that the crucial exercise is to identify and describe the system of government at the relevant point in time.

The evidence of the actual political events strongly suggests that William took the throne as heir.[48] Furthermore, the laws of Edward the Confessor had been confirmed by law, with such modifications as were made. The important matter is that when the king in Curia or the king in Parliament made such laws, they were legally binding on him and on all others within the system of government. There are other reasons to prefer this conclusion of William taking the throne as heir and not as absolute conqueror.[49]

What is ultimately conclusive is that the issue of sovereignty as well as the system of government and its incidents are settled in the law of the constitution at least by the Revolution of 1688, and we need not enter more fully the debate or definitely solve this controversial issue surrounding the Conquest. What is important is to accurately describe the British system of government. What is certain is that parliamentary sovereignty was firmly established in the British system of government by that time and in the law of the

British constitution. Furthermore, this fact provides the determinative background for the former colonies attaining self-government and independence.

What is even more relevant is that common law lawyers sometimes claimed that from William taking the crown as heir and therefore under the law then existing, Parliament was not wholly supreme or sovereign. Even if one accepts the evidence as establishing that William took the throne as heir, this fact does not assist that argument. Also, the scope of power exercised by the king or in a certain manner at a particular point in time in the past does not necessarily mean that the crown is solely limited to such powers – all depends on the system of government.

Matthew Hale argues that William did not obtain his kingdom by absolute conquest, but as successor to Edward the Confessor, and outlines the effect of the laws of the kingdom. First, the subjects, but not the king, are under the coercive power of the laws. Second, *potestas directiva* are laws that oblige the king. For example, the coronation oath confirmed the Great Charter, and other laws and statutes concerning individual liberty. The law could bind the king's acts and make them void if contrary to the law. For example, Hale states the king would act contrary to law in stating that no land grants are permissible except under the great seal, and that granting monopolies would be void.[50]

He argues that the sovereign power of England resided in the king as the only supreme governor. The king's powers of 'sovereignty' are listed, including over peace and war, money and coinage, pardon, the military, and the making of laws, and from the king originally derived all jurisdiction for the administration of common justice, civil or ecclesiastical, ordinary or delegate. It is not certain that Hale is correct that the king held all jurisdiction over ecclesiastical justice, however. This point only becomes certain after Henry VIII took this jurisdiction. Prior to this time, the Church was one with the State, and the view existed in thought and practice that it may not have been subject to the king's power.

Although Hale calls the king sovereign, he sees qualifications to the king's powers.[51] First, there existed substantive limitations. For example, no subject could be forced out of the kingdom. The stipulation that no taxation could be levied without the consent of Parliament[52] was said to be adjudged and declared by the king with the advice and assent of the Lords and Commons in Parliament, which was of the greatest possible weight. Secondly, though legislative power resided in the king, it had to be with the advice and assent of the two Houses of Parliament. Thus, proclamations could not make law; they could declare and publish laws already made, and be used in aid of the king's powers.

Hale's view of the nature of sovereignty is inadequate. For example, some qualifications on the king's power were enacted by the king or Parliament. There was nothing that prevented the sovereign from limiting Parliament's power, for example in stipulating the manner and form of legislating. Furthermore, when William conquered England, he recognized custom, but said he could change it, and in fact did so. These facts nevertheless establish sovereignty after the Conquest. As we will see, Hale misunderstood Hobbes on the nature of sovereignty,[53] rendering his criticisms ineffective. Hale gives sovereignty the meaning of simple supremacy, which is not incompatible with the supremacy of Parliament or the law in their respective spheres. As the king was personally above the law, and the sphere of his supremacy wider or more active than Parliament or courts, Hale speaks of the king as sovereign and his supremacy as sovereignty. As a common lawyer, his political conceptions were of a medieval type (involving limitations on king, Parliament, and human law-making agencies by the law of God and of nature), which shows a fundamental misapprehension of Hobbes' analysis of sovereignty.

Nevertheless, Hale's view represents the common lawyers' view with its medieval influences, and provides valuable insights into the nature and effect of the Conquest. As such, it represents the highest and best case that can be made for this version of the common law view and for its use against the consequences of parliamentary sovereignty.

On the other hand, even Hale's view would not support courts nullifying legislative power based on the common law or otherwise. Hale did not say the common law was a source of authority superior to statute. All laws were created by will and consent, implicitly from custom or explicitly by legislation. Furthermore, it is impossible for an inferior court to have power to nullify laws made by a supreme legislative, as the same power of making laws and the supreme power in the last resort are necessarily vested in the same institution, in the king and in Parliament.[54]

The Legal Basis

This view of the supremacy of legislative power, and of the inability of the common law or courts to nullify laws, is supported by the legal basis of the constitution as at the Conquest. After the Conquest, the Norman kings were the rulers of England, including in law-making. They insisted that they were the undisputed lords of every piece of land.[55] Notwithstanding this sovereignty and aside from the strict enforcement of royal rights, the Norman kings made clear that the customary laws of Edward the Confessor would continue.[56] However, a proper understanding of sovereignty and the law then existing reveals, in light of the new sovereign entity, that these customary laws would have been subject to any new laws of the realm, at least in the form of laws of the Curia Regis, and later Parliament. The Norman Conquest made little change in the general attitude toward legislation, except to enhance the position of the crown assisted by a small and informal council. Legislation still continued.

Newly enacted laws by William I and II, Henry I, and Stephen were few. One important document in ten sections sets out the laws which William and his magnates ordained after the Conquest, such as the Christian religion being inviolate, peace between English and Normans, the laws of Edward the Confessor being confirmed, all free men being included in frankenpledge (see below), and the hundred and county courts being expected to carry on as before.[57] Several important changes were made through legislation, such as abolishing the death penalty for certain offences, abolishing penal slavery, and making radical changes in the constitution of the hundred court, whereby bishops could no longer transact ecclesiastical business there.[58]

The legislation of the three succeeding reigns was more sparse. One example is that Henry I issued a formal Charter of Liberties in 1100 promising to stop the oppressive practices which William II had introduced.[59] The Charter became a frequent form of legislation. While large portions of the Charter withdrew certain oppressive crown claims of doubtful legality, other parts established new rules in the place of old ones, and various arbitrary feudal dues were reduced to reasonable limits, all of which constituted a change in the law.[60] The Charter concluded a grant of the law as it was under Edward the Confessor, "together with those revisions which my father [William the Conqueror] made by the advice of his barons." That is, Henry I maintained the legislative changes which William made to Anglo-Saxon law. Henry I also restored capital punishment in cases in which it was abolished.[61]

A more recently discovered Charter of Stephen (1135–54) refers to a *statum decretum*, which established the rule that if there was no son, daughters would inherit by spindles.[62] As noted earlier, this law was a result of Church teachings and influences.

During the reign of Henry II, the first outburst of legislation occurred. The form of legislation varied, including by ancient and solemn charter, and more frequently by the assize. One example is the Assize of Clarendon in 1166, which was made with the assent of all the prelates and barons of England, and was, in form, an expression of the king's will.

Henry II confirmed the Charter of 1100. Also, as a response to the conflict involving the king and Archbishop Becket between ecclesiastical and lay law, in which the latter had been recently considerably enlarged, a council of all the magnates of the realm in 1164 "recognized" (in the sense of "recognition" or verdict of a jury) a list of customs which they declared were the practice of the reign of Henry I.[63] Some of the provisions repeated practices dating from William I, such as requiring either the king's permission before a tenant-in-chief could be excommunicated, or an appeal from Church courts in England to the Pope in Rome. Some provisions introduced remarkable laws. For example, a lord was held responsible to the king if his servants did wrong to a bishop. A provision also held that certain disputes involving land were to be decided in the king's courts, which had been the rule in Normandy as well. Chapter 15 introduced the important rule that no plea of debt was withdrawn from the king's jurisdiction because it was accompanied by an oath or pledge of faith. Spiritual censures could also be imposed for breach of faith. In this way, the state appropriated a large concurrent jurisdiction over contract, although Church law was for some time more advanced and equitable. Other assizes established new forms of trial by inquisition or jury, and established new forms of action in the law of real property.

As we will see, the Magna Carta of 1215 was largely declaratory of ancient custom, but was in other respects legislative, substituting new rules for old ones in several areas. During the next ten years, the Great Charter was three times revised and much of the first version abrogated. Repeal or amendment is just as much legislation as the introduction of new law.

Legislation became more frequent with Henry III. The Statute of Merton was the product of the continued struggle by the barons to limit the king's power. One provision allowed a lord of a manor to enclose common land if sufficient pasture remained for his tenants, and set out when and how manorial lords could assert rights over waste land, woods, and pastures against their tenants. It quickly became influential for the common law with respect to ownership. The statute also dealt with illegitimacy, women's rights concerning dower, and the right to bequeath crops in land.

The significance of these laws is twofold. First, the laws of Edward the Confessor were recognized in post-Conquest laws, and later confirmed. Second, legislation could change a previous law, such as those of Edward, and this ability was again confirmed by law. Therefore, it cannot be said that the judicial portion of common law or custom necessarily trumps post-Conquest laws, nor that legislation may only declare custom, nor that judges have any power to declare Acts of Parliament void.

As stated earlier, one immediate consequence of the Norman Conquest was that it changed the entire basis of land law in England, which was the most crucial area of law at the time. Even if this development did not wholly supersede the older custom, it did at the very least make fundamental changes to customs and common law. The latest Anglo-Saxon forms of landowning were restated in the form of Norman ideas about tenure, and expressed in suitable relevant technical terms to bring them into line with the system familiar to Norman lawyers. In light of the historical facts, Coke's view that William only brought Norman terms for hunting, hawking, and other plays and pastimes, and that most of the customs of Normandy were derived from English law, is not sustainable.[64] The king's court put into order the chaos of local custom by creating certain types of tenure to which all land ownership had to conform. There was also modification of military duties, such as tenure by knight service. This state of the law again demonstrates that Norman kings had the power to, and in fact did, change customary law, and in fundamental ways. It undermines the view that Parliament may not change any part of the common law, or what is sometimes referred to as the 'ancient constitution,' but may only declare what it says. On the other side of the coin, this evidence undermines the view that there are fundamental laws arising from the ancient constitution (existing from time immemorial) that cannot be changed, except perhaps that under the common law Parliament is sovereign, and hence cannot be abolished or relegated.

Another immediate consequence of the Norman Conquest was that it increased the confused mass of local customs by adding an admixture of Norman laws and customs, as well as fragments of canon and Roman law.[65] An example of one specific addition is that of a fully operational system of frankenpledge. Frankenpledge was a system of compulsory collective bail established for individuals, not after arrest, but as a safeguard in anticipation of it. The state of the law reveals transition.[66]

Furthermore, the jurisdiction exercised by the undifferentiated Curia of the twelfth century also demonstrated a legal power and status above ordinary or customary law. For example, it had characteristics associated with a court of equity. Its process was begun by petition to the king, and its interference in a particular case could result in remedies outside of, and indeed in contradiction to, the ordinary system of justice.[67] The Curia's activities resulted in the superseding of the old law by the common law, which developed into a regular system of law in the thirteenth and fourteenth centuries. The Curia's rules became the ordinary common law of the country, and not something outside ordinary law, which had previously given to them an equitable character.[68]

Therefore, the law of the royal court reflected a fourth species of law superior to the tribal customs of the Saxons, Mercians, and Danes in its universality, stability, and power. Its jurisdiction was strengthened and extended, such that a centralized judicial system administering a law common throughout the country emerged. The expansion of the common law, administered by the king's court, was effected through the invention of new forms of action in the form of writs, which were developed to address wrongs.[69]

Initially the king's court was only concerned with matters of state and matters of special difficulty which could not be otherwise determined. Forms were developed to simplify matters. When it was decided to enlarge the scope of the king's court, new forms were created. Expansion was effected by new forms of action. Civil business first started with land so that the crown through its court should have firm control of land. The earliest writs were not documents directly instituting litigation, but were in form administrative commands to an alleged wrongdoer or some inferior jurisdiction to do justice in a particular matter so that the king should thereafter hear no complaints about it. Disobedience was punished in king's court unless there was a satisfactory explanation.

The crown deliberately encroached on seigneurial jurisdiction when it devised the writ of right *praecipe quod reddat*. This writ completely ignored the feudal lord and was directed to the sheriff of the county where the land lay. It contained instructions for commanding the defendant to render to the plaintiff the land which he claimed, and if he failed to do so, the sheriff was to summon him before the king or his justices to show cause, and the sheriff was to return the original writ with the names of summoners who witnessed its service. The crown invented other writs in the form *praecipe quod reddat*; especially important were the popular writs of entry. Whatever its form, the original writ was not the assertion of the jurisdiction of the court, but rather a royal commission conferring on the judges the power to try the matters contained in it. For every case a separate ad hoc authority was thus conferred.

New writs under Henry II established the principle that no freeman need answer for his land without a royal writ unless he so chose. The effect was significant. It allowed the defendant to choose to have real property cases removed from seigneurial courts into the king's court. This principle and the *praecipe* gave the king's court the basis of a very wide jurisdiction over land. New forms of action were devised that attacked the position of the lords. The assizes were based on the principle that a person who had been recently evicted from the quiet enjoyment of his land was entitled to be restored. The writ of right was difficult and involved heavy proof (as well as the fact that one could be compelled to wage battle). *Novel disseisin* provided the solution. The principle was that the person disseised should be restored at once to his possession, and he need not be called upon to defend his title while he was out of possession. This legal form was introduced from canon law by Lanfranc into England.

A new pattern of writs developed which required the defendant to explain his action or misdeed, such as the action of trespass, rather than his inaction. The writ system was expanded into a very technical system.

Therefore, the crown deliberately encroached on seigneurial jurisdiction by disregarding the lawful rights (property rights, as they then were) of the feudal lords. The result was that the king's court acquired a very wide and general jurisdiction over land without any reference to the existing feudal courts. The position of the lords was further weakened through the use of the assizes instead of trial by battle. This centralized judicial system gradually reduced the local courts to insignificance, and substituted a common law for the mass of local customs.[70] Even with the national uprising against the abuse of this large crown power by John, which resulted in Magna Carta, the power exercised by the king and the activity of the Curia increased, and state administration was strengthened such that in substance a new system of central government was established.[71]

At the same time, the equitable characteristic of immediate dependence on royal power weakened. The Curia acquired writs that litigants could purchase. Secondly, the barons, and later Parliament, understanding that the power to make new writs was in substance a power to make new law, limited the king's discretion to invent new remedies.[72] Courts understood that it was not for them to make new law nor to change existing law. Thus, the system of common law tended to become rigid and technical, especially when controlled at the end of the thirteenth century by royal courts.

Political – King and Curia Regis (Undifferentiated)

The post-Conquest political order was governed by the Curia Regis, which performed all the functions of government, including the judicial. The legal basis for Parliament is evident in this period. The Curia Regis was the place where the king resided, attended by the chief officials of his court and household, and was the supreme central court where government business in all its branches was transacted. There was no separation between legislative, executive, and judicial functions. The Curia was the king's court. It was itinerant. The king often heard suitors in person.

The notion of magnates as the king's partners in government originated in the traditional feudal relationship between lord and vassal, involving reciprocal rights and responsibilities, including seeking and giving counsel on matters of mutual concern.[73] Henry's coronation Charter indirectly acknowledged that the consent of the barons was required before the law could be changed. Paragraph 13 states his promise to restore the law of Edward together with the amendments by the king and his council of barons. A number of other statements were made in support of this proposition.[74] The advice and consent requirement was a legal one, contractual in nature, and not just custom. The customary or practical aspects of that requirement involved questions such as how that advice, summoning, composition, and consent were to be realized.

The composition of the Curia was determined by the principle of tenure from the king. It was different from the vague principle determining the composition of the Witan, but it was always possible for the king, because he was king, to summon a person not his tenant.[75] Thus, while there is general resemblance between the Witan and Curia, there is no institutional continuity.

There was, however, an institutional continuity in the office of the king. The Norman kings regarded themselves as successors of Edward the Confessor, entitled to exercise those governmental or prerogative powers belonging to them as Edward's successors, which they believed were put into their hands for the preservation of peace, the protection of the weak, and the maintenance of justice.[76] These powers were vague and these kings were able to exploit them to the fullest.

After the Norman Conquest, England was governed by a succession of strong rulers in touch with the main currents of Continental thought. They created the centralized institutions in which the English common law originated. The Royal Court, from the beginning of the twelfth century, was beginning to influence the law of the country. The old English customary law was not wholly replaced, but transfigured, making it a system of law appropriate to a modern state.[77] By a combination of the powers of the feudal council and the powers inherent in the royal office, Henry I and Henry II put the law and government on a new basis.[78]

In theory, the Curia was composed of the king's tenants in chief, nobility and spiritual; royal officials; and others the king summoned. In practice, two types of assemblies existed – a large assembly of all leading landowners and officials, and a small body of officials who probably did the ordinary work of government. As the smaller meetings were also Curia, the idea existed that the professional judge in the royal court was the court itself and could act with all its powers.[79] Since there was as yet no formal distinction, both bodies had the same undefined powers of government. The increasing activities and exercises of powers of the Curia Regis resulted in the growth of a centralized judicial system and common law. The large meetings were the feudal councils. The smaller ones were in the nature of legislative and administrative boards, and central courts of law.

The feudal Council was a legislative, administrative, and judicial body. With its counsel and consent, William I made new laws and amended the laws of Edward the Confessor. This counsel and consent of the Council is mentioned by Henry I in his Charter. Council did not have much practical power to oppose the king's will permanently, as the king could almost always carry out the measures he wanted; but, the king was aware that the counsel and consent of the Curia added weight and facilitated enforcement of the law. Council supervised the working of the feudal system, and decided on disputes about tenure. It was consulted on many important matters of state. As a feudal court, it exercised civil and criminal jurisdiction over the king's great tenants in chief. As in communal courts, the members were the judges. They, not the king, gave decision, and the king or other president of the court announced the decision.

The smaller meetings were attended chiefly by officials. In them, we can see the beginnings of a centralized administrative and judicial system. Its financial and judicial business became increasingly specialized. The mass of work became too great for one undifferentiated tribunal. Thus, in the twelfth century, the Curia began to disintegrate, eventually leading to separate departments of state and separate courts of law.

Trial procedures were substantially the older ones. Trial by ordeal existed until the early thirteenth century when the Church prohibited it, which decree of Innocent III was accepted immediately by Henry III.[80] The plaintiff with secta[81] made the complaint which the defendant denied. The court awarded one party the right of going to proof. Later, with the abolition of ordeals, the use of juries and the new mode of proof, including presenting evidence, became more popular until it became the established procedure, particularly in and after the thirteenth century.

As previously noted, medieval conceptions were influential in the development of law and government, and are important in the development and understanding of the meaning of the supremacy of law.

Contribution of the Twelfth- and Thirteenth-Century Legal Renaissance

At the end of the eleventh and beginning of the twelfth centuries, a renaissance of learning, pre-eminently a legal renaissance, took place. There was a revival of the study of civil law based on the Justinian *Corpus Juris*, and canon law was being developed into a rival system. During the Middle Ages, canon law was at least as important as civil law, and exercised its influence over a wider sphere. With a level of order achieved from feudalism, these ideas made for the gradual development of the legal and political knowledge needed to create and administer a governmental machinery, and the state developed the physical force to attain its practical realization.[82] Civil and canon law, as well as feudalism, formed the legal background to legal, political, and intellectual ideas. The Bible and Aristotle were important influences. In terms of law, it made for the theoretical supremacy of right, legal or moral, which through medieval history is manifested in public and private law, in which even the emperor is bound by law.[83] There was also the ability to adapt law to changing circumstances.

Under the strong rule of the Norman and Angevin kings, the influence of the new legal ideas of the twelfth-century legal renaissance was marked. These legal ideas influenced the judiciary and courts, and the technical expression and modes of reasoning pertaining to legal rules more than the substance of the rules themselves, which were based largely on customary law. At this critical point in English law, the government, including the royal courts, was staffed by men familiar with this new learning. They knew civil and canon law, and would reshape, modify, and systematize English law. The judges, like most of the clerks and officials, were drawn from the clergy. There was also significant direct influence on some areas of law, including methods of illustrating and explaining principles of law or working a modified form (writ) into its substance (a rule of law), such as the assize of novel disseisin; the law of procedure, such as making defences to an action in addition to flat denial; the development of the law of pleading; the abolition of trial by ordeal under

Church influence, which made for the growth of jury; matters such as obligation, contract, fraud and negligence, of which the common law lacked rules; the law of bailments; and, the development of the modern law of easements.[84] English reception of Roman ideas was caused not so much by the inadequacy of native rules, as by the inadequacy of the machinery for their enforcement, and the need for more logical and clearer statements of their contents.[85]

Common Law

There are two different and confused usages of the term "common law." First, historically the common law was the law that replaced the old patchwork of customs. That is, common law was simply the law common to England. This common law was, in fact, composed of legislation, prerogative, custom, and judicial decisions. For example, Blackstone states the laws of England were made up of the common law (unwritten law) and statute law (written law). While the common law is now written in reports of judicial decision, their binding power and force of law comes from long and immemorial usage, and by their universal reception; the decision of judges is merely evidence of the common law, albeit held in high regard.[86] Second, there appears a more recent usage meaning judicial decisions (from courts traceable to royal courts), which is separate from legislation or prerogative. An acceptable usage of this sense of the term is illustrated by A.V. Dicey to indicate that the common law is that which judges enforce.[87]

However, today, judges often assert that the common law is judge made,[88] which is not quite so in view of its history, as we have seen. It may be that this shift in meaning has not been fully explored. One possible explanation may lie in the fact that early on, there were uncertainties involved in identifying what was a statute.[89] The courts did not always have a copy of the statutes, nor were they recorded in the national archives in a regular fashion; there were difficulties in proving a statute; and, even when statute was proven, it was not unusual to find statutes seriously misquoted.[90] These uncertainties may have led to other confusions, including to the conceptual indiscriminate melange of judge made law and statute law as common law. Given the inconvenience of a lack of an officially authentic collection of statutes or series of reports, lawyers relied on judicial dicta, books of authority, and works of private persons.[91] Plucknett concludes that it is "therefore not surprising that there have grown up certain legends as to the operation and effect of particular statutes which have no historical basis."[92] This melange may have led some judges to erroneously think they could use the common law to limit or override legislation.

Also, there was an attitude of free interpretation by judges up to the middle of the fourteenth century, in which statutes were sometimes strictly applied, sometimes stretched, sometimes the operation of a statute too widely drawn was restricted, and sometimes the courts even refused to obey a statute. Part of the explanation lay in the fact that statutes were widely drawn, but the main factor was the judges' intimate connection with Council that allowed them to exercise royal discretion, which was the privilege of the king's closest advisors. As we will see, this close connection later ceased. Legislation would then be interpreted strictly according to its terms and according to logic. Furthermore, Plucknett emphasizes two points:

First, the courts undoubtedly did disregard statutes when they thought fit, and secondly, they expressed no principle of jurisprudence or political theory which would serve as an explanation – still less as a reason – for their attitude ... If reasons of however great technicality made it desirable to neglect some words of a statute, then they were quietly set aside, but in doing so neither counsel nor judges enquired into the nature of statutes and legislation, the sovereignty of Parliament, the supremacy of the common law, the functions of the judicature, and all the other questions which the modern mind finds so absorbingly interesting ... We shall be getting nearest the truth, it seems, when we remember that the fourteenth century was in urgent need of good law, firmly enforced, for then we shall understand that the judges' great pre-occupation was to apply the best law they knew as courageously as they could, and that our modern difficulties, whether political or juridical, to them would have seemed, if not unintelligible, at least irrelevant and pedantic.[93]

This conclusion is a reflection of the judicial mind of the time. However, from the point of view of the rules of the system of government, a caution is in order. It would be inaccurate to treat issues of the nature of statutes, parliamentary supremacy, and judicial jurisdiction as being merely interesting to the modern mind, rather than as legal requirements which were properly regarded or disregarded by the judges of the time.

As a practical reality, Parliament's legislative and political functions made it inconvenient for them to interpret statutes pursuant to their jurisdiction as the high court, and as rules of construction were devised by judges and their complexity increased, the practical ability of judges to construe or misconstrue legislation became unimpaired in practice because of the lack of effective parliamentary oversight.

If this second, contemporary meaning of common law is used, care must be taken, as it may lead to the lack of distinction between the different elements making up the 'common law,' including statute. This error, in turn, sometimes leads to the fallacy that courts interpret the common law, perhaps even at their discretion, and somehow the common law may trump parliamentary legislation. There is no necessary link in logic, let alone one based on the British system of government, allowing such trumping to occur. Nor do judges have any sort of jurisdiction to change the common law as they think best, including under statute. The common law comprises a legal hierarchy of elements. The highest is legislation, which courts do not have the power to modify or repeal, and elements originating in judicial decisions, which courts may be able to change, though under certain constraints, for example as a result of the scope or limits of the common law; the nature of judicial jurisdiction; and, professional practices, such as precedent and *stare decisis*. Legislation is superior to judicially interpreted common law.

The definite beginnings of the common law do not occur before the first half of the twelfth century. Many of these rules originated pre-Conquest, but were administered and shaped by Norman lawyers, a process which was often influenced by Roman and canon law.

William and his immediate successors settled that there should be a common law, and fundamental principles began to emerge. As outlined earlier, the newly enacted laws assumed a background of customary law observed in the days of Edward the Confessor. Customary law thus went back to the Saxon period, but restatements and adaptations were made to deal with the new situation created by the Conquest. Attempts were made to state the customary law in a collection of books from the early twelfth century, the most important of which was *Leges Henrici Primi*. A spur to the common law was that, in addition to West Saxon, Mercian, and Danish custom, a new use and custom of the king's court was emerging. This custom was making for centralized government and a common law rendering all the tribal customs obsolete. The *Domesday Book* was the foremost authority for the history of English law at the time. Thus, the king's court was beginning to have a definite relation to the two most important branches of law at that time – land and criminal law.

During the reign of Henry II, royal judges were generally churchmen. They were in charge of declaring the custom of the king's court and constructed a rational, general, and definite system of law out of the conflicting mass of custom. Older law was swept away and replaced by new rules. Enacted law was least numerous, but was important, particularly in creating some of the legal institutions by which the common law was created and through which it did its work.

The king was free to issue what writs he pleased.[94] The Rolls did not yet show a fixed and classified set of actions. The court was not fettered by precedents. Glanvill states that the court was willing and able to act on principles of equity that right may be done.[95] Litigation later became characterized by a number of distinct causes of action, each begun by an appropriate writ.

The remedies given by law in Bracton's time (during Henry III's reign) were not yet limited by a fixed register of writs. There were a growing number of writs which could not be changed without consent of Council, especially if a change would infringe statute law.[96] The writs were original and judicial as they were known in Glanvill's time. Later magistralia were issuable to meet new cases in which it was thought an action should be granted. These magistralia were the immediate and effective cause of the rapid development of law during this period. Their existence meant that law could be developed to meet new cases. However, the Court did not attempt to attain abstract justice at the expense of rules of procedure and pleading. It was not until the common law courts had to compete with the jurisdictions of Chancery, the Council, and Admiralty that there was a development in law comparable to that displayed during this period.

THE NARROWING SCOPE OF COMMON LAW

As distinction within government grew, including between Parliament (as legislature) and Council (the executive), discretionary crown powers ceased to be exercised through common law courts. This distinction involved Council's abandonment of crown discretionary power, which resulted in further limitations on the jurisdiction of the common law. The common law ceased to mean the law administered by all royal tribunals. Rather, the term took on a more narrow sense. It was the law administered by common law courts and the various local courts closely connected with and controlled by them.[97] This is a *foundational point* in the jurisdiction of common law courts. Court jurisdiction became substantially limited at this point from the time that it was part of Council because it no longer shared in the power of Council after becoming separate from it. This point is immediately deducible authoritatively from the system of government. It also is evident from the historical evidence that once the intimacy between Council and judges had ceased, judges no longer felt themselves in a position to exercise royal discretion, which was the privilege of the king's closest advisers, and the common law courts begin to regard themselves as a government department whose function was to carry out its duties along prescribed lines. This entails and gives rise to statements such as that courts cannot change ancient usages; that statutes are to be interpreted strictly exactly as they stand, and are not to be considered suggestions of policy within whose broad limits the court can exercise a wide discretion; and, that distinctions are drawn between strict law and equity.[98] The separation into two functions of legislating and establishing text, and adjudicating and interpreting the text, began to emerge. In time, until perhaps very recently, judges would come to accept the theory of their absolute submission to the word and letter of the legislature.

Over time, the common law was developed and its scope became more certain. By the fourteenth and fifteenth centuries, the sphere of common law jurisdiction had become definitely fixed. There was greater clarity of procedural rules. These changes tended to give a new fixity and rigidity to the rules of common law. The disadvantage was excessive technicality, and even a lack of ability to deal with new circumstances. Courts became preoccupied with the working and management of this complicated machinery. The advantages were also significant. The growth of certainty and system in the rules of law made the common law a uniform system and aided it in establishing its supremacy over the local courts. From a steady working of the common law machinery, the branches within the sphere of common law were systematized and developed.

CONCLUSION

The evidence establishes that the common law is not judge made. In contradistinction to the period in which the Curia was fashioning the common law, including making modifications to local customs, once distinction in government occurred and common law courts could no longer share in the power of the Council, these courts' jurisdiction became substantially limited.

From this point, the common law comprised judicial decisions (that part of customary law systematized into a coherent body of law in the twelfth and thirteenth centuries, and judicial treatment of that body ever since), legislation, and prerogative. Legislation and prerogative are not judge made, and judges can only interpret what law was actually made. The legislature is itself a superior court, and its legislation is superior to judges and their decisions. That judges have assumed the power to interpret prerogative, and thus to define its limits, is not synonymous with it being judge made. Prerogative exists wholly independently in legal source and power from judicial pronouncements.

Even at this stage, it is evident that the legislating body (Curia, and later Parliament) was not merely declaring and enforcing pre-existing natural and common law, as some claim.[99] It was consciously making new law, and even changing common law, modifying or overruling judicial decisions, and creating new areas of common law. The argument that courts were to enforce an immutable pre-existing law is called into question. Even post-Conquest, customs were not venerated as infallible and immutable.[100] For example, in 1100, Henry I in his coronation Charter promised to remove all bad customs unjustly oppressing England, which he enumerated.[101] It was understood that new law could be created by deliberate legislation.[102] The writ of Henry III's Council prohibiting trial by ordeal abolished the one lawful means of trial involving time-honoured methods, which was replaced by the jury procedure. The jury procedure was not yet the trial by jury as we understand it today, which since the sixteenth century has meant a body of twelve impartial people who come to court with an open mind. The older trial by jury involved jurors finding the verdict from their own knowledge of the events or parties. Even the court, at times, was concerned about the compulsory depriving of the right to trial by ordeal.[103] Edward I had established a number of new laws, which constituted perhaps the most extensive reforming legislation until the nineteenth century.[104] In the early fourteenth century, novel law was being made which defeated the common law.[105] Furthermore, courts routinely distinguished between statutes declaring old law and those making new law, which determined for them how the statute was to be interpreted.[106] Thus, it could be said even more afterward that Parliament was not a mouthpiece of pre-existing standards.

Second, the common law was not boundless, and under judicial authority alone it was not expandable, at least significantly, nor was it even capable of dealing with all disputes. Rather, the common law became a bounded and limited jurisdiction as the courts became independent and separated from Curia or Council.

Finally, there is a connection between the common law and the constitution in the sense that the common law contained law relevant to the government machinery and its constitution. Judges' decisions on these matters were not applying a 'fundamental' law in the sense of a written Constitution higher than parliamentary legislation, but were applying statute and common law to governmental bodies. For example, eighteenth-century statutes dealing with local government were interpreted and applied by justices of the peace and courts of common law. Therefore, the statutes were worked into the technical system of common law; and, in cases involving government based on common law principles, statute law and common law were fused together.

Courts

Courts held before royal judges differed from communal courts and the general body of the king's court. Royal judges formed the court. When the king's interests were concerned, royal control was strict. When not, royal judges were influenced by the fact that they began to sit as regular tribunals at a time when the idea became current that the suitors of the court were the true exponents of the law. This idea emphasized the dominant medieval view that law should reign supreme, and led judges to regard the exposition of law as emanating from the court rather than from the king. They were royal judges bound to obey royal commands, but they were also judges beginning to create law, as discussed, which was within their delegated jurisdiction, and at a time when it seemed natural that the court should expound the law. This idea with respect to the position of law tended to give it a practical independence.[107] This change in attitude may offer some insights into why, after hundreds of years, the common law has become regarded as judge made law.

One particular episode of note was the commission of inquiry established by Edward I to hear complaints about judges. Bracton had also noted the deterioration of the bench, and the perversion of the law, in which judges corrupted the law's doctrine and decided cases by fancy rather than by rule. The result of the inquiry was disgraceful to all branches of the civil service, especially judges. Widespread corruption was found and a majority of judges removed, which had a positive effect on future judicial decision-making.

Confusions about Statute

Early on, there were uncertainties involved in identifying what was a statute. These uncertainties may have resulted in other confusions, which in turn led to the conceptual indiscriminate melange of judge made and statute law as "common law." This melange may have led some judges to think they could and can use the common law to limit or override legislation.

Hale[108] calls the statutes made in the time of Henry III and Edward I and II the "old statutes," partly because many of them simply affirmed the common law, and because the rest of them that made a change in the common law were not so ancient as to be part of the common law. Especially considering the extensive judicial treatment of them during successive times, the expositions and decisions together with the old statutes were, in a manner of speaking, incorporated into the common law and became part of it. Older sources of law became so established that it was rarely necessary to cite the actual statute, if there was one, which had made the law.

Holdsworth states that the form for making statutes was not yet fixed at the end of the thirteenth century, and documents existed which were not statutory in form or substance, such as administrative rules regarding the conduct of business in the Exchequer, and a case decided in Parliament on the subject of waste. But, for the most part, the important statutes of the time had parliamentary sanction.[109] In the following century, the role played by the different parts of the legislature in the enactment of statutes was not yet fixed, nor the boundaries between legislature and the executive authorities defined precisely. The result was some obscurity in the number of documents that could be called statutes. Documents on the Statute Rolls were clearly statutes. Other Acts of Parliament were often in the form of charters or letters patent. Coke's view is that any instrument to which the king, Lords, and Commons appear to have assented was a statute.[110] Holdsworth is less certain, as many such entries on Parliament's Rolls were not in any collection of statutes. Thus, given the inconvenience of the lack of an officially authentic collection of statutes or series of reports, lawyers relied on judicial dicta, books of authority, and the works of private persons.[111]

Pocock argues that the real status of laws lies in the fact that they were so often expounded by judges as to be incorporated into the very common law, absorbed by the body of immemorial unwritten law which it was the judges' business to deliver. If the records of the most ancient parliaments still existed, they would show that most of this unwritten law (*lex non scripta*) now regarded as ancient custom was originally statute.[112]

Plucknett argues that while the Provisions of Merton (1236) is treated as the earliest English statute, earlier documents on the public records can be regarded as legislation with equal justice. He states that during Edward I the forms of legislation were varied. For example, the Charter was really a conveyance, and the various charters of liberty, including Magna Carta, were drafted in identically the same form as a conveyance of real property and use the word grant. The Provisions of Merton is in the form stating that it was "provided and granted," which appears to be half-way between a charter that technically comes from the king alone, and later statute made in Parliament. A binding statute in the reign of Edward I simply meant something established by royal authority, whether by king in council, or in a parliament of nobles or in a parliament of nobles and commons as well.[113] He is also of the view that it did not matter what form the statute took, be it charter, or a statute enrolled and proclaimed, or merely an administrative expression of royal will to judicial authorities by letter (writ). The distinction between statute and ordinance appeared in the later fourteenth century as a difference between Acts that obtained the consent of the king, Lords, and Commons, and those that did not.

From the point of view of whether or not these law-making forms constitute law, which appeared to be Plucknett's concern, there may not be much difference. However, from the point of view of analytical jurisprudence or the system of government, there is a distinction. The jurisdiction to make ordinances or to make law through prerogative could be, and was later conclusively determined to be, narrower than statute enacted by king in Parliament. Prerogative was bounded by the common law. Indeed, as we will see, a main point of contention during the 1600s was locating the sovereign in government, and determining who was the predominant partner in legislating. One of the points of controversy would be whether legislation emanated from the king or from the king in Parliament.

Part of the uncertainty of what constituted a statute in this period comes because much depended on the intention of the king and Parliament, which was not always expressed. Also, much depended on whether the measure was assented to by all the estates of the realm, and whether what was enacted was intended to make a permanent and deliberate change in law or was more temporary in character.

NORMAN CONQUEST TO MAGNA CARTA — CONSTITUTIONAL ISSUES

Fundamental questions during the time of Henry III were such issues as the relation of the king to law, and the nature or powers of the body which could control the king. Another important issue was whether the common law was the king's law (given that royal judges were of the king's court, following Roman authorities), or could be adapted to the new situation created by Magna Carta (harkening to older Teutonic traditions and strengthening the old idea that a law was a rule of conduct independent of the king, and therefore was a bond uniting various parts of the body politic). The prevailing thought of the time was that while law was a bridle of state power, there was no legal limitation based on fundamental law, but rather one based on God's or natural law. Any notion of judges, as inferior officials, challenging the validity of law made by the 'king counselled' would have been unthinkable.

Bracton saw the king as supreme in his realm. He could not be sued in his own courts, nor his acts disputed there until the king's pleasure be known, as the king was the apex of the legal system, without equal. The king could not be subject to legal compulsion – no writ could run against him. If he did wrong, he was only answerable to God.[114] As other medieval lawyers and political philosophers thought, royal power should be exercised subject to the law, and the law should be passed with the counsel and consent of the magnates after due deliberation and discussion. The law was the bridle of royal power. Law made the king. However, this was no diminution of power in the sense of being limited by 'fundamental' laws in the modern sense of the word. It was a moral duty to obey, reinforced by baronial council and the threat of divine retribution, but not any form of legal compulsion.[115] Incapacity to err was the mark of deity. Similarly, Bodin states that the sovereign was not subject to another's commands or to the law, but was bound by God's law and natural law.

Principles such as the magnates being partners in government, arising from the feudal relation, gave rise to controversies. For example, it was not clear from whom, how often, or in what forum the king was obliged to seek counsel. It is significant that the barons never attempted to use regular judicial procedures to compel the king to accept their demands. Rather, they resorted to disobedience, armed rebellion, political trials, and as a last resort, deposition. The reason is that the common law offered no remedy. It was the king's law and his judges, which also gave rise to the fear of partiality.[116] There was no judicial method to resolve disputes between king and barons. This fact led to the widespread belief that ultimate authority was in the king alone, for example in making a final decision based on conflicting counsel, because the peace and unity of the realm depended on it. This position depended on the inviolability of his will. Thus, even unjust or incompetent decisions could not be legitimately overruled. Therefore, to submit to judges, who were essentially bureaucrats and subordinate to the king, legal challenges against the validity of laws made by the king with consent of the barons, would be unthinkable to Bracton and later medieval thinkers. No temporal jurisdiction exceeded that of the king counselled.[117]

Holdsworth sees Bracton as conceiving of the king and his servants as ruling according to a law binding all members of the kingdom. The king's servants did not work merely as royal deputies depending solely on the king, but as dispensers of a law which should bind all within the realm.[118] It was a natural idea to judges of courts born in an atmosphere of ideas conceiving law as declared by the court, and not by the king or lord whose court it was.

Jeffrey Goldsworthy says this view did not mean the king's courts functioned independently of his will. Rather, the process began as a petition to the king for amendment of his unjust actions. This view echoes Blackstone, who spoke of petition as an act of grace.[119] The court was able to give redress because the king admitted his errors and submitted to its judgment (voluntarily or under pressure from the magnates). The cases suggest that the jurisdiction of the king counselled was more powerful than that of the king alone, but both were the king's jurisdiction.[120]

Because the constitution was stable as it was based on law, it was possible to distinguish between abstract law and the rulers who were thought to pervert it. Thus, the question was what would occur if the king refused to obey the law. Bracton hints that the barons could restrain the king. As yet, the constitution of Parliament was not fixed. He lays down the main characteristic of English constitutional law as its dependence on common law. However, he could not yet state any remedy for breach by the king. The question remained unanswered, and was perhaps unsolvable since the problem of sovereignty had not yet been envisaged.[121] In fact, the question would remain unanswered until the Revolution of 1688. At that time, the dogmas of the personal superiority of the king to law and the royal prerogative being subject to law were reconciled in English law.

2

Constitutional Settlements: Differentiation within Government, Magna Carta, and the Common Law Courts

DIFFERENTIATION WITHIN GOVERNMENT

During the Middle Ages, there was a tendency to vest the judicial, executive, and legislative government functions in different bodies. From the time of Magna Carta, the nobility possessed the power to oppose the king successfully, and a rift between the larger and smaller assemblies occurred. The larger body became the body criticizing or opposing government, and the smaller body of officials came to be the king's servants.[1] This rift also gave rise to important changes in the juridical system, as we have seen and will continue to see, both in terms of court jurisdiction and of institutions.

However, an earlier disintegration was gradually taking place in the two chief departments of the smaller assemblies, finance and judicature, as they were obtaining increasing control over government administration in their respective areas. Still, there was no complete separation.

With the increased judicial jurisdiction and work of the court during the reign of Henry II, the knowledge needed for the new procedures and growing number of writs increasingly became the monopoly of the official. The system grew more complicated, such that sessions of Curia at which ordinary litigation was disposed of tended to fall apart from the larger meetings of Curia, which discussed policy and important political cases. The need for this differentiation in the twelfth century was also due to the specialization of official members of the Curia, foreshadowing the development of distinct departments such as itinerant justices, and of a special branch of Curia to deal with common pleas at a central location. This differentiation and specialization also became an important factor in establishing and maintaining judicial independence.

This development is significant.[2] First, in the seeds of tribunals with limited jurisdiction, as opposed to large undifferentiated powers of government, the coming split can be seen in the Curia, mainly, though not solely, in judicial work. As proceedings before these tribunals with judicial work were begun by writs, they soon developed a technical procedure, procedural rules, and rules of law, which became the common law because, as with their jurisdiction, they would extend over the whole country. Such tribunals so conducted began to exercise a powerful attractive influence on the as yet undifferentiated Curia. The tendency for Curia sessions of court dealing with ordinary judicial cases was to approximate judicial tribunals, and to diverge with respect to matters of administration and state policy.

MAGNA CARTA, GOVERNMENT, AND THE JUDICIAL SYSTEM

In the national uprising, all segments of society (landowners, ecclesiastics, traders, with barons at the lead) were united against John's tyrannical use of power, which was necessary in order for them to be able to coerce the king. Magna Carta attempted to define the conditions upon which the king must conduct government. It ended a period in which law was developed by crown power alone, and began a period wherein Parliament had the power to take a role in making and developing law. It represented the first attempt to state in legal terms some of the leading ideas of constitutional government. It also familiarized people with the idea that by means of a written document, it was possible to make notable changes in the law.[3]

Medieval people in 1215 understood Magna Carta to be an enactment formulated by the king, Church, barons, and merchants as partners in the legislative powers of the nascent state.[4] It contains clauses which deal with their respective grievances. For example, there were clauses guaranteeing the liberty of the Holy Church expressed as a freedom from government, that is from subjection to a temporal prince.[5] Magna Carta was clearly not a Church-State separation.

Indeed, Archbishop Langton, who mediated between the king and his barons, drafted it by drawing on Church ideas. The Great Charter and the common law guaranteed the position of the clergy in Parliament. There were also clauses placing limitations on arbitrary power, such as with respect to fines, property taken for debt, and the administration of the property of a deceased. This episode also demonstrated the importance of the Church in constraining secular abuses of power. Additionally, to address the king's tyranny, Langton put the barons under oath to restore the rule of law.

A number of Magna Carta's provisions regulated the new machinery of government and justice, such as clause 14, and clause 12 regarding taxation which was later dropped. Common pleas was to be held at a fixed place (clause 17), which emphasized the Court of Common Pleas as a purely judicial court. Other provisions dealt with the local administration of justice. Clause 18, for example, established delegates from the Curia in certain common pleas, which took a range of cases away from feudal courts. Civil assizes were to be held by itinerant justices. Arbitrary and disproportionate fees were to cease.

A number of clauses were aimed at fettering the new machinery of government. First, clause 34 reflected the barons not objecting to the Curia assuming jurisdiction over issues of possession, unless land ownership was in dispute. Second, clause 39 states that no freeman was to be imprisoned, exiled, or in any way destroyed except by lawful judgment of his peers or *per legem terrae*. The meaning of this important clause has been debated. For example, Coke believes that this clause refers to legal processes as due process of law; however, Holdsworth argues that it is aimed at brute force.[6] It did not intend trial by jury (a royal judge and a body of recognitors making findings of fact), which the barons did not want. They wanted an old type of tribunal in which all suitors were judges of fact and law; they did not want to be judged by their 'inferiors.' The issue arose whether *per legem terrae* meant the law of the land. This interpretation is significant constitutionally as it laid down the principle that liberty and property are not to be interfered with without due process of law. Holdsworth is inclined to the 'law of the land' interpretation based on the entire document, and the weight of contemporary statements.[7] The more restrictive view is that the barons only asked for a trial before their peers, which referred to the judicial system in part.

Therefore, at the beginning of the thirteenth century, Magna Carta made clear that law supported royal justice. As such, there would be a law common to England.

By the end of John's reign, there was a clear separation between a court at a fixed location to hear common pleas, and a court following the king with jurisdiction over common and crown pleas. The courts were not completely distinct until 1272, with separate rolls and a separate chief justice for Common Pleas. Still, it was not always possible to distinguish the courts. The special competence of each court was still only vaguely defined.[8] Common Pleas was inferior to the court which followed the king, and appeals could be made to that court from Common Pleas.[9]

COMMON LAW COURTS — THE SOURCE OR BASIS OF THE COMMON LAW COURTS' POWER

The original source and basis of the courts' power was a delegation of power to judges from the king, or from the king and Curia Regis through legislation. As Blackstone notes, the king as fountain of justice and general conservator of the peace of the kingdom gave rise to various powers, including the sole right to create courts of judicature. All jurisdictions of the courts were either mediately or immediately derived from the crown, and the crown appointed judges.[10]

Accordingly, courts of law as legal institutions were bounded by law. First, the basis of their power was delegated authority, and their jurisdiction was confined to the areas actually delegated. Second, the courts could only have as much power as the king could legally delegate, and could not exercise power beyond the king's power, except as legislation otherwise provides.

The king's common law courts were in origin a pre-eminent species of franchise jurisdiction. In the medieval view, prerogative was a species of liberty or peculiar royal law, placing the king outside ordinary law, just as the land over which a franchise existed was outside the ordinary law.[11] The king's courts at an early date became courts of common law. Thus, the king's privileges and franchises were guarded and applied as part of common law.

Even under Anglo-Saxon feudalism, the king gave out various grants of jurisdiction of mixed proprietary, justiciary, and fiscal rights. The landlords imitated this practice and began to sub-grant. Glanvill cites a comparatively new rule of the king's court that those commissioned by the king to administer justice could not delegate this power.[12] Thus, judicial jurisdiction was not only granted by the king, it was only the king who could delegate such power.

Until Magna Carta, the law was developed by crown power alone. Henry II's legislation added significantly to the jurisdiction of the Curia Regis over criminal and civil matters, and gave it wide powers of supervision over the conduct of all local courts and officials.[13] All this jurisdiction was exercised through royal writs. The writ procedure became perhaps the most salient feature of the full-grown common law. It influenced the substance of the law and the development of the legal system. The Curia was a popular court because of the advantages it offered, such as its power to compel a defendant's appearance and the ability to enforce judgments backed by the strength of central government. Its procedure was better than the older courts; for example, trial by combat was replaced by a kind of jury. The king or his justices could also order cases to be heard in the king's court.

The *Quo Warranto* enquiries of Edward I were further evidence demonstrating that the source of court power was in the crown. Bracton stated the theory that all jurisdiction flowed from the crown.[14] An express grant had to be shown. Prescription did not give title, but aggravated the offence.

Holdsworth calls Bracton's theory exaggerated, more prophetic than true in reality.[15] First, he argues, the true meaning of franchises was becoming obscure due to differences in the legal terms used. Second, under feudalism, larger landowners either assumed or procured a grant of the new processes and powers of the Curia.

However, Holdsworth's approach conceptually confuses the nature of sovereignty or law with actual practices, and illegal ones at that. This error demonstrates the dangers of adopting a purely historical inquiry, without a suitable analytic theory by which to assess the historical facts. In fact, Holdsworth states that such 'silent usurpation' of franchises was later prevented.

Plucknett states that the origin of the older jurisdictions is obscure, and not derived from the post-Conquest crown.[16] However, this observation can only go so far in assessing the legal scope of these older jurisdictions. First, as their origins are lost, the source of their legal power is also not precisely known. Practically, many freemen became dependent tenants to a lord as a result of being unable to pay the unbearable taxes imposed by the king. Also, the hundred often fell into private hands, sometimes purchased from the crown, in which case a court leet was held and the sheriff excluded. Second, this view also lacks a theory as to the interface between these older jurisdictions and sovereignty or sovereign authority, particularly in relation to the feudalism then existing, and between these older jurisdictions and their decisions with law. One cannot simply examine, for example, the relation between lord and tenant, as this expresses only part of the overall legal relationship pertaining to feudalism. The lord's lands were likely held of the crown and formed part of the crown's ancient demesne. Furthermore, the customary law as determined by the court of the people was not only subject to new laws, but was being replaced by the common law enforced by royal Curia courts, which recognized and sometimes changed custom that was contrary to natural law or reason, in the course of establishing a common law for England. Finally, in any event, as we will see, these older jurisdictions were abolished or wholly superseded by the royal courts that established the common law. These courts were initially wholly and directly derivative of royal power in theory and fact.

By the time of Edward I, this assumption of private jurisdiction was considerable. The *Quo Warranto* proceedings enquired by what warrant landowners were exercising their *jura regalia* (adopting Bracton's theory). However, as a result of the resentment among the barons and other landowners, the king was obliged to compromise. The two Statutes of Gloucester of 1290 allowed a possession without interruption from the beginning of Richard I's reign as conferring good title.[17] Thus, the king's theory that no franchise could exist except by royal grant was established as law for the future. It was rigidly enforced in litigation before ordinary courts,[18] and at the general Eyre.

The franchise had to be proven, could be lost, and could not be assigned. It was settled that a franchise would not be allowed if, in the opinion of the court, it could not lawfully be granted by the crown.[19] This point is most interesting and significant given that the common law court's authority was also established and granted by crown power, and *a fortiori* this limitation must have also applied to it. The only exception must be legislation expanding court jurisdiction beyond what the crown conferred or could legally confer. Finally, as the jurisdiction of franchise was determinable by common law courts, the large-scale silent usurpation of franchises was eliminated. Nevertheless, many franchises continued to exist by being proven by charter; by action under the statutes of 1290; or rents were paid for them; and, grants may have been made or confirmed by the Norman and Angevin kings, including the grants of large territories and jurisdiction by the Anglo-Saxon kings, such as that of Durham under a bishop. This confirmation also supported the view that franchise authority came from the crown.

The jurisdiction of the various common law courts was limited. This fact undermines the position that common law courts had such jurisdiction as to enable them to deal with all disputes between parties – a view perhaps arising from notions of deemed or inherent jurisdiction.

With respect to subject-matter jurisdiction, Common Pleas was the only common law court in which real actions and older personal actions of debt, detinue, account, and covenant could be commenced. Its jurisdiction could only be ousted by express words of exclusion in a charter or other instrument granting this jurisdiction to another court.[20] Common pleas involved civil matters which were distinguished from crown pleas, involving criminal and mortal matters, although the king could be a party to common pleas. The older forms of action, real and personal, became obsolete because they were too technical, causing delays. New actions, such as trespass, had taken their place, and could also be brought in King's Bench. King's Bench and Exchequer offered several practical advantages, particularly by the former employing legal fictions. For example, the plaintiff was not as likely to be defeated by the wrong writ or technicalities, the presence of the defendant could be secured, and the process could be swifter and less costly. The rivalry in concurrent jurisdiction resulted in King's Bench eventually taking the great proportion of business.[21]

The second area of jurisdiction related to supervising or correcting the errors of the older local courts by the use of various writs. This jurisdiction became gradually less important as these local courts declined, beginning in the fifteenth century. Their supervisory place

Constitutional Settlements

was taken by justices of the peace, who were controlled by King's Bench. Third, Common Pleas acquired a general jurisdiction to issue prerogative writs of prohibition and later habeas corpus. Finally, this court had exclusive jurisdiction over its own officials or other persons privileged to sue or be sued before it, as did other common law courts.

It was not until a century after Common Pleas became a distinct court with distinct judges and records that King's Bench attained its position. King's Bench followed the king (*coram rege*). While Henry III was a minor, there was no *coram rege*. That is, it was not yet a court of King's Bench, but a continuation of the undifferentiated Curia Regis performing executive, legislative, and judicial functions. King's Bench was a court of first instance for 'great men' and causes, and it supervised and corrected the errors of other courts.

While the court followed the king, the king was not necessarily present at its sessions. It was also beginning to sit more at fixed places. It still drew much of its authority from the fact that it was held in the presence of the king. Its jurisdiction in error and over criminal cases originated in its close connection with the person of the king.

Signs of divisions in this court *coram rege* appeared by the end of Henry II's reign.[22] The procedure of the common law was becoming more fixed and technical, especially with respect to appeals or review for error, including from Common Pleas. Cases heard in accordance with common law procedure tended to separate from cases to which this procedure was not applicable, and from the sessions of the court at which the non-legal element predominated. Also, after the civil war, during the reign of Henry III, the writ of trespass became common (criminal and quasi-criminal in nature), and the common law procedure used. Thus, sessions of court at which the professional element predominated tended to be occupied with the correction of errors of inferior courts, and with the trial of criminal or quasi-criminal cases. This differentiation of the court grew during Edward I's reign. Its competence was limited to amending false judgments and criminal cases. An overriding power was reserved to the king (in his council, or his council in Parliament). These bodies were only beginning to split at this time.[23]

King's Bench gradually became a separate court of common law as it lost, during the fourteenth century, its former close connection with the king himself. Cases heard before King's Bench, like those heard before Council, were said to be heard before the king, but by the end of the medieval period, the king as a general rule ceased to be present in court. Coke refers to the cases of Henry IV and VI for the proposition that as the king entrusted judicial power to his judges, he could not himself pronounce judgment, especially where the king would be a judge in his own cause.[24] Holdsworth disagrees with Coke's assertion.[25] There is no such clear statement contained in the Year Books. Furthermore, it is improbable that this view was held during the later part of the fourteenth or fifteenth centuries, because it was contrary to the medieval idea of the supremacy of law, which was strongly held by common law judges: namely, that the king could interfere with the rules by his own discretion. In the old Curia, it was not the king, but the court that gave judgment. In these specialized courts of common law, judges formed the court. When Coke states that James I could not give judgments in his court of King's Bench, he could not cite any decision precisely on point.[26] Finally, there was legal and political expediency in Coke's position.

The separation of King's Bench from the king was also aided by the fact the king had another court to deal with cases arising in geographical proximity to him (Steward and the Marshal), and pertaining to his household (Marshal of the Marshalsea).

King's Bench also lost its former connection with the king's Council from the end of the fourteenth century. Council was tending to become more the organ of executive government, Parliament the organ of legislation, and King's Bench was becoming simply a court of common law concerned with the judicial side of government.[27] This separation of organs contributed to friction between Council and Parliament.

The common law courts were affected by this separation. They recognized Parliament, whose consent was necessary to make the laws they applied, while Council sometimes acted, in the courts' opinion, beyond statute and common law. Common lawyers began to think errors in King's Bench ought to be corrected in Parliament, not Council. King's Bench ceased to be connected with or even to be directly controlled by Council.

King's Bench became simply a common law court. But it preserved in its style and jurisdiction traces of when it was a court of a

Constitutional Settlements

different kind. Thus, it exercised wide powers of control over other courts and officials; and, in exercising a wide criminal jurisdiction, it retained the quasi-political powers from when the court held *coram rege* was both King's Bench and Council.

This court exercised a jurisdiction which was general and universal. Coke states that its jurisdiction involved crown pleas; reviewing errors of fact or law of all judicial proceedings; errors and misdemeanors extra-judicial tending to the breach of the peace, oppression of the subject, or misgovernment; trespass; personal actions; and, the criminal justice system.[28]

King's Bench did not ordinarily try criminal cases, unless it transferred the matter by *certiorari*, for example if a fair trial could not be had before an inferior court, or some difficult question of law was likely to arise. Also, there was a procedure to question the correctness of inferior court decisions (in the form of a criminal or semi-criminal proceeding against the jury or judge).

Originally, civil jurisdiction belonged to Common Pleas. King's Bench always exercised jurisdiction where personal wrong or force was alleged,[29] including trespass, which was exercised concurrently with Common Pleas.

In legal terms, the inter-court rivalry demonstrates that judges acted unscrupulously and even illegally in the attempt to expand their jurisdiction. King's Bench invented a process giving it concurrent jurisdiction with Common Pleas over all personal or mixed actions based on the fact that the defendant was in the custody of the king's Marshal of the Marshalsea. This functionary kept the prison of the court, and the court had general jurisdiction over him. A person could bring any sort of action over the Marshal except real actions. The first step therefore was to get the defendant actually or constructively into the Marshal's custody.[30] The proceedings were fictions begun by alleging a fictitious trespass to give the court jurisdiction, which did not set forth the true cause of action. Thus, a statute of 1661 required that the true cause of action be set forth, which restored some part of the ancient jurisdiction to Common Pleas. King's Bench circumvented the statute by using trespass to give jurisdiction to itself. Common Pleas resorted to a similar device to compete. In both cases, the commencement of the proceedings was a document whose contents were completely fictitious.

As I argue elsewhere:

The essential dynamic that arises from this element [government apparatus] is that governments and bureaucracies will seek to expand their responsibilities and compete with other governments and bureaucracies to expand and to fight challenges to their 'jurisdiction.' If demands for their services decline, they must find new justifications to exist. Their jurisdiction and the expertise of these organizational complexes constitute their power and create their permanence. The politics of competitive organizations affects relations not only within a specific level of government (intragovernmental relations), it also affects the interaction between different governments within a polity ... This process holds profound implications for the relations between the different levels of constitutionally recognized governments ... and not just for their bureaucracies.[31]

In the thirteenth and early fourteenth centuries, jurisdiction in error belonged almost exclusively to King's Bench. By the end of the thirteenth century, a higher court was emerging, the king's council in Parliament, which could correct errors in King's Bench. The highest court in the land was the high court of Parliament.

The jurisdiction involved superintendence over due observance of law by officials and others. When King's Bench was indistinguishable from Council, it shared with Council this superintendence. One branch developed in the procedure in the writ of error. Another branch developed into jurisdiction to amend extra-judicial misdemeanors, chiefly by prerogative writ. Writs included habeas corpus, certiorari, prohibition, mandamus, quo warranto, and *ne exeat regno* (to forbid a subject from going outside the realm). In this way, King's Bench, and through it the common law, gained a large degree of power to prevent the commission of illegal acts with respect to local and central government and officials.

The Court of Exchequer became a separate organization in the twelfth century. A slow and gradual separation between the financial and judicial sides occurred, and it became a distinct court. This court was gradually assimilated into the other two common law courts.

Its jurisdiction during the fourteenth to the first half of the sixteenth centuries was primarily the hearing of revenue cases. The court began to exercise supplementary equitable jurisdiction, and jurisdiction over common pleas when its judges grasped at jurisdiction, together with its profits. When statute was passed to prevent the court from holding common pleas, it made crown right the foundation of a fiction to secure jurisdiction by stating that if the plaintiff could not recover his debt, then he would be less able to satisfy the crown.

As Parliament was seldom summoned during the sixteenth century and the Exchequer was the only court that could amend errors of King's Bench, it was desirable for another court to hold regular session. The new court of Exchequer Chamber was created in 1585 to amend errors of King's Bench, and statutory appeals established.[32]

A number of points of significance are evident. First, King's Bench, as a court of common law, was not the highest court after its separation from the king and from Council. Second, statute could determine the jurisdiction and the status of the courts. Third, while the courts dealt continually with certain subjects, such as appeals, ultimately judges were not capable of fashioning an effective system in some areas of law, notwithstanding significant experience. Legislatures had to remedy the defect, such as with respect to the writ of error by the Criminal Appeals Act, 1907.

One other group of judges that played a role in the common law world was the itinerant justices. In the twelfth century, itinerant justices travelled the country. They were commissioned to perform various government functions, both judicial and administrative. Oftentimes, they inquired into the conduct of local officers and held royal court. The character of the commissions varied. In the thirteenth century, commissions were regularly issued at definite dates, and the forms were fixed. Some commissions came to be integral parts of the judicial system, closely linked with common law courts. Therefore, the source, existence, and jurisdictions of itinerant judges were a specific delegation from the king through commissions.

Overview

The courts of common law and itinerant justices were vested with almost all the common law jurisdiction of the country, civil and criminal. There were still left to the old courts and officials certain police duties, and criminal jurisdiction over small offences. Royal justice in the fourteenth and fifteenth centuries picked up these last remnants through common law courts introducing newer remedies and more efficient procedures; by the creation of justices of the peace; and, by statutes adding to the justices' duties, including supervising the administration of local government.[33]

The Bounded Jurisdiction of Common Law Courts

It is, therefore, inaccurate to state that common law courts had complete, let alone exclusive, authority to hear and decide cases involving disputes between parties. Furthermore, the common law courts' authority was bounded categorically in a number of ways. It was bounded both substantively and procedurally.

There is a distinction between the necessity of government to be able to adapt laws to new circumstances and the claiming of this power by the courts. The question is one of jurisdiction. The fact that central courts did not *exercise* jurisdiction over commercial disputes, for example, does not mean they did not *possess* that jurisdiction. Within their jurisdiction, courts may be able to develop law and procedure and their own institutions to effectively deal with new problems. It may also be that the courts' jurisdiction does not allow these matters to be brought abreast of new developments, and other powers must be invoked in aid, such as legislation, or legislative reform of courts as institutions.

SUBSTANTIVELY BOUNDED JURISDICTION

The common law had a substantively bounded jurisdiction. Stated positively, there were areas of law or jurisdiction outside the common law. The content of that bounded jurisdiction was furthermore illuminated by what powers the king did not delegate, including the power to legislate, dispense, suspend laws, and pardon.

With separation growing in government, including between Parliament (legislature) and Council (executive), discretionary crown powers ceased altogether to be exercised through common law courts. The distinction involved Council's abandonment of crown discretionary power, which resulted in further limitations on the sphere of common law. These limitations included equitable and extraordinary powers, as well as foreign trade, which was a matter for government, that is for king and Council, and later for Council and Admiralty. The sphere of common law tended to become limited and fixed.

The Law Merchant in earlier times involved both maritime and commercial law. Merchants were a distinct class in the Middle Ages and customary laws developed. These laws, having a basis in Roman law and tinged significantly with canon doctrine, differed from common law and were administered in courts that were distinct from ordinary courts. These mercantile customs progressed to meet the needs of expanding trade, and were developed into technical rules of law influenced and aided by juridical concepts derived from civil and canon law. Generally, civil law influenced the technical development of the law, whereas canon law influenced the substance of law and the machinery applying it. A system of mercantile courts and a body of mercantile law developed. To a large extent, a uniform commercial law was made and administered by the merchants for themselves. While some English doctrines of commercial and maritime law were traceable to the Middle Ages, most of the modern law was due to reception of these Continental doctrines in the sixteenth and seventeenth centuries. Common law courts had no jurisdiction over contracts made or torts committed abroad.[34]

Later, in their jealousy and coveting of jurisdiction, the courts of common law confined the court of Admiralty to maritime causes, and appropriated to themselves jurisdiction over commercial cases. They then assimilated commercial merchant law, and constructed our modern system of commercial law.

Judges were aware of the advantages of enlarging their jurisdiction, and were ready to adopt any workable expedient to do so, even an illegal one. The judges of Henry VI and VIII's reigns adopted the principle that if the contract was made in England, the action could be brought there.[35] By supposing a fiction that these contracts or offences were made or committed in England, common law courts captured jurisdiction[36] over the growing commercial business of the country regardless of the fact that the common law and its procedure were less suited to it than Admiralty, and were even incompetent to deal with such cases.[37] The devious device was that when the contract stated that it was made at a certain place, for example in Bordeaux, the judges would claim that this was actually a place in the county of Islington in Middlesex, and that the question of whether or not there existed such a foreign place could not be challenged in the case. On this basis, the fabricated claim was not considered by the common law judges. Admiralty court had historical truth and substantial convenience on its side, and the opposition of Coke and common lawyers was unscrupulous.[38] This capture of jurisdiction by the common law courts resulted in a slower development of commercial law. Many points of maritime law that were afterwards painfully elaborated by the common lawyers had for at least a century been familiar to the civilians; for example, the liability of a carrier for loss because of thieves was discussed at Westminster in 1671, but was settled in Admiralty as early as 1640; so were many questions with respect to Bills of Exchange, Bills of Lading, General Average, and Insurance. To the litigant it meant much inconvenience. Commercial litigants attempted to avoid the common law courts where possible. Modern legislation restored to Admiralty many powers and much jurisdiction of which it was deprived in the seventeenth century, but by that time admiralty law had lost its international character.

After the Revolution of 1688, the courts of common law and equity obtained complete jurisdiction over all commercial cases, and most maritime ones. Thus, in England, commercial and maritime law became a branch of ordinary law, founded on the principles and rules of cosmopolitan Law Merchant introduced into England.

Ecclesiastical law covered a wide sphere of jurisdiction governed by canon law. Its courts have a long history. William by ordinance insisted bishops not transact ecclesiastical business in the hundred, but hold their own Courts Christian, which was done from that time. However, it appears that the bishops continued to administer canon law in the county courts as late as the time of Henry I.[39] Later, friction with the common law courts arose and the common law courts produced decisions that narrowed the scope of ecclesiastical law.

A number of other areas were outside of common law. For example, common law would not recognize or enforce the Use or even a chose in action. Thus, the common law could not control the kinds of estates that could be and were created in equity by Chancery.

PROCEDURAL-SUBSTANTIVE LIMITATIONS: THE WRIT SYSTEM

In addition to the common law's substantively bounded jurisdiction, there was also a procedural-substantive limitation inherent in the writ system. The jurisdiction of common law courts was bounded by technical writs corresponding to various causes of action. After the Conquest, the rules of the king's court for the foundations of the common law were being established. The forms of action and procedure were the most important part of the law during Henry II's reign. Many of these writs obtained substantially the form which they would permanently possess. The writs indicated the extent of jurisdiction already appropriated by the king's courts.

The writ of Prohibition was later used to enable the king's court to make good its claims to jurisdiction against many of its rivals. Writs of pone, justicites, and recordari facias were processes by which king's court was able to control local jurisdiction. Numerous writs with respect to land held by free tenure were attaining fixity. There were possessory assizes and various forms of writ of right. The writ of entry was beginning. The king's court was assuming jurisdiction over personal status. Writs of debt, detinue, covenant, and *de plegiis acquietandis* show the court was beginning to assume jurisdiction over property other than land, but such actions were rare compared with those relating to land. A distinction between original and judicial writs emerged. Original writs originated an action. Others were issued during the proceeding to sanction or compel parties to take necessary steps.

The king was free to issue what writs he pleased, which determined the extent of the jurisdiction of the king's court.[40] The growth of parliamentary powers in the thirteenth and fourteenth centuries made it clear that in Parliament legislative power was vested. Through the Provision of Oxford of 1258, the Chancellor could not seal any writ, except writs of course, without the command of the king and of his Council. By 1294, it was established that every writ brought to the king's court ought to be according to common law or statute. Indeed, as we will see, even in the terms of the Statute of Westminster II, 1285, the common law courts' lack of jurisdiction to create new writs was evident. Thus, the register of original writs became practically closed, as every new writ had to be provided by Parliament. This final result was obtained gradually and was tied to the decay of equity administered by courts of common law.

For example, action on the covenant ceased to be of much importance after Edward I, when it was established that covenant would only lie on a deed under seal. The writ of *novel disseisin* was an improvement over the law, given that an action for title carried a heavy burden and might lead to trial by combat. However, there were some technicalities to this assize, given that it lay only between the disseisor and the disseisee, or the actual parties involved. If the person wrongfully taking possession of land died and his heir entered by descent, the assize could not lie against the heir. If the person whose land was wrongfully taken died, the assize was not available to the heir. New writs of entry had to be developed to overcome these situations. Problems requiring this sort of technical writ and procedure made parties seek equitable relief in many cases involving estate administrators and executors, and on some other issues statute was necessary.

To some extent, the excessively technical development that constricted the common law was the fault of common lawyers and judges during the fourteenth and fifteenth centuries, notwithstanding that judges could no longer exercise royal discretion once they became separated from Council. As the procedure of common law courts grew more elaborate and unreasonable, statutes dealing with procedure became more numerous. Further constraints on the courts arose later with the development of *stare decisis*, particularly when law reports became more systematic and reliable.

EQUITY

As is evident from the foregoing discussion, common law court jurisdiction decreased when the king was no longer present in his courts of law and the courts ceased to be closely identified with the person of the king. They could not assume his prerogative to administer equity. Between the twelfth and fifteenth centuries, the king administered this justice through the Council and the courts immediately connected therewith. In the twelfth and thirteenth centuries, King's Bench and Eyre[41] were closely connected with king and Council. In the fourteenth and fifteenth centuries, the Eyre ceased and King's Bench lost its close connection with king and Council.

The equitable jurisdiction was more connected with the intimate relations of the Chancellor and Chancery with the king's Council.[42] The Council was a direct descendant of the Curia. The separation of the common law courts and the growth of parliamentary powers deprived the Council of much jurisdiction in different branches. However, it still continued to be the executive government and exercised wide judicial powers due to its close connection with the king, including extraordinary powers above and beyond ordinary law.

From the fourteenth century, the need was apparent for a court with extraordinary jurisdiction to temper the rigidity and technicality of the common law administered in common law courts. Other defects of those courts included slowness, expense, inefficiency, abuse by the over-mighty, antiquated methods of proof (refusing to allow parties or any interested persons to testify, and the continued existence of wager of law), their suspicions of volunteer witnesses, and their inability to compel one party to an action to disclose evidence useful to his adversary.

The theory behind this equity power was that the prince was the immediate minister of justice under God, sworn to deliver justice. Thus, besides his court of law, the king must either reserve to himself or refer to others a "certain sovereign and pre-eminent power to supply the want and correct the rigour of positive or written law, which of itself cannot make a perfect rule."[43] The principle underlying the Chancellor's equity jurisdiction was that people's actions are so diverse that it is impossible to make any general law aptly meeting every particular act without failing in some circumstances. The general law administered by common law courts was often very narrow and technical, making the Chancellor's interference necessary. This foundation underlying equity jurisdiction was vague, but tended to become more fixed with time. This idea is common to many systems of law, and came naturally to the medieval mind, which sought to establish justice as the ideal to be aimed at by rulers. This system of government, including equity jurisdiction, demonstrates that (common law) courts do not have all powers to deal with all aspects of legal disputes before them, but may only deal with the 'law,' and only within the bounds set by that law.

There were well marked lines of a purely equitable jurisdiction exercised by the Chancellor or Chancery, such as in relation to contracts and matters of account.[44] First, Chancery dealt with cases falling outside the common law, such as alien merchants, and maritime and ecclesiastical law, in which the common law courts had no jurisdiction. While the common law could not enforce contracts that were not written and under seal, nor contracts not already executed in which goods or land were already delivered, equity would enforce them on the basis that contracts were based on consent and a breach of faith was a sin, therefore faith should be kept and agreements of good faith and honest dealing enforced.[45] Second, Chancery became involved where the common law gave a remedy but the ordinary courts could not act, such as due to the disturbed state of the country or the power of the defendant. The court could order parties to do or not do something in order to ensure justice was done, such as the writ of subpoena and the power to cite in contempt. The nature and scope of equitable jurisdiction became more definite when the Chancellor was relieved of cases calling for equity because enforcement was impossible. The court gradually confined itself to giving compensation in such cases, leaving culprits to be punished by the courts of Star Chamber or common law. As early as the second half of the fifteenth century, the purely equitable jurisdiction was showing signs of becoming distinct from the criminal or quasi-criminal jurisdiction of Council. Third, Chancery had jurisdiction to deal with cases which could not be dealt with by ordinary courts because the law itself was at fault. For example, the rigidity of law resulted in the enforcement of strict legal rights that was contrary to equity, such as due to fraud, forgery, duress, or mistake; and an equity of redemption was established during the reign of James I. Fourth, the Chancellor dealt with matters of a chiefly quasi-ministerial character regarding writs, and claims affecting the king's interests. Some specific matters equity dealt with were trusts; family law, including equitable control over infants and guardians; administration, or accountings, such as estates administration; specific relief; and, mortgages.

Chancery was making important additions to many branches of law. In terms of substantive and procedural law, influences of the rules and conceptions of canon law, and thus to some extent Roman civil law, can be traced. Canonists were willing to give relief on the grounds of abstract justice, based on the principles and rules of civil and canon law considered fair and just in suitable cases, in order to satisfy the demands of conscience, even though this involved a dispensation with the rigid rules of common law.[46] Sixteenth-century Chancery's equitable principles were based on strictly medieval conceptions. No human law contrary to these universal laws of God or nature was valid, given that their existence and validity were presupposed by all human laws. However, a human law might be consistent with these laws, which would make it a valid and fair general rule, but when applied to a particular case, might work manifest wrong. Reason and conscience (the laws of God and of nature) decided how and when injustice caused by the generality of rules of law was to be cured. Thus, the ideas of canonists were important. The actual law of the state was the starting point of equity, which would be called upon in cases of some hardship arising from the law. In its final stage, equity tended to become less based on principle supplementing or setting aside law to do justice in individual cases, and more a settled system of rules supplementing the law in certain defined ways. As Nottingham stated, the conscience of the Chancellor was not his natural and private conscience but a civil and official one, and therefore equity was a matter of rule and not of discretion.[47] A closer coordination with the common law thus came about.

JURISDICTION ADDED BY LEGISLATION

Given that the jurisdiction of common law courts was bounded, and even excessively so, it was extended, from time to time, by crown power exclusively before Magna Carta, and later by legislation. The existence of legislation over a new area meant that common law courts attained jurisdiction over the matter, unless such jurisdiction was assigned exclusively to another court or body. Legislatures also had to remedy difficulties arising from court decisions, or, as with the Statute of Uses or bankruptcy legislation, when courts otherwise demonstrated an inability to deal with the subject matters within their jurisdiction.

One important example of legislation adding to the jurisdiction of common law courts is the Statute of Westminster II. The statute gave the Chancellor power to vary slightly the forms of writs in order that justice might be done in similar cases.[48] One significant effect of the Statute was that it was the principal means used to extend the scope of civil trespass. Common law judges assumed the ultimate decision to quash or sustain a novel writ, but could not do so if Parliament allowed the writ to be made.

Statutes of the thirteenth century were significant in shaping the development of the law. Legislation influencing the technical development of law on this scale did not occur again until the nineteenth century. For example, the Statutes of Westminster I[49] and II[50] covered the whole field of law – procedure, real property, criminal law, and 'constitutional' law. Such statutes were both amending and constructing in nature.[51] Chapter 18 dealt with the writ of eligit, in which the judgment creditor could in alternative to *fieri facias* elect to take all the debtor's chattels and to hold half of his lands until the debt be taken out of the chattels and rent. The Statute of Gloucester (1278) made important amendments to land law, and involved landlord-tenant matters, killing in self-defence and by accident, and fixing the jurisdiction of local courts. The Statute of *Quia Emptores* was a pillar of real property law. It gave tenants in fee simple of land held by free tenure the power of alienation, and defined the effect of such alienation. A number of other statutes were passed. The Statute of Merchants (1278) established a system of recording debts and making land liable to execution.

The statutes of Edward I can be seen as the greatest development of common law and the settling of its jurisdiction. Statute was the most significant basis upon which to create additional common law jurisdiction. With that jurisdiction, the courts have been the body most responsible for the actual development of the law: that is, through applications or usage of the principles or jurisdictions established.

During Tudor times, legislation became more detailed and flowed at a more rapid rate. A great many significant changes in the law were made. Legislation dealt with matters such as uses, Wills, charities, conveyancing, bankruptcy, commercial law, and criminal law.

COURT JURISDICTION CAN BE TAKEN AWAY

Whereas legislation can add to common law court jurisdiction, it can also take away from it. A number of instances of statute taking away court jurisdiction can be cited. For example, Common Pleas was the only court of common law in which real actions and the older personal actions of debt, detinue, account, and covenant could be commenced. Its jurisdiction could only be ousted by statute, or by express words of exclusion in a charter or other instrument granting this jurisdiction to another court. This monopoly lasted until the abolition of these actions by statutes passed during the years 1833–73.

During Edward I's reign, the scope of tort law administered in royal courts was narrowed in 1295 when Parliament declared that no action for defamation could be brought there; instead, it was left to ecclesiastical courts.[52]

An ordinance of 1311 stated that Parliament must be held once a year or twice if necessary for hearing pleas, including those in which judges were divided. In a case arising soon after, Judge Bereford stated: "And because the new Ordinances direct that when Justices are in doubt about their Judgment the cause shall be sent into Parliament, to Parliament you must sue."[53]

Edward III's Statute of Treasons directed that judges were to send a case to the king and his parliament for treason or other felony.[54]

As stated, the new court of Exchequer was created to amend errors of King's Bench. In 1830, statute also deprived King's Bench of the jurisdiction to amend errors of Common Pleas.

Legislature could add to or decrease the scope of the jurisdiction of courts, affect their status and hierarchy, and determine to what bodies appeals may go, even to Parliament itself.

Legislation could also require courts to do certain things in the course of their judicial duties. For example, the Statute of Westminster II, chapter 31, dealt with bills of exception to overcome the problem faced by a party who attempted to appeal a decision by writ of error because a court did not enrol the exception which it overruled. The higher court could not address the matter because it was not "on the record," and judges could thereby thwart the unlawfulness of their rulings. The statute allowed such exceptions to be written in a "bill," to which the trial judge must affix his seal. Many judges were very unhappy with the statute, and one judge was prepared to act illegally in refusing to seal bills.[55] This statute shows that while the roll was under the absolute control of the court, legislation was higher than any lawful judicial action or decision.

Even within matters acknowledged or granted to be under court jurisdiction, legislatures could bound that jurisdiction. The almost conversational style of legislation under Edward I resulted in a wide scope of discretion in its interpretation by the courts. Tudor legislation, representing the newer approach, restricted the courts much more narrowly to the text of the statute itself. As a result, the text became longer, with more fulsome enumerations, exceptions, provisions, saving clauses, and so on. The Tudor period marked the age of the preamble. The preambles to Henry VIII's most drastic statutes were accompanied by a vigorous defence of their policy.

Conclusions Thus, even as at the time of Edward I and in the later thirteenth century, when there existed no clear separation between the branches of government, there was a limitation of the jurisdiction of the common law courts, and the judges themselves were very much aware of and accepted this fact. Furthermore, the fact that courts may have taken over a jurisdiction, does not mean they in fact possessed it. Some, like Hart, assume that law is a political process, that is, that government is what the highest officials agree upon. However, jurisdiction is determined by the actual system of government, and rules emanating legally from that system. Where courts have taken over a jurisdiction without authority (or illegally), and have kept it for a long time, there may be an argument for recognizing these decisions as law (de facto, not de jure), and at most developing this into a prescriptive jurisdiction, although that latter proposition is very doubtful indeed. Thus, the question, in such circumstances, is not whether the court's exercise of power was legal, as it was not, but what is to be done about it by legally constituted institutions, such as courts and legislatures. This analysis does not lead to the conclusion that judges' interpretation is always law unless changed by appeal or by legislature. Such a view improperly substitutes for the law and system of government the results of an event or a particular decision. It would also substitute the supremacy of law for the supremacy of persons.

THE SIMULTANEOUS EXISTENCE OF OTHER COURTS AND JURISDICTIONS

The simultaneous existence of other courts and legal jurisdictions demonstrates that common law courts were not the only bodies settling disputes, and that they did not have all the jurisdiction to settle disputes. These other courts exercised rival and inconsistent jurisdictions. Different component parts of the legal system developed during different periods in different courts, and acted on different principles. In addition to courts of common law, a proliferation of other courts including equity, Admiralty, ecclesiastical, Council, Star Chamber, local courts communal, franchise, and feudal and manorial were all contributing something to the general body of English law, especially Admiralty and commercial courts. During the Middle Ages, there were many different royal courts, such as Exchequer, courts of common law, and Council.

Local Courts The common law, by statute or court decisions, defined the sphere of local court jurisdiction. Common law courts also controlled the exercise of that jurisdiction, including by prerogative writs. This common law control produced a uniformity of rule. The communities of the land still had an independent life and performed many government functions subject to the law, which resulted in the development of the two fundamental characteristics of the constitution: self-government and the rule of law.[56] The superiority of the king's court and the controls it exercised over local courts is understandable and flows from the obvious legal fact that the king's courts were superior in law. That fact does not mean that courts of common law did not act illegally in taking over certain jurisdictions from time to time.

There was a tremendous amount of competition and rivalry between these various courts. In the end, the common law courts gained superiority, secured by their close association with Parliament.[57] The common law courts were particularly jealous of all other jurisdictions.

Plucknett also points to the fact that the common law courts offered better remedies: notably, trial by jury.[58] The courts held that in almost all cases the suitors were still the judges and a collection of archaic rules and procedure had to be observed.[59] This ruling was even applied to actions brought under a writ with a *justicies* clause, which implied that the sheriff was a judge in the modern sense of the word.

Once the common law courts won complete victory over older local courts, they then attacked courts with greater powers of resistance because these central courts sprang, like themselves, from the crown. Their theory was that a court could not be a legal court unless its jurisdiction was based on either parliamentary Act or prescription. Thus, the court of Chancery and Council were by prescription held to be legal courts, but not the more recent committees of Council or the Court of Requests.[60]

Central Courts Chancery was a central court. It was discussed previously in terms of its equity jurisdiction. After the Conquest, Chancery was a secretarial bureau, and the Chancellor was secretary of state for all departments. The separation of Chancery from the Curia as a distinct department dates from 1238.[61] Henry dispensed with baronial chancellors holding office for life, and took the office in his own hands. The Chancellor became an important official because he kept the Great Seal, which put him at the head of the English legal system, and made him the legal centre of the constitution. As stated earlier, the English legal system became a system of royal justice initiated by original writs, which had to be sealed by the Chancellor. As well, all important government acts, treaties, and royal grants were sealed, and therefore came under his review. So too did actions before common law courts, as well as petitions to the king, Council, or Parliament either for original writ, or for execution of the answer on petitions.

The Chancellor and Chancery had a close relationship to the judicial system, and from that relationship much of their jurisdiction arose, particularly from their close connection with Council and the Chancellor's control over the issue of original writs, as well as from Chancery's organization and efficiency as a department of state. Also, because Chancery was closely connected with the common law courts and Council, it was able to give any relief ordered, either by ordinary writs or orders by Council. Thus, it was natural for petitions asking for the redress of legal or moral wrongs to be referred to the Chancellor.[62]

As a result, the Chancery assumed some characteristics of a court as well as court procedures, such as affording a hearing. During the fourteenth and fifteenth centuries, its new position as a court became marked and supported by statute.[63] From the sixteenth century on, Chancery became a separate court, with common law and equitable jurisdiction, of which the latter was more important.

Conflict between the courts of Chancery and common law intensified in the sixteenth century. The common law courts recognized in a practical sense that law could not be modified by equitable principles, unless the Chancellor had the power to restrain parties from proceeding at law or to enforce their judgment. For example, some judges stated that if the Chancellor imprisoned parties for disobeying an injunction, they would release them using habeas corpus.[64] Common law judges themselves did not like being the subjects of injunctions (they were accustomed to granting orders of prohibition to other courts). They saw that their supremacy was at stake. During the reign of James I, Coke decided several cases wherein he held that imprisonment for disobedience to Chancery injunctions was unlawful, on the basis that a court of equity may not interfere with matters properly triable at common law or freehold.[65] Chancery responded that their injunctions did not interfere with the common law as the judgment stood; rather, they looked at the conduct of the parties. James I settled the dispute in favour of Chancery based on Bacon's report in 1616, and from that time on, this power was not successfully challenged.

When business increased in this court, there were increased complaints about defects in its organization.[66] Before 1688 and with the Restoration these complaints involved inadequate judicial staff, the resulting backlogs and delays, and abuses amongst officials. It was sometimes said that even the Lord Chancellor could not always be trusted, and the actual work was done badly by underpaid deputies (staff), while the suitor paid enormous fees to sinecure officials who regarded their offices as property. Indeed, Lord Macclesfield was impeached for corruption after an inquiry in 1726.

Council and Star Chamber in the Sixteenth Century   The growing organization and jurisdiction of Star Chamber, the creation of the various subordinate provincial Councils, and the development of the court of Chancery, Court of Requests, and Admiralty, all threatened the supremacy, but not the existence, of the common law system. They used different principles and procedures. Common law courts attempted to attack their rivals and engaged in a number of self-interested decisions. Because certain branches of Council were founded on statutory authority, it was impossible to go behind this authority, and the only attack was excess of jurisdiction. Thus, the courts recognized that they must obey legislation, and that there was no fundamental right to a case being heard before common law courts.

The common law courts had an even weaker case against Star Chamber. Star Chamber's jurisdiction was exercised, and the exercise of some of its jurisdiction had many precedents. In this period, many new courts and councils either came into existence or enlarged their jurisdictions, and encroached on the courts of common law. An umpire was needed. Council and Star Chamber claimed this jurisdiction. In the sixteenth century, the claim was conceded. Star Chamber issued orders to judges of different courts with respect to the conduct of cases; it stopped, delayed, and expedited an action, and gave directions for the hearing; it issued injunctions; and it gave directions regarding the issue of prerogative and other writs.[67] This fact again shows the common law courts were not the highest bodies on questions of law. The common law courts could not deny, for some purposes at least, that Star Chamber was a legal court. Thus, the strategy of attack was to try to limit its jurisdiction. For example, the court stated that Star Chamber owed its origin to a statute of 1297, which only defined some branches of Council's jurisdiction important at that time. This theory was not in accord with historical fact, and was condemned by leading lawyers of the day irrespective of political party and professional bias.[68] The Act did not create a new court, as there already existed a court of Star Chamber and all privy council judges were part of it. Thus, it had jurisdiction over offences in addition to those listed in that statute as a result of its former jurisdiction.

With the victory of Parliament over the king in 1641, legislation[69] was passed abolishing the Council and Star Chamber, and requiring matters of property, real or personal, to be tried in ordinary courts by the ordinary course of the law. The result is that English law follows the theory of ministerial responsibility and not a system of administrative law; and, the *foundational result* is that the common law courts permanently enlarged their civil and criminal jurisdiction.

Courts of Record Status   "Court of Record" is a term based on the proposition that when a king asserted his own word as to what had taken place in his presence, it was incontestable and conclusive. The king communicated this privilege to his own special court, therefore the formal records of the king's court could not be disputed. The proposition that it alone could fine and imprison was the latest to be developed. It was thus based on sovereign privilege.

In competing with rival jurisdictions, one device was to make the distinction between a court of record a real and not a technical one, by stressing the manner of keeping the record and other consequences which the status of a court of record came to involve. This technical construction was mere trickery, as the powers of the court were determined by how much power was delegated legally.

Coke deduced, from some vague dicta in the Year Books about powers of courts of record, the new rule that it was only a court of record which could fine and imprison. This new rule was intended to cripple these rival courts. Holdsworth finds the proposition questionable with respect to the power to fine, and wrong with respect to the power to imprison.[70] During this period, Coke's exaggerations or misstatements had little or no effect, as the power to fine and imprison was habitually exercised by Council, Star Chamber, Chancery, Admiralty, and High Commission. This power was essential to their efficacy, and historically justified. These courts were as much royal courts as the courts of common law were. During most of the fourteenth century, King's Bench and Council were intimately related, and Council could control the proceedings of King's Bench. Furthermore, the relations of these courts with the crown were more intimate than those of the crown with common law courts. Thus, these courts came within the original principle which also gave to courts of common law their superior status of courts of record.

These other royal courts possessed superior status as courts of record, regardless of the fact that their records did not meet the technical test devised by common law courts. Not only is there no authority for making the possession of a Latin plea roll the basis of the status of a court of record, but this is contradicted by both fact and law. Furthermore the proposition is indefensible on other grounds. The inadequacy of the formal record as an account of the most material parts of the trial is recognized.[71] These other central courts kept formal and more adequate records in English. The absurdity of making possession by a court of a Latin plea roll the crucial test of status of a court of record is revealed by Shower's argument in *Rex v. Berchet* (1691) 1 Shower at 119–20: if that is an objection, than all the ancient Parliament Rolls and Acts of Parliament before Henry VI, mostly enrolled in French, not Latin, and many Charters, writs, and commissions enrolled in French, and statutes since Henry VI, must not be records. To this point, one must note that Parliament was also a court, and the highest one at that, higher than all common law courts.

By the end of the fifteenth century, there were signs that competition from these rival courts was making for a freer development of the common law, rendering it not so constrained by excessive technicality. This period also shows that the development of a law-abiding instinct is acquired after periods of efficient rule. This instinct, in turn, supports other principles, such as the rule of law and even democracy.

Conclusion While in some cases, the jealousy, coveting, and usurpation of jurisdiction by common law courts led to good long-term results such as the supremacy and rule of law (and not 'administrative law'), there were also great inconveniences in a number of areas, such as the common law courts' mishandling of commercial matters. The common law did not even arrive at a systematic law of contract until centuries later than the rest of the Western world, which caused difficulties for people and commerce in the meantime, and this deficiency had to be addressed by Chancery, as well as by the Law Merchant previously mentioned. Another example of this is that the motive of the court seemed to have been to enlarge the powers of common law courts at the expense of local tribunals.[72] The result was not infrequently confusion and injustice; for example, parties committed to prison for debt obtained release and defrauded their creditors. Therefore, legislation was necessary to restrict the common law courts' scope. This coveting and jealousy also demonstrated that courts can and in fact do act without authority and usurp jurisdiction illegally, and even resort to deliberate deceptions to achieve whatever result judges may wish, which supports arguments such as Blackstone's that the law is not simply what judges may say it is. It also supports the imperative, as with all government bodies and officials, to scrutinize these power holders, to never be wholly and blindly trusting, to 'check' such bodies or officials when necessary, particularly on the occasions when they act without authority (or illegally), illegitimately, or inappropriately, such as through misconduct or improper motives. The above are not the only examples of judges acting unscrupulously or illegally. Other examples of illegal judicial behaviour include the courts sometimes adopting the principle that they were not bound to apply a statute if it had never been enforced. Not only was no attempt made to explore the theoretical implications of the principle, but the system of government, including royal prerogative, definitely left no room for any theory that statutes become obsolete by non-use.

OTHER LIMITATIONS OF JURISDICTION: MATTERS OF
HIGH POLITICS AND SUCCESSION

Another limitation on the jurisdiction of common law courts involved matters of high politics and succession. The common law did not apply there, and the courts were to remain silent.

The king was not thought to be amenable to the law.[73] The twelfth- and thirteenth-century law books state that such fundamental political questions lay with king and magnates.[74]

At the time of the Wars of the Roses, judges declined to give an opinion with respect to the Lancastrian and Yorkist titles to the throne because they saw that their proper business was to do justice between party and party, and this matter was said to be too high and touched the king's estate and regalie, which was above the law and passed their learning.[75]

The courts were not competent to render opinions in the area of high politics. Thus, when James II was in substance deposed and Parliament created a new king, even though this was stated in terms of abdication, the judges and lawyers, when consulted by the Lords, admitted that none of the rules of common law were applicable.[76] It was a Revolution, and the people through their representatives in Parliament assumed the right to make and unmake kings.

PART TWO

Parliament

3

Parliament's Development through the Reformation and Its Relation to Courts

This chapter continues to outline the broad picture of the major building blocks and elements of the British system of government, with a greater focus on Parliament and its development toward parliamentary sovereignty. Chapter 3 builds upon previous ones, including establishing the superiority of Parliament's status over all other bodies and in law-making, as well as the inability of any actor to challenge its laws, except through appeal to higher divine or natural law. Courts lack jurisdiction to challenge the validity of statute or to compel Parliament to do anything based on unwritten law, be it common law or other principles. This description is accurate even when Parliament was not supreme in the most complete sense. That is, Parliament was at all times supreme, even though it was not sovereign in the sense of having the jurisdiction to exercise the fullest extent of sovereign powers. At no stage in the development of parliamentary supremacy were common law courts anything but inferior bodies. At best, courts had the authority to use natural law as a basis of statutory interpretation, but not to go against legislative intention.

The first section describes the foundational constitutional settlements up to the Reformation. With the Reformation and the annexing of supreme authority over the English Church, the king in Parliament became omnicompetent in a manner omnipotent, except perhaps with respect to succession and full control over prerogative, which were established with the Revolution. The legislation of the period and the understandings of state officials demonstrate Parliament's freedom from limitations even with regard to the most precious and inviolable rights. Parliament's superiority of status and power over courts is further illustrated by its power as a reviewing body, or by its ability through legislation to review, modify, or annul court decisions.

The Rebellion and Revolution completed the main foundations of the law of the constitution, which are discussed in Chapter 4. The constitution's content was determined by what the actors in these events intended to establish, which was complete and unlimited sovereignty. The only question was whether the king or Parliament was the sovereign law-maker. The latter view prevailed as a consequence of war and rebellion.

FOUNDATIONAL CONSTITUTIONAL SETTLEMENTS — PARLIAMENT UP TO THE REFORMATION

Magna Carta altered the position of the Curia. The king's defeat meant he was no longer practically absolute. From the various experiments evolved the Model Parliament of 1295. From the union of feudal and elective and representative principles, the modern Parliament was obtained, comprising the House of Lords and House of Commons. For example, the idea that magnates could speak for the community was ancient, based on the feudal idea that they could speak for their tenants in chief, and so on down the line.[1] During Edward I's time, representatives of other estates of the realm, such as knights and smaller landowners, towns, and clergy came to be established in Parliament. The wording of the writs of that year was interesting because it used words taken from Justinian's Code: "what touches all should be approved by all." However, even previously during the reign of Henry I, the Commons were called to Parliament, but were not constantly or regularly elected by writ until Henry III.[2] Of course, as we have seen, parliamentarians such as Petyt attempted to show that the origins of the Commons were pre-Conquest and dated from time immemorial, and that this was known to be so during Henry III's reign. In Magna Carta, the barons claimed to be the community of England. At least by the end of the thirteenth century, Parliament was regarded as having full power to bind their communities, and their Acts were regarded as being made by common consent.[3] On the other hand, the legal authority of court rulings only bound parties to the litigation.

The highest court became Parliament, where "doubtful points of law are determined, new remedies for new wrongs created, and justice distributed according to every man's deserts."[4] It might be recalled that the common law courts had no such authority to create new remedies. Also, judges could be called into Parliament to give advice, and their advice could be followed or not. This high court of Parliament was above all other courts, including those held in theory *coram rege*, and it cannot be denied that that court was the king in Parliament, or that the court's sessions were parliaments.[5]

From the earliest period in the history of Parliament, the principle was accepted that the wishes of the majority were decisive.[6] This principle was probably derived from canon law.

Parliament at this time had a fluctuating composition. The addition of representatives from counties and boroughs in time led to a complete separation of the king's council in Parliament from any other council or court. In the fourteenth and fifteenth centuries, the same process of differentiation, occurring with respect to courts of law, also divided Parliament from Council, and Parliament itself into two Houses. The activity of Council became separate, probably before Richard II, when separate records began. By this time, the machinery of government was practically complete, with separate courts of law, a court of chancery, Council, and Parliament.

The rise of Parliament has foundational significance for the organs and sources of law. It involves the final ascertainment of some of the most characteristic features of law from Parliament as a settled body possessing certain powers, the exercise of which tended to grow rapidly and became more definite.

Both Magna Carta and Bracton's *Treatise* make it clear that the council of the nation should be consulted with respect to the passing of the laws. The consultation requirement had been a vague restraint on the crown because the manner and form in which the nation should be consulted was uncertain. There was no clear distinction between legislative and administrative acts. It was growing clearer during Henry III's time, but the increased use of Parliament's legislative power was the cause of the distinction.

At this time, the king's council in Parliament, assisted by judges, was the basis of Parliament. The king and the king's council in Parliament were the body which made laws or ordinances. Consent of the Commons was not yet necessary.[7] The chief justices, as members of Council, still had real input into the making of laws. This fact and the cases indicate that an inquiry into framer intent in passing

94   Parliament

a statute was in order, as the judges knew what the statute was intended to mean because they participated in writing it.[8]

Also, the king and his justices, sometimes with the counsel of the bishops, earls, and barons, could authoritatively interpret a statute after it was made.[9] Canonists had a maxim, restricted somewhat, that interpretation properly belonged to the power that ordained, which alone could authoritatively interpret its own acts; and, civilians were of the same mind. In this way, Henry III decided disputes about the interpretation of Magna Carta, which were published by letters close. Nor was this merely a royalist theory. When Henry III was at the mercy of his barons, they wrote a warning to the Bishop of Durham that the interpretation of laws and customs belonged to the king and the nobles, and none other. Edward I frequently put this principle into practice. The king and his justices published an extra-judicial 'exposition' of the Statute of Gloucester in 1278, and in 1281 the king in Council made a 'correction' in the same statute. The common law courts acknowledged this principle of appealing to the legislator when faced with difficulties of interpretation.[10] The practice or pattern later developed that interpretation would be left to the court. This result came about because of parliamentary history and the concentration of parliamentary activities in politics and legislating made it inconvenient for Parliament to become a permanent organ for the interpretation of statutes, although those who considered the issue admitted to the inherent reasonableness of the principle that the legislator was the best interpreter.[11]

The beginnings of the change in which judges ceased to be equal with other members in Council probably occurred around the commencement of Edward III's reign. In the case of Judge Tresilian, during the time of Richard II, involving questions put to judges concerning Chancellor de la Pole's condemnation, it was clear that judges were mere advisers and were no part of Parliament, and that the declaration of treason belonged to Parliament. On the basis of these opinions, Parliament declared the condemnation of de la Pole erroneous and revocable, and reversed the sentence against him.[12] Smith confirms that judges sat on woolsacks, together with the master of the rolls and secretaries of state, and had no voice, but only sat to answer or advise upon the law when asked, if doubt arose.[13]

Only the king had prerogative powers. The king or Council individually were inferior to the king in Council, and, as we will see, inferior to Parliament. Judges were inferior to both king and Parliament. When judges were a part of Council, they had a share in law-making. The king or the king in Council or Parliament could make law, and in hearing disputes could also make law. But even in antiquity, judges could not decide contrary to or change that law, which required the consent of the Witan. When the judges separated from the Curia, much power and jurisdiction was lost. The common law was limited substantively and procedurally, and subject to parliamentary statutes.

In the following century, Parliament became a distinct body and antagonistic to Council. Common law courts only allowed parliamentary enactments as law. Only direct parliamentary action could change law. The king agreed in 1377 that statutes made in Parliament could only be repealed in Parliament. At Richard II's deposition, he was accused of violating that principle. Henry IV in 1407 and Henry V in 1419 informed the Pope that even statutes condemned by the Church could only be repealed with the assent of the three estates in Parliament.[14] It could no longer be expanded by administrative acts. The discretionary powers of the crown ceased to be exercised through common law courts, though the crown still possessed discretionary powers. This supreme court split into Parliament (legislature) and Council (executive), which tended to more clearly differentiate statute from ordinance.

At this point, the common law attained a commanding position. It could be changed by Act of Parliament alone.[15] In Parliament alone could the decisions of its own courts be pronounced to be erroneous.

During the fourteenth century, Parliament gradually became more than an assembly where the king and his council met the estates of the realm to discuss the state of the nation. It was becoming an essential organ of government, separate from and often antagonistic to the king and his council. For example, the ordinances of 1311 forced on Edward II by the barons required the king to make appointments and certain kinds of decisions – such as war, leaving the country, grants, and coinage – only by the counsel and assent of his barons, and later in Parliament.[16]

In 1349 it was said that the king made laws with assent of the peers and commons, and not through the instrumentality of the peers and commons.[17] The king acted on advice of Council or Parliament, but initiated and framed laws. In so doing, he could act on the information of any considerable body of subjects, such as merchants or the clergy on petition of these classes. As the head of executive authority, he also had the power to make ordinances. While he could, as part of his executive functions, delay or perhaps suspend the operation of law for adequate cases, he could not deliberately repeal that which had become accepted as part of the common law.[18]

Gradually, due to the growing importance of Parliament, statute came to be regarded as an enactment of the king and Parliament. Parliament's action gradually separated those enactments to which it consented from those to which it had not consented, and Parliament gradually asserted a right to initiate legislation and to control the framing of statute. Parliament prevented ordinances by the king on petition of the clergy or merchants from being considered as statutes unless Parliament's approval was received. Petitions of Parliament that were assented to became Acts of Parliament, which were separate from other petitions.[19] The change in the mode of enacting statutes introduced a clear test of what was a statutory enactment.

In the fourteenth and beginning of the fifteenth centuries, the king on the advice of judges and others in council framed and enacted statute on petition of Parliament. As the fourteenth century advanced, the initiation of legislation was gradually made by the Commons, and sometimes the Lords.

Petitions of the Commons outlined grievances and asked for a remedy. When Parliament was not sitting, Council considered these requests, and if it thought legislation necessary, Council would prepare such legislation according to its discretion and publish it as a statute with parliamentary authority. As the Commons grew more powerful, it expressed dissatisfaction with this method. Sometimes the government failed to act on the petition, and sometimes Council legislated along different lines from that which was approved. Henry V promised that nothing would be enacted contrary to the Commons' petition, but even after a statute was passed the crown sometimes assumed the power to alter or suspend it.[20]

The change in procedure from legislation by petition to bill emphasized that Parliament had become a partner with the king in legislating, and that it was acting as a true legislature. Both the House of Lords and the House of Commons acquired an independent corporate character, as is evident from their numerous privileges,

Parliament's Development

successfully asserted and recognized by courts in wide and ample terms. Thus, the High Court of Parliament attained an important place among the many courts, and possessed attributes differentiating it from them.[21]

By the mid-fifteenth century, Parliament's right to control taxation was undisputed. Previously, the 1297 Great Confirmation of Magna Carta had forbidden the king from levying an aid (taxing) without the consent of the council.

Parliament became further developed during the sixteenth century. Henry VIII knew that he must work with Parliament to raise supplies. Important measures instituting the Reformation were passed by Parliament between 1529 and 1536.

Throughout this period, crown and Council exercised a large control over Parliament. Council was to deliberate and propose, and Parliament to discuss. Permanent government was by the king and Council. They determined policy, and initiated all important legislation. The infrequency and shortness of parliaments made it impossible to control the executive and prevented the growth of any organized opposition. Towards the end of Elizabeth's reign, the Commons began to act contrary to the limits of speech she wanted, such as debating monopolies despite her efforts to stop them.

All writers of this era, such as Smith, Lambard, Crompton, and Coke, as well as courts, speak of Parliament as the highest and most authentic court.[22] For example, Smith states that Parliament is the "highest and most authentic court of England ... and no other means available to make any new forfeiture of life, member, or lands where there was no law ordained for it before" and speaks of Parliament as the "most high and absolute power of the realm."[23] Lambard states:

> It hath also jurisdiction which have need of helpe, and for which there is no helpe by any Law, already in force; And whereas the erronious Judgements of any other Courts must be reversed by a higher authority; this Court doth not only reverse the errors of the Kings Bench, which is superiour to all the other; but it may also amend the errors committed in the Parliament itselfe, if any such shall at any time appeare.[24]

Finch, a highly regarded legal mind of the period, states:

The Parliament is a Court of the King, Nobility and Commons assembled, Having an absolute power in all causes. As to make Lawes, to adjudge matters in Law, to trie causes of life and death; to reverse errors in the Kings Bench, especially where any common mischiefe is, that by the ordinarie course of Law there is no meanes to remedie: this is the proper Court for it. And all their Decrees are as Judgements. And if the Parliament it selfe doe erre (as it may) it can no where be reversed but in Parliament.[25]

Furthermore, as stated in the *Case of Captain John Streater* (1653),[26] involving a parliamentary order imprisoning Streater, the judges asserted the inability of any lower court to question what Parliament had done. To the objection that Parliament did not have the power to make laws, Roll C.J. replied that Parliament had legislative power and may alter and order as it pleased, and may make new laws. To the objection that the order was not read three times, it was replied that the judges could not question it.

A large part of government was carried on by courts acting under judicial forms. Thus, the idea of all governing bodies having the nature of a court was a natural idea to those discussing public law. There are several reasons why Parliament continued to be called a court.[27] However, too much stress should not be placed on this fact.[28] Also incorrect is the claim that Parliament as a court was understood to be an institution in which judges determined pre-existing legal rights and duties. Particularly prior to the differentiation within government, there was an overlap of functions, and even courts with primarily adjudicative functions had legislative or administrative functions as well. Even during Henry VI's reign, lawyers were discovering that conceptions borrowed from the law with respect to the jurisdiction of courts could not easily be applied to taxation and legislation, which after 1327 were becoming the most important functions of Parliament; whereas, the judicial functions diminished in importance. As with local government, Parliament's non-judicial functions rapidly developed. Parliament was as much comparable to Council as to a court.[29] Thus, the old institution of Parliament was adapted to meet the requirements of the modern state, and developed to become a true legislative assembly. Finally, Parliament had come to be regarded as a representative political assembly, with attributes and powers far exceeding those of an ordinary court and possessing omnicompetence. Parliament's exercise of a fusion of judicial and legislative powers was supreme. It was not limited to enforcing immutable pre-existing law.[30]

The change in the mode of enacting statutes at the end of this period introduces a clear test for the statutory quality of an enactment as distinct from an ordinance. In the fourteenth and beginning of the fifteenth centuries, the king on the advice of judges and others in council framed and enacted statutes on petition of Parliament. As the fourteenth century advanced, the initiation of legislation gradually passed from the crown to the Commons and sometimes the Lords. Allowing the king to frame the law was found to be inconvenient. Parliament effectively asserted its position through the change in the mode of enacting statutes, which became usual during the time of Henry VI.[31] The practice of legislating by bill came to substitute for the practice of legislating by petition; this was an important component of Parliament's transformation into a true legislative assembly. If legislation took the form of a petition to the king, it did not differ materially from petitions resulting in judicial decree. The bills of this period did not involve petitions, and as they required consent of both Houses, their passage emphasized Parliament as a partner in legislating.

By 1365, it was recognized that as Parliament represented the whole kingdom, its law presumed that all were privy and knew it, even if it was not proclaimed in the counties or published.[32] This notion confirmed ideas that Parliament's authority was superior to any judge, and that its decisions embodied the consent and combined wisdom of the community. Now Parliament stood as representative of the kingdom, consisting of two corporate bodies with equal rights, which was the firm foundation for equal positions, or, in money matters, a preponderant position of the Commons in legislation and policy.[33]

By the end of the sixteenth century, the English Parliament was recognized as the highest and most authentic court of England.[34] Indeed, the agreement that Parliament could do anything except that which was impossible was recognized in many ways, including in the Act of Dispensations, 1534, proclaiming Parliament as the most high court with full power and authority. Under Coke's leadership, the common lawyers were claiming that the common law administered in their court was supreme law, to which even crown prerogative was subject. Parliament was recognized as the supreme legislative and taxing authority in the state, with adequate procedure and privileges.

From the early fourteenth century, it was maintained that only in Parliament could there be any legislation, or any alteration of the common law or statute. Parliamentary statutes could not be repealed without its consent. The Statute of York (1322) was passed in order to repeal a set of 'ordinances' made by a group of barons in 1311 for the purpose of dominating the crown. That statute made the declaration that matters relating to the estate of the king and country must be agreed upon by the prelates, earls, barons, and commons in Parliament. It is often considered to be the first express recognition of Parliament as a legislative assembly. From the statute of 1322, it was steadily maintained that legislative power was in the whole Parliament alone.[35] This view united both Houses with common law courts and judges. One result of Edward II's reign was the established practice of regarding a parliament which contained representatives of the commons as a true parliament.[36] During the fourteenth century, Parliament's composition became more definite, and it gradually became the ultimate court in the land, the national legislature, and the representative body of the nation.

Smith spoke of Parliament as the most high and absolute power of the English realm. The king is present, as are the nobility, gentry, and yeomanry. The king speaks for the highest, the barons for the nobility and higher; knights, esquires, gentlemen and commons for the lower; and bishops for the clergy. They consult and deliberate together. It is the consent of all as all are deemed present in person or by representative, it is firm and stable, and taken for law.[37]

By the later fifteenth century, legislative acts with Parliament's authority were distinct from those without it. The distinction between statutes as opposed to ordinances or proclamations was made clear. Thus, subordinate power included the law-making power of the king (prerogative), and also the by-laws of the older communities, including parishes, which performed governmental functions. These were subordinate to statute or common law. The limits of the king's vague prerogative power remained unresolved for a long time.

One limitation from the end of the thirteenth century was that a law made by Parliament could only be changed by the same authority. Law could no longer be expanded by administrative acts. Crown discretionary powers ceased to be exercised through common law courts, however the crown still possessed them.

At the end of the medieval period, Parliament had large powers over legislation and finance. Through its control over finance, it obtained a wide ability to criticize and control the conduct of the executive, and by impeachment to try and punish royal officials who broke the law.

After the deposition of Richard II, Parliament's exercise of powers increased, and it exercised constant control over the composition of Council and its conduct of government.

Role of Common Lawyers

As Parliament was emerging during the fourteenth and fifteenth centuries, an alliance between Parliament and common lawyers came about. Common lawyers helped to develop the capacity of the Commons to control government, thereby enabling the Commons to become an integral part of government. Lawyers recognized Parliament as the highest court the king had, which could grant relief not obtainable anywhere else, exercising powers which the king or any other body in the state could exercise, and in which the errors of their own courts could be redressed.[38]

SIXTEENTH-CENTURY REFORMATION AND RECEPTION OF ROMAN IDEAS

England came under some of the same legal, political, and religious influences as the rest of Western Christendom. Of particular importance was the legal renaissance of the twelfth and thirteenth centuries, which had substantial effects on the growth of centralized government and of a common law capable of expanding with changing society. The other important wave of Continental influence occurred during the sixteenth century's Renaissance, Reformation, and reception of Roman law. These influences not only affected the law and government of England, but they had a profound effect in changing public opinion. Holdsworth argues that the achievements of the strong kings of the twelfth and thirteenth centuries, and of the Tudors in the sixteenth century, enabled the assimilation of enough Continental ideas of law and government to overcome disorder and

102 Parliament

to make England a modern territorial state, without losing its medieval past, thus allowing for a predominantly native and continuous development.[39] When the Tudors restored order, a new order of government was not needed. The result of the Renaissance and Reformation was that the territorial state became in theory supreme. Part of the reason was the denominational split in Christianity, as well as new theories of sovereignty, contract, and government, but it would be an exaggeration to say that Christianity did not have a significant influence.[40] Now, the state had to realize that supremacy. Violence was conspicuous in medieval times. Feudalism was the compromise which subjected armed force to the rule of law, and increasingly the latter was winning.

English law in the sixteenth century was affected by the revival of Roman law. Unlike in other countries, in England there was both a suppression of canon law and some depression of the study of civil law. The serious limitations of medieval common law were its rigid technical rules and cumbersome procedure. The problem was partially remedied by new courts and councils which created new bodies of law, supplementing or rivalling the common law. It was inevitable that these new bodies of law were influenced by Reception, which administered the civil law as on the Continent.[41] Common lawyers and judges tried to counteract the new courts' wholesale reception of the principles of civil law. This influence led to an extension of common law. Continental principles made an important and lasting influence on English law, although the new did not supersede the old. During the sixteenth century, Roman influence helped make English law sufficient for the needs of a modern state.

To maintain order, a strong and efficient central government had to be built. The chief organs of government were the Council and its various branches: Star Chamber, Chancery, and Court of Requests. This body was beginning to exercise its powers to a greater degree.

At the close of the Middle Ages, the functions of government were already to some extent specialized, including with respect to judicial power. The common law courts were independent of Council, and other parts of judicial power vested in Admiralty, Chancery, and the Court of Requests. Parliament controlled tax and legislation.

Thus, Council tended to become primarily an executive and administrative body. It did not cease to exercise other powers, however, and it had wide judicial powers whenever it saw fit to use them.

There was a tendency to delegate its wide judicial powers to Star Chamber. Council and Star Chamber were composed of practically the same officials. It was on this identity that the legality of the wide and indefinite powers of Star Chamber was based. This fact supports the conclusion that the court's power comes from delegation by the king, or legislation, as does the authority of other state power holders. Smith argues that the prince was "the life, head and authority of all things done in the realm of England," and Council was the chief agency for carrying out his will.[42]

The Reformation

Prior to the Reformation, Parliament was generally recognized as being supreme on all matters except spiritual affairs. The State and Church were separate sovereign entities, each supreme within its own sphere, and the relations between them akin to the parliamentary inability to legislate over foreign sovereignties.

For example, the Pope held jurisdiction on matters of religion and the Church throughout Christendom, and had authority to punish temporal rulers violating divine law by excommunication and even deposition. During the "Investiture Contest" the Church was concerned about the rapid rise of powerful monarchies which were apt to use the Church for their political ends. William compelled cathedrals to elect his nominees as bishops and he delivered to them the emblems of spiritual and temporal authority. Gregory VII prohibited lay investiture by 1075, holding that the Church was independent of the State, and that no temporal ruler could confer ecclesiastical authority. This episode led to compromise in 1107. Plucknett argues that the conflict had important results on the political theory of the state, including the nature of kingship, the limits that ought to be put on the power of temporal rulers, and criticism of the state in terms of the highest ideals of government which then existed – the universal Church.[43] Another conflict between Innocent III and John erupted when the former refused the king's candidate for archbishop, and substituted his own and better choice, Stephen Langton. John confiscated Church property in response. It was a political conflict of principle, in which John saw the bishops as higher civil servants and the Church as subservient. Langton supported the separate spheres of Church and State, attacked John's shifty conduct, and proclaimed that John's vassals were not bound to him after he had broken faith with the King of Kings (and the high principles of law to which all human law should conform). John then submitted to Rome and did homage to the Pope's legate. Archbishop Langton then undertook to require the king to make amends, and produced Henry I's Charter as the basis of what was normal and just, adding a list of more recent grievances. In 1215, John put his seal to the Great Charter.

With the Reformation, supreme authority over the English Church was transferred by force from Pope to king through the legislation of the Reformation Parliament (1529–36). That Parliament terminated the immunity of the spiritual realm from statute, and in so doing overrode the custom of the realm.[44] With the Reformation Parliament, Henry VIII worked out the constitution of a national church with him at the head. For example, the Act of Restraint of Appeals, 1523, declared England to be an Empire whose king possessed full and plenary jurisdiction in all cases, secular and spiritual, and prohibited appeals to Rome. The king became the head of the Church. Only then could the king in Parliament be called truly omnicompetent in a manner omnipotent. However, that description is probably best reserved until the Revolution, when Parliament's power over all aspects of royal prerogative and succession was undisputably determined. There was then an enormous consolidation of state legislative power. Ironically, the king's despoiling of Church lands contributed to and hastened the monarchy's own decline in relative power to becoming a figurehead *vis-à-vis* Parliament, in that the dissolution of the monasteries and the resulting redistribution of assets contributed, together with other economic changes, to making the freeholders more powerful.[45]

At the beginning of the sixteenth century, Parliament had not yet acquired full legislative sovereignty. This status was not because of the medieval view that human laws were subordinate to God's or Nature's law. In the absence of an institutional means of enforcing these superior laws, there is no difference between that belief and the modern conviction that Parliament is morally bound to act justly.[46] The reason, rather, was the existence of a rival institution in the form of the Pope claiming independent and superior authority to enforce God's law, at least over exclusively spiritual matters.

The English Reformation resulted in an enormous consolidation of state legislative power. It settled by force, whether illegally or legally, that ecclesiastical jurisdiction was under the king's power. Under Henry VIII, England's position towards the Reformation was settled. The Church was 'reformed' and made an integral part of the state, thus strengthening the central government. This was also a period of prerogative rule.

Henry VIII knew he could use the growing feeling against ecclesiastical jurisdiction and that of the Pope. He asserted his power over the clergy. Henry's threat of trial and punishment for premunire (recognizing a foreign jurisdiction inconsistent with the crown) resulted in the clergy's submission to Henry's demand for the Church to surrender its legislative independence. All future ecclesiastical legislation was subject to royal veto and revision, which led to further statutes abolishing the Pope's jurisdiction in England. The divorce episode only determined the way it would go, and since Henry could not get it at Rome, it had to be in England and the authority of the Pope eliminated. Ironically, the English Church was still the historic Catholic Church, but changed along Henry's lines. The Pope's authority was replaced by the supremacy of the king. The destruction of the monasteries followed. This episode itself demonstrates Parliament's freedom from limitations by overriding title to property, which was universally regarded as one of the most precious and inviolable of all the rights subjects possessed.

At this point, both the parliamentary and royalist sides agreed that no other human institution could authoritatively judge any statute invalid. The courts enforced the most radical Reformation statutes without questioning their legal validity. The judges conceded this authority claimed by the king in Parliament, notwithstanding its violation of the most fundamental of rights – property rights – and even of Magna Carta itself. The statutes passed were regarded as binding until formally repealed. Even Mary, believing the statutes contrary to divine law, accepted legal advice that they had to be repealed nonetheless.[47] Also, Elizabeth acted on legal advice that only limited changes to the recently restored Catholic Mass could legally be made without Parliament's consent. Thus, she secured statutes reinstating royal supremacy over the Church, and Protestant doctrines and observances.

Parliament was now supreme. Henry VIII recognized that law could be changed by Parliament alone, and thus that England was a constitutional monarchy.[48] Elton notes that supreme law-

106   Parliament

making power was by now vested in the king in Parliament.[49] While Goldsworthy concludes that Parliament was now supreme, following or extending the view of those such as Elton, he sees the unresolved issue being the nature of Parliament and its authority. That is, was legislation made by the king alone, which he chose to exercise only in Parliament, or by a composite institution – the king in Parliament? As we will see later, the constitutional disputes of the sixteenth century were not settled until 1688. The unresolved issue was whether the king or Parliament was the sovereign lawmaker. The battle was between royal prerogative on one side and parliamentary legislation and the common law on the other. Both sides agreed that no other human institution could authoritatively judge any statute invalid.

PARLIAMENTARY CONTROL OVER COURTS AND COURT DECISIONS

Parliament's superiority of status and power over courts is further illustrated by its ability to consider and review court decisions. Through legislation, Parliament also has the ability to modify or annul court decisions, to state that a court's decision does not accurately reflect the law, and to declare the law. Therefore, there is not only no evidence to support the proposition that it is improper for Parliament to consider or override judicial decisions; the opposite is true.

In the early seventeenth century, the committee system was extended and important developments occurred. There was clear precedent for standing committees on courts of justice. Charles complained that the growth of the committee system made criticism by the Commons more effective and searching, thus allowing them to extend their privileges by standing committees. He specifically complained that they sent for and examined officials, including judicial ones, such as the barons of Exchequer and some judges. He complained that the enquiries produced an unsufferable disturbance and scandal of justice and government.

The connection between King's Bench and Council lasted to the end of the fourteenth century. Parties were routinely summoned to appear before the whole Council, and errors were redressed by King's Bench and by Council.[50] All proceedings of lower courts at all stages were within Council's cognizance.[51]

Council and Parliament could interfere with proceedings of Common Pleas and King's Bench.[52] Both Council and Parliament were regarded as courts. Power was largely undifferentiated. Both possessed wide judicial powers. As the separation of the organs was occurring, particularly the separation of Council from Parliament, common lawyers began to think that errors in King's Bench ought to be corrected in Parliament, not Council.[53] Thus, it was accepted not only that King's Bench decisions could be reviewed and corrected (that it was not the final word on the law), but that it ought to be done in Parliament and not Council. After a 1366 decision,[54] the jurisdiction to amend errors of common law courts was left to Parliament.[55] While such jurisdiction was said to be in Parliament, it was generally regarded as vested in the Lords, and never judicially questioned. However, Hale,[56] Coke,[57] and Holt[58] assert that the right of the Commons to share in the judicial powers of the Lords was a disused but a subsisting right.[59] Holdsworth believes the Commons never seriously claimed to share the judicial powers of the Lords.[60]

Parliament had not ceased to exercise a number of judicial powers that had belonged to it since the time when the king in his council in Parliament was regarded as an enlarged meeting of the old undifferentiated Curia. As the Lords was more immediately connected with this aspect of Parliament, it came to exercise these powers to review the decisions of common law courts. It was thought the power of finally declaring law should be entrusted to the parliamentary body which made law, and not to an executive Council concerned mainly with the application and enforcement of law.[61]

Parliament could also control common law courts through legislation. From the early fourteenth century, it was maintained that only in Parliament could there be any legislation, or any alteration of the common law or statute law. From a 1322 statute, it was steadily maintained that legislative power was in the whole Parliament alone.

In the fourteenth and fifteenth centuries, as the procedure of common law courts grew more elaborate and unreasonable, statutes about procedure became more numerous. Parliamentary criticism and amendment of the common law tended to modify its technicality and keep it in touch with the realities of life.[62] Legislation often solved problems judges were unable to solve, and legislatures improved the state of the law. Early examples include the Statute of

Westminster II, statutes related to Uses, and statutes that dealt with the problem of demonstrating fraudulent intent. Following the Black Death, lords who could not find servile labour either leased lands to free labourers or tacitly conceded to their peasants the benefits of ownership in their holdings. For a long time, the common law refused to recognize these property rights being acquired in custom, and therefore these tenants or copyholders had to go to courts of equity to enforce their rights. In fact, it could be said that the courts of common law, along with the manorial courts, played an important role in inventing the dogma that the freehold in a villein's lands was in the lord. This legal invention lowered the inhabitants of the manor, who were originally free, to the position of serfs. Another example is that with respect to jury trials in libel prosecutions, judicial opinion rejected the political ideals and opinion of the time. Thus, in 1792, the legislature overruled the courts after explicitly considering judicial decision. Legislation provided that juries had the right to give a general verdict; that is, to decide on the fact of publication, its truth, and whether publication had the meaning alleged, and the judge could not direct a guilty finding merely on proof of publication. Such legislation also helped put the right of liberty of discussion on its modern basis. This Act was in declaratory form, in order to convey the idea that the law the courts pronounced ought to have been made otherwise.

As we have seen, statute provided for the relative status of courts, and established to which courts appeals could be made; for example, it indicated that appeals from King's Bench went to Exchequer Chamber. In 1830, statute deprived King's Bench of the jurisdiction to amend errors of Common Pleas.

4

The Great Rebellion and Revolution of 1688

The Great Rebellion and Revolution of 1688 completed the main foundations of the law of the constitution and the system of government. The end of this period legally established parliamentary sovereignty, and the supremacy of the law. These foundations are directly relevant to the systems of government of the former Dominions. In order to understand precisely the meaning and content of those foundations comprising the British system of government, we must know what the actors or law-makers involved intended to establish as their intention largely determines what they actually established. In order to understand their intention, we must examine the new theory of sovereignty, the historical background, the ideas of the competing parties, and the events themselves.

THE NEW THEORY OF SOVEREIGNTY

Rival theories of state were being developed at the end of Elizabeth I's reign. The parliament/common law theory was based on the supremacy of Parliament and the common law, which competed against the theory of the Council, based on royal prerogative, and against the views of those wanting strict compliance with Church of England rites. Some commentators believe that until then, English lawyers could state no certain law regarding the position of the king, and English political philosophers were unable to grasp Bodin's theory of sovereignty.[1]

The legal renaissance of the thirteenth century tended to give the king a higher position than that of a mere feudal lord. When the theory of the Holy Roman Empire was becoming unpractical, there was a tendency during the fourteenth and fifteenth centuries to put the king into the place of the emperor over his dominions. The idea arose that a state recognizing no superior was an imperium. Royal power grew in the sixteenth century, and central government was strengthened. Ideas arising from the revival of classical studies were unencumbered by the medieval view that kingship involved duties and rights. The Reformation brought changed ideas of Church-State relations. The result was that the king as representative of the State began to clothe himself in the divinity attributed to the Church in medieval times, and claimed accountability only to God.[2] These ideas struggled with the older theories, which were not lost, but were adapted to the new territorial state and influenced modern political thought.

The new omnipotent state needed a new political theory to explain it. Bodin's theory of sovereignty and its application to the king became important. It was not just a new theory of the state; it was a new theory of sovereignty, in which the sovereignty of its ruler was the essence of the state. The existence of the sovereign ruler distinguished the state from other associations.[3] The sovereign could be a person or a body. There was also the idea that sovereignty must be absolute, and could not be the fettered by merely human laws (as law depended on his willingness), by coronation oaths, or by any conditions.[4] The sovereign alone could make and repeal laws, and impose and remit taxes. The subjects could have no legal rights against the sovereign, nor the sovereign legal duties to them.

Holdsworth says Bodin is a little inconsistent in admitting such rights might exist, as the sovereign was bound by rules of morality and religion (this phrase is perhaps misquoted, as Bodin states "natural and Divine law"), but was accountable for breach to God alone.[5] As we have seen and will continue to see, any such inconsistency is more apparent than real.

This theory answers the extent of state powers, and the nature and binding force of law. Law was no longer a rule of conduct. Law was the command of the sovereign. Customary law was only law as long as the sovereign recognized it and allowed it to exist.[6] The old conception of a state made up of a head and members, existing to execute justice and maintain truth, was substituted by the idea that the state's existence was embodied in the sovereign to carry out the sovereign's will based on the force the sovereign could command.

The expression of these higher claims in England was the restoration of the idea that subjects had certain moral or natural rights

Other theories, political and religious, arose in opposition to Bodin's, as many feared this gift of unfettered and unlimited powers to the state ruler would be fatal to liberty. These opposing theories were based on both historical and analytical grounds, developed particularly by Roman Catholics and, later, Calvinists, denying the divinity claimed by the state and asserting the higher claims of their respective churches. Indeed, from the beginning of Christian history, the assertion of Christ's lordship over the world and over history implicitly recognized that people should not submit their personal freedom in an absolute manner to any earthly power, but only to God and Jesus – Caesar was not "the Lord."[7] There were important precedents of the Roman Catholic Church upholding these limits to state authority, which achieved a kind of check and balance on arbitrary authority. For example, the Holy Roman emperor Henry IV (1050–1106) was excommunicated by Pope Gregory VIII for insisting that as he was God's divinely appointed ruler, he could appoint bishops. The mighty ruler had to humble himself. He was forgiven and readmitted to the Church. Pope Gregory drew on Manegold's arguments that a king's office was by consent for the definite purpose of government, based on contract with the people. If the king broke his *pactum*, the people were set free from that tyranny or subjugation.[8]

The expression of these higher claims in England was the restoration of the idea that subjects had certain moral or natural rights (based on the supremacy of the Church or on a theory of tacit contract) of which they could not be deprived by state power, and that a breach of those rights would justify resistance. For example, the Jesuit view, later taken up by the reformed churches, was that man was naturally endowed and born with freedom from all subjection, and was at liberty to choose a form of government. The power which any one man had over others was at first bestowed according to the discretion of the multitude. Indeed, it is sometimes thought that notions of ancient liberty and lawfulness of resistance had come into England through the influence of clerics such as Langton. The historical school sought the restoration of institutions which could check the king's power, such as the king not being able to legislate without the consent of his estates. Therefore, these theories stated that the command of the sovereign was not necessarily binding law; there were limits. For the former, his command must not infringe natural or moral rights which state law could not override, and for the latter, the king could not legislate without consent of his estates.

The territorial state made the problem of sovereignty the political problem of the century. It tended to make the medieval ideal of securing the supremacy of law decline, such that it was no longer an end in itself. The debate was about the balance of power or the location of sovereign power in the state, which was argued on the basis of the supremacy of a version of divine or human law. This change gave rise to further changes. The analysis of sovereignty tends to separate morals from law, and draws lines between moral and legal right. Insistence on the legal supremacy of the sovereign tends to banish ethical ideals from political reasoning. Rather, the considerations that came to the forefront were utility or expediency, and making the dominant aim of politics the securing of the greatest material advantage.[9]

The position of the English king was different because, as a result of the development of English institutions, the whole authority of the state was not conferred on the king. Particularly relevant was the growth of Parliament's powers and privileges, which gave salience to the medieval ideas of supremacy of law, limited prerogative powers, and the position of common law. Therefore, the king was not the sovereign power as Bodin understood it. Parliament was or became that sovereign body.

Even Henry VIII respected the powers and privileges of Parliament. In *Ferrer's Case*, the king's powers when acting within Parliament were recognized to be far larger than when acting outside it. These powers of Parliament were recognized by all writers of the constitution during that period. The Tudors respected the law, even if they occasionally perverted it. For arbitrary acts, they always endeavored to obtain legal sanction. King and Council frequently took the opinion of judges and their law officers, implicitly admitting their acts should be governed by law. The supremacy of law, stating that the king had no prerogative but what the law allowed, was the view of the courts and all the leading lawyers, statesmen, and publicists of the Tudor period.[10] The correctness of the *Case of Proclamations* was not generally doubted. The rules followed directly from Parliament's legislative supremacy, which was by then fully established.

Thus, the idea arose that there was a distinction between the natural and politic capacities of the king. This distinction was supplemented by the deduction from it of another distinction, namely, between prerogatives inseparable from the person of the king (that thus could not be granted to another person, such as the appointment of justices of the peace, pardon, and dispensation), and separable prerogatives that could be conferred on others.

The king's prerogative was subject to law, but there was a wide sphere within which the king could act as he pleased. It was absolute, not in the sense of free from legal restraint, but free discretion, the exercise of which could not be called into question by any legal process, nor in a law court. Otherwise, the extent of prerogative and mode of use were subject to certain legal limitations, which the law courts must interpret.

Therefore, the king was not the sovereign power as Bodin understood it. Parliament was or became that sovereign body.

Holdsworth argues that during the Tudor period, no one could say where sovereign power lay, nor was it directly grasped until conflict made it necessary to determine who could, in the last resort, enforce one's will. He refers to a debate about the views of Smith.[11] Pollock states that Smith intended to assert that the king in Parliament was the sovereign power. Alston disagrees. He claims that Smith, in declaring Parliament to be the most high and absolute power of the realm (at least, in time of peace), was not considering the question of sovereignty in the modern sense, nor statements bearing on the great controversy of the next century. The king had the most power when at the head of his army, or when presiding over Parliament. Figgis thinks Smith's standpoint was nearer to Bracton's than Bodin's. Gook, in considering the development of English institutions in the sixteenth century and the legal doctrines underlying them, agrees with Alston, but does not think Smith thought of Parliament as a judicial court, on this point agreeing with Pollock. Holdsworth goes on to characterize Smith correctly when stating that Smith asserts that the king with Parliament could exercise supreme authority in the state. Indeed, after listing a number of Parliament's powers, Smith goes on to state: "[T]o be short, all that ever the people of Rome might do either in *Centuriatis comitijs* or *tributis*, the same may be doone by the parliament of Englande,

114   Parliament

which representeth and hath the power of the whole realme both the head and the bodie."[12]

On the other hand, Holdsworth's assumption is inaccurate that the sovereignty of any particular country can only be determined through conflict, when people are driven to consider the precise extent of the ruler's power, or whether it is shared by any other person or body within the state. The difficulty stems from an inadequate conceptualization of sovereignty. Any state government has a content, that is a particular system of government in existence. To say the actual sovereign or system of government does not exist until it is consciously decided by a great conflict is incorrect analytically and historically. Even in great conflicts, the majority of people may not be directly involved in making such choices, or their choices may not be respected – the history of marxism and communism provides ample illustration of such a proposition. Another difficulty in Holdsworth's argument is linking habitual obedience with people considering the precise extent of the ruler's power. Analytically, every system of government, at any time, can be described. This is so whether or not the actual sovereign, in Bodin's sense of the word, is locatable. The distribution of sovereign powers within the state is identifiable, even if there may be difficulty in precisely stating the extent of powers and their allocation. This issue will present itself whether or not there has been a great conflict. It may even be true that at a given time, it may be difficult to describe the system of government, for example in situations in which none is firmly established. Thus, his view does not match legal reality. Furthermore, his view is also inaccurate in a practical sense. Revolution and conflict may not clarify the sovereign in the system of government in existence, but may overthrow it and call forth another sovereign or system of government.

The fact that Parliament might be able to exercise supreme authority in the state, which was true after the Reformation, and undoubtedly by 1688, does not mean that no other bodies could legally exercise state functions, even law-making ones.

COMPETING THEORIES OF THE STATE'S SOVEREIGN

A determining factor in accurately describing the British system of government is that throughout this period it was always believed or assumed that there was a sovereign. All agreed that the king's authority was highest in Parliament and controllable by none.

The growing independence of Parliament raised the question of the relation of the crown to Parliament, which in turn raised the most fundamental question of the seventeenth century – the location of sovereign power in the constitution. Eventually, the contest came down to the split in the nation between two parties: on one side, the parliamentary party, common lawyers, and Puritans, against prerogative supporters, those supporting rival courts, and those wanting strict compliance with the rites and ceremonies of the English Church. The main political question was the position of royal prerogative and whether or not it was the sovereign power in the state. Relevant thereto was the issue of whether the king or the king in Parliament made law. All agreed that the king's authority was highest in Parliament and controllable by none.

Royalist Theories of the State

The Reformation settlement was founded on royal supremacy. Accordingly, there was a leaning in favour of the divine right of kings. Under this theory, authority was transferred from Pope to king, and theories of blind obedience to the king and non-resistance arose, which gave a theological colour to mystical legal doctrines about prerogative. Bodin's doctrine of sovereignty was used to support a theory of royal absolutism.

The divine right of kings stated that the king was the supreme ruler and supreme judge; was above the law; could make, mitigate, or suspend laws; and, was answerable for his acts to God alone. Henry VIII declared this proposition and Tyndale agreed. The *collectaea satis copisosa* was a collection of biblical passages, precedents, and other historical evidence compiled to justify royal supremacy. Some royalists maintained that royal prerogative was based on immemorial custom.

The language of the authorities was uncertain and conflicting. In some of the more recent precedents, the language used about the king and his inseparable and absolute prerogatives seemed to support James. Other precedents and the powers and privileges of Parliament seemed to prove definite limitations on the king's prerogative.[13]

116 Parliament

James' theory was adapted to support his position that he claimed as king to be the predominant power, without being wholly contrary to English public law principles. The new royalist theory focused on the distinction between absolute and ordinary or private kingly prerogatives. He claimed an overriding absolute prerogative to deal with matters of state; that is, applied to the general benefit of the people and not guided by rules of common law.[14] The king did not obtain this prerogative by law, but immediately from God, and this sovereign power could not be questioned or subject to legal challenge.[15] The king was subject only to the directive, not coercive, force of law. All laws owed their original and continued existence to absolute crown prerogative, including the common law. The ordinary power was said to be for particular subjects, exercised by equity and justice in ordinary courts to aid the king in keeping his voluntary undertaking to comply with law in ordinary cases ('just' prerogative), which was called common law, and these laws could not be changed without Parliament. In this way, James claimed to settle conflicts of jurisdiction between courts; to stop pending cases in which he was interested; to issue proclamations; to stop discussions in Parliament on matters he considered outside its jurisdiction; and, to arrest persons dangerous to the government. The general conduct of government belonged to the king, although he could not pass a statute or tax without Parliament's consent. Thus, even the royalist theory did not establish the king as sovereign, but it would have made him the predominant partner in the state. All royalists agreed that if the two Houses assented to the king's exercise of law-making, it could not be legally challenged. They agreed that the king stood in highest estate in Parliament. Given the royalist understanding of the relation between king and judges, they could not have held the view that the king's laws could be held void by those he appointed to administer them. If the exercise of his other absolute prerogatives was a matter of his discretion, then all the more so was his exercise of the power to make laws with the consent of Parliament.

As the conflict between king and Parliament grew under Charles I, prerogative supporters had to claim that the king was the sovereign power. Serious encroachments were made on Parliament's power with dissolutions of Parliament; there was a claim that ministers were not amenable to law for acts done under the king's authority; the liability of MPs' conduct in the Houses before the ordinary

The Great Rebellion and Revolution of 1688 117

courts was asserted; and, the prerogative supporters attempted to use proclamations enforced by Star Chamber as a substitute for statute, and even resorted to taxation by devices to raise money, such as 'ship money.' Ship money was defended on the basis that in time of necessity, of which the king was the sole determiner, he could tax or do as he pleased. In *Hampden's Case*,[16] the court upheld this claim, and the logical consequences of the theory of prerogative were attained. In effect, some judges declared the king to be the sovereign power in the constitution, and even declared that the king could not be divested of his sovereign power even by an act of legislature.[17] Berkeley J. stated that the king did not need parliamentary consent under law. He relied on the maxims that the king was trusted with the state of the commonwealth, and the king could do no wrong. These maxims were said to ground the *jura summa majestatis* in which only the king, and not the high court of Parliament without his leave, may be involved in many matters, including the common prerogative in cases of necessity over his subjects for the defence of the commonwealth. Otherwise, the king's majesty having majestical right and the power of a free monarch would be lacking.[18] Neither James I nor Charles I observed the limitations of prerogative set out in the *Case of Proclamations*. Therefore, royalists saw that the king had many prerogatives, which through their extension could secure sovereignty, and render parliamentary control nugatory or enable the king to dispense with Parliament.

Charles I was determined to rule without Parliament. To do so, he needed to acquire a power over direct taxation, which he attempted to do by extending *Bates's Case* (prerogative over foreign trade, prerogative over trade, and the claim that the power over impositions belongs to kings to maintain their crown and dignity), and by trying to use the prerogative over national defence.

In terms of individual liberty, even after the Petition of Right, the king's ability to commit and keep a person in prison was large so long as he had a court such as Star Chamber to enforce his commands. In this way, he disregarded the judges and evaded the Petition of Right. The cases of Strode, Long, Seldon, and others committed to prison by Star Chamber for the part they took in the riots after the dissolution of Parliament in 1629 amply demonstrate the point. The accused persons successfully obtained bail in the common law courts. However, Charles managed to keep them in prison longer

118 Parliament

by not allowing them to be produced in court when the judges were ready to give their decision. Then, to avoid defeat in the courts, he allowed them bail, but insisted on security for future good behaviour.

Accordingly, at this time, the crown's contentions prevailed in the courts. The courts held that the king had large powers to imprison dangerous persons,[19] to regulate trade,[20] and to act as he pleased to secure the safety of the country.[21] The last two powers could be used to raise revenue. These courts ignored the *Case of Proclamations* and extended the proclamation power to support the system of prerogative rule.

The hypothetical case of abuse or tyranny did not undermine sovereign power under either the royalist or parliamentary theories. There was no superior jurisdiction, thus no legal remedy. As absolute security was impossible, some person or body must be the trusted authority in the end, and both camps held their trust differently.

Parliament's View

The parliamentary party sought the modification of prerogative, leaving Parliament free to exercise the powers it had won. It also sought to preserve and extend individual liberty, and to reform administrative abuses. It resisted change toward the new modern ideas of 'progress' represented by the royalists, who saw a sovereign king, backed by an army and trained civil service, as the most effective means to achieve important policy goals, such as to counter lawlessness, develop trade, and encourage learning, all of which royalists thought made for rapid progress and for an ordered civilization. Royalists thought that when the law was doubtful, it should be interpreted in accordance with modern needs. Incidentally and ironically, this approach can and often does lead to backward thinking. It is an interpretive approach that contemporary Canadian courts take in Constitutional decisions. Ironically, also, in the modern period, as in other times, it is the self-regarding progressive thinkers that are backward, and conservatives that are the real 'progressive' thinkers. Parliamentarians drew their inspiration from the medieval past and the central political idea of the medieval rule of law.

Parliament's ideas were strong where the crown was weak. It stood for individual liberty, control over tax and legislation, and the supremacy of law. It had the support of most common lawyers, country gentleman (which included justices of the peace), and the mercantile classes, and represented the ideals of the nation. It was weaker where the crown was strong because it was slow to understand the nature of the sovereignty question, and some have argued unable to suggest a workable solution, at least at first.[22]

Whitelocke was first to elaborate a complete theory complementary to supremacy of law.[23] Parliamentary supremacy became the accepted principle of modern constitutional law. First, the rule and ground of the state was that there exist rights of sovereignty, *jura magestatis*, which regularly and of common right belonged to the sovereign power of the state. Unless custom or the provisional ordinance of the state disposed of them, the sovereign power was *potestas suprema* – a power that could control all others and could not be controlled. Sovereign power lay in the king twofold: in Parliament, the king was assisted and he ruled with the consent of the whole state, which was the sovereign power of the state; and, in the king alone.

The idea was that the king in Parliament, representing the entire community, possessed a law-making authority that was legally supreme and beyond challenge. This power was delegated by the community, subject only to the condition (contractual or by natural law) that the king made law and imposed tax only in Parliament, and exercised other power in accordance with the common law. Otherwise active resistance could be the remedy.

Cromwell followed Marsiglio of Papua's ideas that the source of state authority was the citizenry, constituting the faithful of the Church, and attributed the law-making of the people to Parliament, which some authors state tends toward a positivist conception of law, bringing Cromwell's views closer to legislative sovereignty than those of any other medieval writer.[24] Law was analyzed in terms of legislative will and coercive sanction, and Marsiglio suggested neither divine nor ecclesiastical law were law because of their other-worldly character, or because they lacked coercive sanction. Therefore, Cromwell conceded the validity of unjust laws. He also dismissed the relevance of divine law and believed Parliament possessed legislative sovereignty.[25]

Hooker's argument became the best known sixteenth-century parliamentarian theory, becoming common in the next century. Parliament was the essence of government, the body of the whole realm, which spoke for everyone. Therefore, all were bound to obey. Sovereign power exists at the apex of any legal system, from which all jurisdiction derives. Without a supreme authority, the course of justice should go infinitely in a circle. Hooker attributed legislative sovereignty to the king in Parliament, as the representative of the community.[26]

Prynne, commissioned to provide a justification for the Civil War, stated in 1641 that Parliament was the absolute sovereign power, the sole law-maker, with absolute sovereignty over the laws themselves, including Magna Carta, and had altered the common law in many cases.[27]

Parker, the principal parliamentary advocate, agreed. There is an arbitrary or absolute power in every state. This power must exist or all suits will be endless. The power could nowhere rest more safely than in Parliament.[28] He defended the unorthodox view that sovereign power ultimately lay in the two Houses, not in the king in Parliament, because in emergency situations the Houses could legitimately act without the king's assent. In normal circumstances, sovereign power lay in statutes passed by the two Houses with the king's assent. This view may seem ahistorical. During the Middle Ages, in the case of emergencies, it was the king who could act foremost under custom.

The 1642 Resolution of both Houses provided that the king could remove himself (his natural body) from his councils and courts. He could not lawfully remove his politic body from them.[29] His legal will continued to be expressed by his regular councils and courts. Since Parliament was his highest council and court, the two Houses could continue to act in his name despite his refusal to co-operate with them. Thus, the maxim 'the king can do no wrong' applied not to his personal actions, but to his official ones, which could never be unlawful.[30]

The proposition that Parliament possessed an absolute and unlimited power to make and change the law was neither new, nor disputed by the king or most of his supporters. They rejected the claim that the two Houses could exercise that power without the actual assent of the king.[31]

It was agreed that ordinary judges did not need the king's personal assent to decide legal controversies because their power was strictly judicial, and confined to applying laws to which the king

The significance is that the courts must interpret what the legislature intended by the words used.

had already assented. Parliament exercised a legislative and judicial power not limited by any earlier power. It could change or overrule the laws at its own pleasure. Therefore, the king's personal assent was required: the legislative act in any community must be confirmed by such person(s) in whom the sovereignty of that community resides. The significance is that the courts must interpret what the legislature intended by the words used.

There was a confidence that Parliament would not abuse its great powers based on the representative element and the checks and balances of mixed government (Commons, Lords, crown). The notion of infallibility was influential. As the community had no corporate form apart from Parliament, and as no person or group outside it could speak or act on its behalf, parliamentarians generally condemned rebellion against Parliament. Such action was thought to defy one's own nature, or to elevate one's private interests above the community's and threaten anarchy.[32] Also there was a recognition of a necessary final authority, and that no other court ought to enter into competition with the high court of Parliament, which gave laws to other courts, but from them received neither laws nor orders.[33] In the 1640s, similar declarations were made by both Houses to deter judges from heeding royal proclamations contrary to their ordinances.[34]

That inferiors should respect and obey their superiors was generally held as the law of nature, and was used to reinforce the authority of the community as represented in Parliament. Thus, a high court could not appeal to an inferior, but could only be reversed by another, later parliament.[35]

The idea that supreme judicial and supreme legislative powers are the same can be found in the writings of royalists and parliamentarians, as well as those of eminent lawyers such as Hale. Parliament was supreme. Furthermore, many would agree on the need for flexibility to respond to changing circumstances, which meant that Parliament could not be bound by law.

The notion that Parliament was the fountain of law was a parliamentarian theme during the Civil War. Thus, Parliament, not the courts, was regarded as the principal guardian of the liberties of the subject. A major disagreement involved in the Civil War was whether the king in person was an essential part of Parliament.[36] Furthermore, Parliament could be more trusted to maintain liberty. Parliament has a definite self-interest in it, while judges could be tools of royal absolutism. Freedom is in the law and not in the judges, who apply a different reasoning and their own reason. Furthermore, the common law was the king's law and thus favoured him.

Therefore, the theories of parliamentary sovereignty propounded during the Civil War were not novel. The novelty lay in attributing sovereignty in extraordinary cases of necessity to the two Houses alone. In ordinary cases, the king in Parliament was sovereign.

The royalists objected that there would be no sovereign unless the king and Parliament agreed. It could be argued that both contending theories were unworkable practically if neither side could in fact assert its position successfully.

Common Law Theories

Some common law theories saw the king and Parliament deriving their powers from an 'ancient constitution' comprised of the most fundamental principles of common law, which maintained a proper balance between both and were therefore legally antecedent and superior to both.[37] This view is not inconsistent with sovereign power, in which such power is conferred by law. For example, parliamentary supremacy based in common law disqualifies Parliament from impinging upon that sovereignty; however, this is a different matter from empowering any judicial review, which it does not. As Thomas Hedley stated in his speech to the Commons in 1610, after discussing the plenary powers of Parliament, including over judges, and Parliament's reversing errors in courts:

> But then you will say, the parliament, which is nothing else in effect but the mutual consent of the king and people, is that which gives matter and form and all complements to the common law. No, nor that neither, for the parliament hath his power and authority from the common law, and not the common law from the parliament. And therefore the common law is of more force and strength than the parliament, *quod efficit tale maius est tale* ... The parliament may find some defects in the common law and amend them (for what is perfect under the sun) yet the wisest parliament that ever was could never have made such an excellent law as the common law is. But that the parliament may abrogate the whole law, I deny, for that were includedly to take

away the power of the parliament itself, which power it hath by the common law. And no parliament can take away the power of any one succeeding parliament or make a law for certain years, which may not be revoked by parliament within those years, much less can it take away the power of it forever.[38]

This common law view differs from that of sovereignty theorists, such as Hobbes, who believed sovereign power stood above and created all law. Many people combined common law and parliamentarian views in this way, providing for a common law or legal basis of parliamentary supremacy;[39] for example, the parliamentary leaders Parker and Pym, who helped lead the nation to civil war.

Whitelocke's 1610 speech in the Commons reflected his view that the sovereignty of the king in Parliament was not incompatible with fundamental law. He thought of fundamental law as the constitution itself, which decided the location of sovereignty. He thought of the constitution as 'natural,' and an important part of it was the law that guaranteed the fundamental right of property.[40]

There was little disagreement that the legislative power of the king in Parliament, whether belonging to the king alone or to the community as a whole, was sovereign. Common law theories could accept this view on the grounds that the common law restricted the prerogative of the king outside Parliament to protect the rights of his subjects, but did not restrict the powers of the king and his subjects in Parliament. Pocock states that no issue as between legislative sovereignty and judicial review troubled anyone's mind; the antiquity of law underwrote the authority of the king in Parliament.[41] Therefore, the sovereignty of the king in Parliament could only be regarded as one of the most fundamental principles of the common law.

THE GREAT REBELLION AND REVOLUTION OF 1688

As the king refused Parliament's claim to being the predominant partner of the state, civil war ensued. Charles I carried out his threat to use new counsel when he dissolved Parliament in 1629 for trying to 'usurp' control over government belonging to the king. Charles I attempted to rule without calling a parliament. He impeached five members of the Commons before the Lords, which

124   Parliament

the Commons claimed was their sole privilege. In a practical sense, the lack of money was crucial, making Parliament needed, and the king's schemes to get money only aggravated the situation. Parliament claimed to be sovereign, and to support that claim, it extended its own privileges significantly.

In response to Charles I's proclamation forbidding militia activity pursuant to order or ordinance of one or both Houses of Parliament without the king's consent, the two Houses made the Declaration of 27 May 1642. It stated that "[i]t is acknowledged that the King is the Fountain of Justice and Protection, but the acts of Justice and Protection are not exercised in his own Person, nor depend upon his pleasure but by his Courts, and by his Ministers who must do their duty therein, though the King in his own Person should forbid them: and therefore if Judgments should be given by them against the King's Will and Personal command, yet are they the King's Judgments." Furthermore, it was declared that: the High Court of Parliament was not only a court of judicature enabled by laws to hear and determine the rights and liberties of the kingdom, it was also a Council to provide for necessity, to prevent imminent dangers, to preserve the public peace and safety of the kingdom, and to declare the king's pleasure in this regard, "and what they do herein hath the stamp of Royal Authority, although His Majesty seduced by evil counsel, do in his own Person oppose or interrupt the same, for the King's Supreme and Royal pleasure is exercised and declared in this High Court of Law and Council after a more eminent and obligatory manner, than it can be by any personal Act or Resolution of his own." The two Houses separated the politic from the natural capacity of the king, and declared themselves to be the sovereign authority of the state.

In these circumstances of impasse, the only solution appeared to be an 'appeal to heaven,' which transcended the constitution by affirming the immediate sovereignty of the sword and the ultimate sovereignty of God. Another side of the debate was how far the injunction of Romans 8 – "let every soul be subject to the higher power, for the powers that be are ordained of God" – obliged one's conscience to obedience when "the powers that be" exercised authority *de facto* and not *de jure* according to law.[42]

The Revolution finally established the supremacy of Parliament, and attained the framers' object for the Act of 1641. Whitelocke's

The Great Rebellion and Revolution of 1688   125

theory became the accepted theory of the constitution, and in the eighteenth century, the growth of constitutional conventions made it workable.

The logical culmination of the parliamentary opposition until 1628 was the Petition of Right. It set out the law in the sense that the opposition understood it, the infringements of the law that had occurred, and enacted that no such future infringements were to occur – the law was to govern. It set out a number of statutes and provisions of Magna Carta and a list of grievances. For example, it declared arbitrary imprisonment to be unlawful and that taxation was to be with the consent of Parliament; also, it denounced forced loans, the unreasonable billeting of soldiers, and the trial of civilians by martial law. A purely legal opposition to the crown became evident. That is, the approach was to secure the law's observance as interpreted by parliamentary leaders. Giving the Petition of Right a declaratory form made it easier for the king to evade, on the grounds that nothing new was granted but only ancient liberties confirmed. It became clear that more was required than just opposing the king's policy by remonstrances, impeachments, and appeals to existing law. New laws were needed to curtail royal power, and to make it impossible for the king to rule without Parliament.

For its own safety, the Long Parliament impeached Strafford and other agents of prerogative rule, as well as some judges. This action settled the parliamentary doctrine that all ministers, including judges, were answerable according to law for their illegal acts. It also introduced the practice that all royal acts must be countersigned by the secretary of state, to ensure there was always a minister who could be held responsible for them.

Legislation was passed that embodied some of the most important principles of modern public law. For example, legislation established the Commons' absolute control over direct and indirect taxation.[43] The Star Chamber was abolished, which deprived the Privy Council and various courts derived from it of all extraordinary jurisdiction, and established the common law as supreme.[44] The abolition of the Court of High Commission removed it from persecuting theological opponents. The Triennial Act controlled the prerogative to summon, prorogue, or dissolve parliaments.[45] It was not until after the Revolution that the supremacy of Parliament was finally established, and attained the framers' object for the Act of 1641.

126 Parliament

Parliament claimed to guide state policy by controlling the appointment of ministers. Ministers had to be responsible to the king and Commons, and ministers whom the Commons did not trust had to be dismissed. This position, in effect, asserted a right to be the predominant partner in the state. There were a number of relevant precedents, including the Grand Remonstrance, establishing this constitutional convention.

The Great Rebellion / Civil War

The 1642 Civil War ended with Parliament under Cromwell victorious along with the New Model Army. After further intrigues, Charles was executed. However, the legislation of the Commonwealth was swept aside at the Restoration. The monarchy was restored, and, with it, the sovereign law-making authority of the king in Parliament. The king's position was restored to what it had been after the legislative changes of the Long Parliament in 1641 and before the outbreak of the Civil War, but with material differences in laws and the practice of the constitution.[46] In particular, legislation made the personal monarchy as the Tudors and Charles I understood it impossible for the future, and made it impossible for Parliament to perpetuate itself in defiance of public opinion. Therefore, when the monarchy was restored, the position of the monarchy and Parliament was altered.

Another interesting aspect of the discourse at this time, which illustrated the idea of parliamentary sovereignty as opposed to that of the king, was the debate surrounding *His Majesty's Answer to the Ninteen Propositions of Parliament*. This involved a doctrine of mixed and conjoined power put forward by the royalists in June of 1642. It maintained that law-making was in the king, Lords, and Commons jointly, and warned the Commons about demanding more power and upsetting the balance. Weston and Greenberg locate this controversy about the *Answer to the Ninteen Propositions* within the debate about the co-ordination of sovereignty.[47] As stated earlier, the concern of many parliamentarians, like Petyt, was that any position denying the antiquity of the Commons was to deny them a share in legislative power, and to leave them only with the authority named in their writs of summons. This period featured debates over

The significant result of the Great Rebellion and Revolution of 1688   127

the antiquity of the Commons and the feudal interpretation of the Norman Conquest.

The significant result of the Great Rebellion was that Parliament became a permanent part of government, able to take its own initiative, and possessing the acknowledged right to freely consider political action. It was no longer a body to be called occasionally to assist the king's government by sanctioning new legislation, or voting supplies the government considered necessary. In future, neither the king nor the state church could use their powers to pursue a policy of which the nation disapproved.

The development of prerogative was now subject to the will of the nation as expressed in Parliament. The Long Parliament's legislation abolishing the Star Chamber secured this result. Permanent alterations in the relations of king, Parliament, and courts to one another had been made. The executive, legislative, and judicial powers began to assume the legal position which they hold in modern law. This development is of *foundational* significance, and is relevant as a legacy to the systems of governments of the other Dominions, including Canada's as established in 1867.

The first half of the seventeenth century marked a turning point in constitutional history. It decided that government was conducted by the king and Parliament, and not the king alone. This result was achieved by parliamentary opposition, which compelled the crown to submit to modifications or limitations of prerogative, leaving Parliament free to exercise the powers it had won.

After the Rebellion, the effect of the Petition of Right was to deprive the executive of all power of arrest and detention in prison, unless a definite charge could be brought. The Declaration of Breda laid down four principles as conditions under which a Restoration was to be effected: general amnesty, liberty of conscience, security of property, and payment of arrears to the army. The application of the principles was left to Parliament.

The first and important Act of the Convention Parliament regularized its existence by declaring the Long Parliament dissolved, and claiming that it was a true parliament notwithstanding any lack of the king's writ or writs of summons or any other defect.[48] Furthermore, in 1661, to prevent any possible doubt pertaining to the validity of the most important Acts of the Convention Parliament, several statutes passed by it were confirmed,[49] although such action was not, strictly speaking, legally necessary.

The legislation of the Convention Parliament (which was disbanded before completing its work, and taken up in new spirit by the next parliament) reflected certain principles.[50] First, the general principle on which these parliaments acted was that all Acts of the Long Parliament receiving royal assent were valid, and all other legislation invalid. There were some modifications, as illustrated by some Long Parliament legislation being repealed, and there was some legislation without royal assent existing on the grounds of necessity, such as the continuance of judicial proceedings and ordinances under the Commonwealth. Second, new laws were passed to deal with the new situation created by the repeal or enactment of some statutes to settle certain controversial matters in favour of the king. Third, Parliament agreed to carry out the principles contained in the Declaration of Breda. Fourth, legislation was enacted to settle royal (hereditary crown) revenue, that is, revenue to pay the current and normal expenses of government. Parliament voted taxes to produce an amount estimated to meet such expenses. These taxes were insufficient and a growing deficit continued.

These actions demonstrated constitutionally that the king was not the essence of Parliament, which had an independent and lawful existence and, in the end, was supreme even without the king.

There is a distinction between parliamentary sovereignty, which has existed for some time, and Parliament as a predominant and effective partner in the state. For example, if rule by prerogative had been successfully asserted, it could have left England in the situation in which parliamentary sovereignty existed, but Parliament rarely exercised its sovereign power. The distinction is between a legal description of the system of government, and government as actually exercised in a practical sense or the relative position or influence of the parts making up the system of government.

At this point, the Commons was as necessary a part of government as the king. It became familiar with all branches of government, and directed state policy. As a result, it thought itself competent to supervise and criticize the conduct of all branches of government. The difficulty it faced was that it still had little real knowledge of the detailed work of government, and lacked the means to maintain constant and effective control over its policy. In practice, government was by the king and officials responsible to him, without direct communications between departments and the Commons.[51] The House was not yet organized into parties, it lacked discipline from party organization, and it was unable to act effectively. It was able to impeach a minister or stop supplies, but was as yet unable to undertake calm and in-depth analysis.[52]

Revolution of 1688

It has been argued that the idea of Parliament's legislative authority limited by unchangeable fundamental laws probably was more influential after the Restoration than before, due to the fear of unpredictable and violent social upheaval. This view was represented particularly by 'constitutional' and absolutist monarchists. Only some Tories believed the common law included an 'ancient constitution' of unalterable, fundamental laws. Absolutists such as Figgis denied this proposition, other than in the area of succession. Even with this invocation of 'fundamental law,' the formal repeal of Long Parliament statutes occurred, including the Triennial Act, the Attainder of Strafford, and the Act Excluding Bishops from the House.

In terms of Whig ideas, Parliament was the principal guardian of liberties, which justified its having unlimited authority.

In the early 1670s, some Protestant nonconformists claimed that statutes impinging on their religion's practices were contrary to divine law, and thus void. They tended to favour parliamentary action to repeal the statutes or to authorize dispensations by the king. They never sought relief by judicial invalidation, or even suggested it was possible.[53]

As before the Civil War, judicial decisions undermined public confidence in judges' willingness or ability to protect the liberties of subjects. The 1680 House of Commons declared that judges were guilty of usurping legislative powers. Also, there was a distrust based on judges being officers of the king, and also due to the prescient fear that judges would evolve into a separate political species accountable to no one. Finally, there was also the Whig view that Parliament was supreme and absolute, giving life to government; it could be more trusted.[54]

One may also point to the views of Locke, *infra*, Sidney, Petyt, Disney, Hunt, and Atkyns. Petyt, the eminent constitutional historian, argued that Parliament had absolute power in all cases to make law and judicially determine matters in law. He undermined and saw as pernicious judicial pretensions to make new law in important cases, or to declare Acts of Parliament void.[55]

Nenner discusses Parliament's authority during the seventeenth century:

> The rhetoric of fundamental law had only a small effect on the seventeenth-century understanding of how law was or ought to be made. For the most part, politicians and jurists alike recognized that the positive law of England, although forged in custom, could be originated, altered, and repealed in Parliament ... By and large there was little if any question about Parliament's wide-ranging legislative function.[56]

During the Restoration and the Revolution, the final settlement of English public law on its modern basis was established. The immediate causes were the ecclesiastical and foreign policy of the last two Stuart kings. These causes allowed for the Whigs, Tories, and even the Church of England to oppose the king together, resulting in a bloodless revolution.

William was invited to preserve the Protestant religion and liberties of England. The Convention Parliament was summoned. It made the Declaration of Rights that was read to William and Mary, who accepted the Declaration. The Convention declared itself, as did the Convention effecting the Restoration, to be a true parliament.[57] It turned its Declaration of Rights into the Bill of Rights.[58] It passed other statutes, such as the Mutiny Act[59] and the Toleration Act,[60] which laid the foundations of the Revolution settlement. The Revolution was formally completed and regularized by an Act of the succeeding parliament, recognizing all Acts of the Convention Parliament as valid.[61]

The Revolution was primarily a Whig victory, but with the assistance of the Tories and the Church. The Whigs won a parliamentary settlement of the succession to the throne, and consequently the final rejection of the idea that the king's title depended on divine right superior to the law of the land. It was Parliament that created the king. This fact is of *foundational significance*, as Parliament had thus established its legal control over succession. Now, it was firmly established that there was nothing superior to Parliament's law. The Revolution permanently secured in final form a large number of the most fundamental principles of public law. The constitutional positions of the Church, king, Parliament, and courts were defined. Especially important was the supremacy of Parliament in the constitution. Also, the Whigs secured the supremacy of law administered by independent and impartial judges, which was seen as a very important safeguard for individual rights and liberties.[62]

As a matter of political reality, the settlement made possible the development of a system of government under which parties could peaceably contend in Parliament for their views.

With the legislative supremacy of Parliament, the definite restrictions on prerogative were complete and prerogative limited to the sphere of the executive. This restriction laid the foundations for affirming the ultimate sovereignty of Parliament. Proclamations continued to be made with respect to overseas crown possessions and colonies, which were related to the management of foreign affairs. Otherwise, proclamations were restricted to executive government, such as enforcing Acts or exercising powers these Acts conferred on the crown, including in relation to commerce, trade, and industry. Executive power decreased generally, for example with the abolition of Star Chamber and other branches of Council, which meant that Council lost almost all of its coercive power.

BILL OF RIGHTS[63] AND ACT OF SETTLEMENT[64]

It is of *foundational significance* that the Bill of Rights and Act of Settlement provisions were designed to stop any future king from relying on the expedients used between 1660 and 1688 to, in effect, make himself and his prerogative the supreme or dominant power in the state.

First, the fact that James II was in substance deposed and that Parliament created a new king destroyed the theory of divine right, even though, as Blackstone notes, this deposition was stated in terms of abdication. The judges and lawyers, when consulted by the Lords, admitted that none of the rules of common law were applicable. It was a revolution, and the people through their representatives in

Parliament assumed the right to make and unmake kings. The Whig position was further emphasized when the Tory Parliament passed the Act of Settlement and entailed the crown on a family that had no claim to it except by virtue of an Act of Parliament.[65]

Second, clauses in the Bill of Rights, Act of Settlement, and Triennial Act dealt with various ways in which Charles II and James II tried to influence or muzzle Parliament. The Bill of Rights declared that the election of members of Parliament ought to be free; and, freedom of speech, debate, and proceedings ought not to be questioned in any court or place outside of Parliament. The Triennial Act of 1694 declared that parliaments should be held frequently and prohibited an intermission of more than three years. Stopping corruption was also a main object of the Act of Settlement. Other ways toward this goal involved securing the legal responsibility of the king's ministers for their acts by requiring that all matters cognizable in the Privy Council had to be transacted there, and all resolutions had to be signed by the Privy Councillors who advised and consented to them. There was also the prevention of any interference by the crown with criminal proceedings instituted by the House against ministers or others because no pardon was pleadable to impeachment. Also, the exclusion from the Commons of persons holding office under the king or receiving crown pensions was aimed at reducing corruption.

Third, a number of provisions addressed the perversion of judicial prerogatives. The Bill of Rights prohibited excessive bail, excessive fines, and cruel or unusual punishments. Jurors were to be duly impanelled, and grants and promises of fines and forfeitures of particular persons before conviction were declared illegal. An important measure was an Act regulating trials for high treason. As well, the Act of Settlement secured judges' tenures of office on condition of good behaviour, with removal being made on joint address of both Houses of Parliament. Salaries were to be ascertained and established by Parliament. This clause removed the Bench from the political arena; made it impossible for the crown, Commons, or Lords to exercise pressure on the Bench; and, thus guaranteed the impartial administration of the law. The result was that supremacy of law became the best security for the liberties of the subject against both the claims of royal prerogative and of parliamentary privilege.

The Great Rebellion and Revolution of 1688 133

Other parts of the Bill of Rights dealt with prerogatives that had been abused. The suspending power was condemned as illegal. The dispensing power was not condemned absolutely; however, no dispensation was permitted except as allowed in statute. Regulating this power by further legislation was found too difficult and was abandoned. As a result, recent dispensations were declared invalid, and no future dispensation was valid unless it was specially provided for in the statute to be dispensed. Standing armies were prohibited within the country in times of peace without the consent of Parliament.

Other clauses of the Bill of Rights and Act of Settlement dealt with matters such as requiring a Protestant dynasty, obligating the monarch to be a member of the Church of England, and denying a right to petition the king.

Holdsworth argues that the most fundamental principles dealing with the position or functions of the king and his prerogative, Parliament and the courts, and individual rights and liberties had already been settled by the legislation of the Long Parliament and the results of the Great Rebellion. These principles were not matters of controversy since the Restoration. What was in controversy was the relative weight in the constitution of royal prerogative and Parliament, control of the courts, and the manner in which rights and liberties should be secured. It is of *foundational legal significance* that "Parliament, as the result of the Revolution, had finally won the contest for predominance in the state": prerogative was subject to law.[66]

SECOND GREAT ACHIEVEMENT: SUPREMACY OF LAW ESTABLISHED

The second great achievement was that the supremacy of law was established, and Coke's view won out in this respect. Coke's writings set out the medieval doctrine of the supremacy of law, in which law, divine in its origin and sanction, was the basis upon which civil society is built, and that this law was supreme above the king and people equally.[67] When the Second to Fourth Institutes were published after Coke's death in 1641, the victory of the common law and Parliament had been achieved. The accuracy or validity of Coke's arguments of the common law and Parliament being supreme in the state were accepted, and his writings were made the basis of modern constitutional law and of the common law.[68] In this fact, we can see bedrock. This foundation of the constitution was in fact the views adopted by the successful parliamentary party with respect to the nature of the sovereignty of the state – these views and intentions of the parliamentary party were the established law and foundation of the constitution. The Revolution disproved the theory of the king's sovereignty.

While it is clear that the Revolution established the supremacy of the common law, it did not vindicate or approve *ex post facto* all the instances in which common law judges had acted outside their jurisdiction. To determine the extent to which there was any legalizing of illegal decisions, one must look to specific legislation prior to and after the Rebellion or the Revolution.

It is clear that Coke's ideas influenced the development of English law. His work was important in restating the law to bring the medieval basis of the law into harmony with the new situation. There were unfortunate results in form and substance related to the retention of obsolete common law rules and doctrines, and case law in commercial and maritime cases was slow to reflect and inadequate to deal with commercial reality. However, the common law did produce a more uniform system than if a more variegated system of different courts had existed. If Coke had not restated and adapted common law principles to modern needs, even Parliament's victory might not have enabled the common law to gain decisive victory over its rivals.

Further Evidence of Parliamentary Supremacy: The Control of Succession Although further evidence of parliamentary supremacy is not needed, that supremacy is both suggested and illustrated in parliamentary statutes dealing with the highest matters of state, especially succession. Notable are statutes making it treason to interfere with the order of succession as established from time to time by statute.[69] Indefeasible hereditary divine right was dead.

This control is also evident through coronation oaths. Election by the Witan, normally from within the sphere of the royal family, was the rule in Anglo-Saxon days. The survival of these ideas is illustrated in that part of the coronation ceremony in which the king is presented by high officials to the people, and is recognized by the people as king.[70] Theological influences tended to emphasize the fact that king inherited something different from an estate in the Land.

The Church insisted that the king, like other rulers, owed duties to his people,[71] which is plainly set out in the oath from earliest times taken at the coronation. The coronation oath indicates the contractual character of English sovereignty. While the wording of the oath was settled immediately after the Revolution, it dates back to the eighth century: to keep the Church and all Christians in peace, to restrain rapine and wrong, and to temper justice with mercy. The Coronation Oath Act (1689) states that the king was to govern the people according to the statutes in Parliament, and the laws and customs of the kingdom. It emphasized the primacy of statute law, and removed any suggestion that laws were granted by and subject to crown prerogatives.

The rise of Parliament in the fourteenth and fifteenth centuries and its control over crown actions gave new meaning to the ideas that the crown was subject to law, and that the king owed duties. A number of pre- and post-Conquest precedents supported this proposition and dealt with parliamentary statutory settlements and resettlements, concluding with the bestowing of the crown on those with no hereditary right, but with only the right conferred by purchase, as in the case of William, Mary, and Anne after the Revolution.[72] These circumstances depended on Parliament being able to act independently of the king, perhaps by deriving authority from the whole community, as well as from the king who summoned it. By the 1530s, it was widely accepted that Parliament had unfettered authority to dispose of the crown. This is an important point in the development of the doctrine of parliamentary sovereignty. Blackstone states that at present title to the throne is hereditary, but not as absolutely hereditary as formerly. The common stock or ancestor for descent was also different. The descent was no longer absolute; it had conditions.[73]

Statute was needed to provide against the fact that when the king died so too did his delegations, leading to the dissolution of the executive, the army, and Parliament. For example, by statute, judges' tenure of office was no longer affected by the demise of the crown.[74]

Finally, there were provisions for the minority, mental incapacity, or absence of a king. Before the rise of Parliament, these events fell to Council as the governing body of the kingdom. Later, Parliament asserted the right to make the necessary arrangements, but did so with respect to particular emergencies.

Dispensing and Suspending Powers of the King   In the Middle Ages, the suspending and dispensing powers were vested in the king, who was supposed to possess a reserve power to enable him to correct the deficiencies of the ordinary law.[75] The jurisdiction of the courts of common law and Chancery owed something to this power. Throughout the Middle Ages, this power was needed to correct defects of the common law and statute, as Parliament sat irregularly, and the language of older statutes was brief and careless.[76]

The medieval lawyer would say the power was not unlimited. It was limited by the king's incapacity to dispense with or suspend the law of nature or of God. It could deal only with human laws and offences created by them (*mala prohibita* and not *mala in se*).

However, in the sixteenth century, this limitation became less distinct. The Reformation caused a divergence of opinion concerning the law of God or nature. The state was assuming the power to determine the content of these laws. English legislature established relations between the Church and State thought contrary to the law of God.[77] This enlargement of legislative power *indirectly enlarged the king's power to dispense and suspend* as it weakened the one restriction on it based on the law of God and of nature.

Prerogative was enlarged as a result of the conditions of the Reformation with a subservient parliament of a despotic king. The king destroyed the power of the Pope over the Church, but as that power was useful, he transferred it to himself to the extent it was possible and consistent with the new settlement.

Tudors and early Stuarts did not make great use of the suspending power, but rather the dispensing power, which gave rise to debates about its limits. For example, the king could not dispense before the Act of Parliament was made. In the *Case of Monopolies* (1602)[78] a dispensation defeating the whole spirit and intent of the Act was held void. The basis of the dispensation power is that a general law may be inconvenient to particular persons, and so the king may dispense. In the *Case of Penal Statutes* (1605),[79] it was held that the crown could not delegate its power to dispense a particular statute. The *Case of Non Obstante*[80] held that any Act of Parliament attempting to bind the king not to exercise a prerogative inseparably annexed to his person, such as to command any subject to serve him or to pardon, could be dispensed with, and even an express clause in an Act restricting this dispensing power was invalid. In debates about the Petition of Right, the existence of a side dispensing power was admitted by the Commons.[81]

The vagueness made prerogatives convenient for kings attempting to make themselves predominant partners in the state. On the positive side, Charles II and James II tried to invoke the power to secure some measure of toleration for Catholics and Protestant nonconformists. In *Thomas v. Sorrell* (1674),[82] a distinction was drawn between dispensations that inflicted a special and particular damage on a private person, which were void, and dispensations that did not. *Godden v. Hales* (1686)[83] held that the king's power to dispense with the Test Act was practically unlimited. The case was correct if the *Case of Non Obstante* was good law. The Test Act deprived the king of his power to command the service of his Catholic subjects. Although there may have been an argument that the *Case of Monopolies* supported the opposite conclusion, Holdsworth favours the technical correctness of Herbert C.J.'s decision.[84] Thus, such a dispensing power could negate any restrictions on prerogative the king did not like, especially those restricting him from furthering his political and religious policy.

Evidence respecting the authority to control or diminish royal prerogative is scarce, but it must have been accepted. Prerogative was generally believed to be defined by the common law, which Parliament was free to change.[85] Guy states that Elton overlooks the crown's absolute prerogative to override the law to preserve the realm in an emergency; but, this was not regarded as a creature of common law.[86] Holdsworth says this emergency power was part of the common law and limited by it.

The idea that the crown possessed certain 'inseparable' prerogatives that not even Parliament could restrict was a development of the early seventeenth century, when the Stuarts claimed the indefeasibility of their divine hereditary rights.[87]

As we have seen, the 'inseparable' crown prerogatives, especially the dispensation power, were put under Parliament's control after the Revolution. No statute could be dispensed except as allowed by the statute, or by a special provision of a bill to be passed during the present session of Parliament. No such bill has ever been passed.

5

Parliamentary Sovereignty
(and Its Doubters)

Although parliamentary sovereignty was conclusively established as the pre-eminent law of the constitution, and as the main component of the British system of government, there have been some hesitations about it and even expressions of doubt. This chapter will examine these challenges.

First, some misconceptions about sovereignty that have led to confusions are discussed. These misconceptions also highlight the need to first describe the system of government accurately in order to bring clarity and precision.

Some hesitations or concerns that arose about parliamentary sovereignty or its implications are then discussed. Next, the parliamentary supremacy doubters are examined. Particular attention is focused on McIlwain, given that his book is regarded as a leading source for those who doubt parliamentary supremacy, and is often used to support judges declaring statutes void. Yet his work provides no authority for either proposition. It is precisely because such authors do not first describe the system of government that these sorts of errors arise. A discussion on Coke follows, particularly in relation to a case involving statements that might imply a belief that courts may be able to overrule Parliament, as well as other cases and expressions of views of the period reflecting such possible implications. Further myths and fallacies are examined with respect to parliamentary sovereignty, particularly the view that it exists because of court recognition.

A misunderstanding about sovereignty is evident in the statement that as the location of sovereignty was not effectively determined, the existing law as administered by the courts was supreme.[1] For example, Holdsworth states that the question of the location of sovereignty was not effectively solved during the last two Stuarts' time as neither king nor Parliament could lay claim to it. Nor, to his mind, was it solved by the Revolution, nor by legislation settling the law of the constitution on its modern basis. Rather, he believes that all the legislation established was Parliament's view in the early part of the century that the sovereign power in the state was the king in Parliament.

However, the Revolution established sovereignty. Holdsworth is correct to say that none of the king, Lords, or Commons is sovereign, but does not recognize that by their acting together in Parliament, Parliament is sovereign. The assumption in his definition appears to be that one of the component parts of Parliament must be sovereign, which is not so. Even Bodin's definition recognized that sovereignty may reside in a person (his preference), or in a body. Holdsworth provides no argument as to why Parliament cannot constitute such a body, nor any other particular body; nor would it be possible to do so. Furthermore, sovereignty theory has been much refined since Bodin, who is regarded as the father of modern sovereignty theory.

Holdsworth goes on to say that if these three partners could not agree, there would be no active sovereign. This statement is correct as a practical reality. However, that is the case for all existing sovereignties. While particularly a problem for (composite) bodies, it is also an issue for a king who is successfully opposed by the people. The argument Holdsworth probably really had in mind was an argument about practical politics. However, it displays some confusion on a number of levels. First, he takes an extreme case of hypothetical non-workability to deny the existence of sovereignty, although such a concern might have been a more realistic one at the time just preceding the Revolution. Second, his reasoning is based on a theoretical misunderstanding of the legal nature and underpinning of sovereignty and of the system of government. Sovereignty is a legal concept. The law establishes sovereignty and sovereign powers. Sovereignty does not, and in reality has never, come from judicial decisions, but comes from the law itself. In fact, there are clear precedents that courts cannot decide political questions of sovereignty. He seems to assume, incorrectly, that the sovereignty of Parliament is not compatible with the supremacy of law. Finally, the statement that existing law as administered by the courts is supreme is technically not accurate given that the courts are servants of the law and Parliament is higher than the courts, and also in light of Parliament's legislative jurisdiction. Furthermore, even historically, it would be absurd to say that the administrators of the law, that is judges, were higher than the king, Curia, Council, or Parliament.

Even if one accepts his premises, he is disproved by his own argument. His syllogism is that the sovereign power in the state is in Parliament. If the members of Parliament cannot agree, there is no active sovereign. Therefore, the law administered by the courts is sovereign or supreme. In any event, because the sovereign Parliament is not paralyzed by the inability to pass legislation, but is active, therefore, the law administered by the courts is *not* sovereign. Incidentally, his conclusion does not even necessarily follow from his premises.

Having denied that Parliament is sovereign because it may hypothetically not be able to work together, he then states that while the result of these events was the supremacy of law, it was politically an impossible idea. Between the three partners, he claims, despite the evidence, no enduring harmony could be expected. If they fell out, then a stronger actor's will would prevail. The logical conclusion from his premises must be that the supremacy of law cannot exist. As well, the characterization is problematic. If there were such a falling-out, in which the will of the stronger prevailed, it might occur by revolution (which then would create a new sovereign, and not one necessarily representing the three partners), or by convention (in which case the old sovereign would continue, but the practices of governance would be determined by convention). It may also be inaccurate to say the political sovereign is one of the component parts of the existing constitution; it could be society at large, particularly the voters. Dicey's explanation of the political sovereign is better.[2] In this way, sometimes the word 'sovereignty' is used in a political sense. The body politically sovereign or supreme in a state is the one whose will is ultimately obeyed by the citizens of the state. The electors are the most important part of, and even perhaps the totality of, the sovereign power in this political sense, since their will is under the present constitution sure to obtain ultimate obedience.

The source of these particular errors is not inadequate historical inquiry as Holdsworth's work is held in the highest esteem. Rather, they stem from an inadequate conceptualization or understanding of legal concepts such as sovereignty, constitutional conventions,

Parliamentary Sovereignty 141

and even practices. These errors demonstrate the necessity of first describing the system of government, including its components, which will result in clarity and precision.

Holdsworth goes on to make the observation that at the close of the century, the repeal or modification of some clauses of the Act of Settlement shows that statesmen were beginning to see the necessity for fresh developments. This was a precondition for the beginning of the last stage in the history of the relation of prerogative to Parliament, which rendered possible the development of cabinet government, and which in turn settled the controversies of the seventeenth century by placing prerogative powers at the disposal of the majority of the Commons. Thus, it led to the growth of constitutional conventions regulating the workings of the cabinet.[3] This part of the argument identifies constitutional conventions properly.

PARLIAMENTARY SOVEREIGNTY AND SOME LATER HESITATIONS

Parliamentary supremacy was recognized and established at this point, particularly as reflected in the ideas of the victors. The views after the Revolution recognized this fact, even if some writers had hesitations with respect to all the consequences of the theory.

It was generally recognized that the sovereign power in the constitution was the king, Lords, and Commons. It was generally recognized also that the doctrines of non-resistance and passive obedience applied not to the king, but to the legislative power in the state, or Parliament.[4]

Burke notes how George III and his ministers used the sovereignty of Parliament to cover their misdeeds. In Parliament, they had the absolute power to obtain their object, and could do so in perfect safety, without rules to confine them or any reckoning afterward.[5]

Holdsworth notes:

But, though the theory of sovereignty was an accepted theory in the eighteenth century, and its attribution to the King in Parliament was a well-recognized principle of constitutional law, all the consequences of the theory were not so firmly grasped as they had been grasped by Hobbes in the seventeenth, and as they were grasped by Austin in the nineteenth century. In fact, just as

142 Parliament

the continuity of the development of English constitutional law long caused certain doubts as to the extent of the powers inherent in the prerogative, so the same causes caused some hesitation in the acceptance of all the consequences of this theory of the sovereignty of Parliament.[6]

The common law lawyers' hesitation was twofold. First, some thought no justification for this theory of sovereignty could be found in older cases. Hale misunderstood Hobbes' theory of sovereignty. Hale interpreted sovereignty as simply a supremacy, which was not incompatible with the supremacy of Parliament or the law in their several spheres. He attributed this sovereignty to the king, then showed that Hobbes' version of sovereignty was contrary to the rules of English law. Hale represented the traditional view of English lawyers, and support for that view was found in medieval and later authorities, especially Coke. Second, distinct authority contrary to the modern theory of sovereignty could be found in medieval and modern books. During the Middle Ages, no one would have asserted the power of Parliament to enact a law contravening those moral rules, which were superior to merely human laws because they were directly derived from the laws of God or nature.[7] In the sixteenth century, St. Germain thought Parliament had no direct power over the laws of God or nature; all it could do was "to strengthen them and to make them more surely kept."[8] In the seventeenth century, Vaughan C.J. stated, "no human authority can make lawful what divine authority hath made unlawful."[9]

Some political thinkers also held reservations. With the Revolution settlement, Parliament became the predominant partner in the constitution. The constitutional rights of the subject, for which Parliament had always stood, assumed a position of greater importance than the theory of sovereignty,[10] which was safeguarded by, and state sovereignty balanced with, judicial independence secured by the Act of Settlement. Locke's view was that political society was founded to protect these constitutional rights, and if government failed to safeguard them, and acted tyrannically, it was *ipso facto* dissolved.[11] This view was in harmony with Whig tradition. For example, both Milton and Sydney believed that laws contrary to the laws of God, reason, or nature ought not to be obeyed. Milton deduced that the execution of Charles I was legal, because it was in accordance with the law of God to kill a tyrant, and even a statute giving tyrannical power to the king had no validity. Locke's view is consistent with the theory of sovereignty existing in law, but the people have ultimately inalienable rights of rebellion, and a sovereign entity may voluntarily reduce the scope of its power. Blackstone disagrees that government would be *ipso facto* dissolved and goes back to the people. For him, laws do not contemplate such a desperate event, which would render all legal provisions ineffectual.[12] Blackstone agrees that the principal aim of society is to protect the rights of men given by the law of nature,[13] which eighteenth-century thinkers identified with the law of God. In addition, the division of powers in the constitution tended to prevent the composite sovereign from acting so frequently or regularly as in states where the king was sovereign. This situation helped relegate the theory of sovereignty to the background, and put rights or liberty to the foreground.

Most medieval theorists held that the limitations imposed on rulers by divine, natural, or human law were not legally enforceable. Many recognized that public officials on behalf of the community had a right to disobey or even resist tyrants.[14] Only the more extreme supporters of the divine right of kings, such as Filmer, denied the right of active resistance even to a tyrant. God could be relied on to remove or punish a tyrannical king acting in violation of God's laws. This idea was defeated in constitutional law terms after the Rebellion, and certainly after the Revolution. Hobbes allowed a small scope for resistance to a tyrant if one was threatened with death. Thus, theorists such as Blackstone, Austin, and Dicey were closer to medieval theorists and to later resistance theorists such as Locke, than to absolutists such as Hobbes and Filmer. That is, they considered popular resistance to be the only appropriate remedy for gross violation of natural law by the sovereign. Blackstone states that if the "sovereign's unconstitutional oppressions threaten desolation to a state, mankind will not be reasoned out of the feelings of humanity, nor sacrifice their liberty by adherence to political maxims originally established to preserve it."[15] If safety of the people required, they could exert inherent powers. Austin speaks of governments being bound by positive morality and divine law, and lacking moral legitimacy to the extent that they failed to comply. People would not obey if they thought they could achieve better government by resistance.[16] Similarly, Dicey describes Parliament as sovereign without

144 Parliament

legal limits, but bound by external forces, in that subjects may disobey and resist, which is an internal consideration.[17]

Those questioning Parliament's sovereignty in the eighteenth century never suggested its authority was subject to limits enforceable by judicial review.[18] The relation of Parliament and inferior courts was never in question. Acts of Parliament were not disputed in any court. There was no higher power to appeal to than the supreme power.

The issue was the relation between Parliament and the people. Parliament's duty to act in their interests was widely thought to implicitly limit its authority, which was enforceable at elections, and by rebellion in the last resort. As the tension between parliamentary and popular sovereignty became clearer, it was never suggested that judges could invalidate 'unconstitutional' legislation. The obligation to obey Parliament was not absolute nor unconditional. The people entrusted their power to their representatives, but this consent or delegation could be revoked, whereupon power would revert to the people – the remedy was extrajudicial.

After 1710, lawful resistance was denied, even if in extraordinary circumstances it could be morally justified. This understanding became the standard defence of parliamentary sovereignty.[19] Court Whigs and Tories used Hale's principle that no human constitution could provide perfectly for every possible eventuality. Government was therefore to be modelled on the common and ordinary state of things and not extraordinary circumstances. It was seen as better for law not to recognize any limits to the legitimate authority of Parliament enforceable by popular resistance, as in the vast majority of cases likely to arise, such limits would be interpreted too broadly and encourage unjustifiable resistance; this outcome was thought far more likely than that the crown or Parliament would in fact exceed them.[20] Cases of necessity, such as revolution, were implied, but it was improper for them to be expressed. Law would not suppose the possibility of a wrong as it could not give a remedy, and it would be distrusting those invested with supreme power. But history would give an answer, as it did in 1688. Blackstone adopts this argument, as we have seen.

This view resolves the tension between human laws contrary to the law of nature being invalid and Parliament being supreme. The only remedy was disobedience or rebellion. Parliament was fully sovereign according to positive law, even though its authority was truly limited by the law of nature, because those limits were enforceable only by extra-legal means and not within the legal system. No court had the power to defeat the legislature's intent. There was a power outside the constitution, but the power of Parliament was legally absolute and uncontrolled so long as the English constitution lasted. Those affirming that Parliament was legally sovereign did not deny that morally its authority was limited, nor that in extreme cases limits were enforceable by resistance or rebellion. The only debate was about what those limits were, and whether particular measures exceeded them. But these disagreements were moral or political, rather than legal. To the extent there was a legal disagreement, it was of terminology as to whether the limits to Parliament's authority could properly be described as legal limits.[21] This resolution was not a denial of parliamentary supremacy. Since the seventeenth century, British constitutional thought has held that Parliament is both legally sovereign and subject to customary restraints. Statutes violating these restraints could be called unconstitutional (in a colloquial sense) even though they were within Parliament's sovereign authority and thus legally valid. The distinction between legality and constitutionality was controversial, and the notion that something could be unconstitutional despite being legal was popular, although confused.

Thus, disagreements about parliamentary sovereignty were more apparent than real, and counter-productive because substantial agreement was concealed by divergent terminology. For example, such divergent terminology included whether those principles (natural law and fundamental customary principles that might justify resistance) were properly termed 'constitutional' if not 'legal,' and what an extreme case might be. The confusion thus generated inspired Bentham and Austin to propose a sharp distinction between legal and moral terminology. Most recent historians agree that the doctrine of parliamentary sovereignty was firmly entrenched in British constitutional thought by the mid-eighteenth century.[22]

Interestingly, the idea of resistance is also contained in Magna Carta, in which a committee of resistance acting as conservators of the Charter was to be elected and work by majority votes. On the Continent, the idea existed that the individual vassal was self-competent to pronounce on whether the feudal lord had infringed

146 Parliament

his duty of protection based on the mutual relationship of feudal protection and fealty. Hence, the idea is contractual in nature. This idea reflects the customary right of distress (contractual) against the king.

Many of those holding that natural law rights were superior to legislation hesitated to accept all the consequences of the theory of sovereignty. They would deny that human laws could take away from these rights. Sometimes, there were echoes of these views in Parliament.[23] Holdsworth sees these suggested limitations on parliamentary sovereignty in the nature of survivals. They were inconsistent with the theory of sovereignty clearly stated by those such as Halifax, Swift, and Blackstone with respect to the powers of Parliament and the binding force of statutes:

> In practice, little stress was laid on them except to provide debating points. Substantially the theory of sovereignty of Parliament was accepted and acted upon.[24]

INTELLECTUAL INFLUENCES: LOCKE AND HOBBES

Locke's views had significant influence in England and abroad. They reflected the political ideas of the Whig party of the period.[25]

In his *First Tract on Government* (1660), Locke argues that the supreme magistrate of every nation (supreme legislative power) must necessarily have an absolute and arbitrary power over all actions of people (other than those specifically prohibited or commanded by scripture).[26]

In the *Second Treatise of Government*, Locke uses contract theory to explain and justify the Revolution settlement. Locke's view was similar to the Jesuit view discussed earlier. Locke starts with the condition of mankind in a state of nature, having perfect freedom and equality, but governed by the law of nature which is reason. It teaches that as all are equal and independent, no one ought to harm another in life, health, liberty, or possessions.[27] While all men are responsible to execute the law of nature, in the state of nature there is not much security that it will be done. Therefore, they agree to join into a community for peaceful living in secure enjoyment of their properties, and for greater security.[28] In entering civil society and making the contract, people give up some liberties, but are not deprived of other natural rights which are inalienable. The state must govern in accordance with laws securing these natural rights of life, liberty, and property, and the state is limited by them.[29] Accordingly, law or authority for civil society was not derived from the will of any sovereign, but from the natural rights of every individual and from his will, as a rational and sociable being, to set up machinery to secure them.

The legislative authority is bound by the law of God, and the limited nature of the authority people conferred on it. A legislature cannot act absolutely arbitrarily: it can never destroy, enslave, or designedly impoverish the subjects.[30] It is bound to govern by general, promulgated laws equally applicable to all; it may tax only with the consent of the people; it cannot transfer its power to another legislative body; and, it must legislate for the good of the people.[31] The ultimate guarantee against a sovereign's will is contained in the principles of nature and reason, which lie outside history and do not change with its changes.

Thus, natural rights are above the law of the state. If government acts contrary to the trust, it is *ipso facto* dissolved,[32] and the people are the ultimate judge of whether a government has so acted. While human laws contrary to natural law are invalid, the remedy is not judicial nullification. The first and fundamental positive law of all commonwealths is establishing a legislative power which is the supreme power. The legislative power must be superior and all other powers derived from it and subordinate. Therefore, the judiciary is subordinate to the legislature, and it is impossible that an inferior power should prescribe to a superior. No other edict can have the force of law. Therefore, there can be no appeal on earth for a tyrannical legislature, no judge between the legislature and people, except an extra-constitutional resort to arms, or 'appeal to heaven.' This is reserved to the people by law antecedent and paramount to all positive laws.[33] Thus, the community in this respect is always the supreme power. However, while government subsists, the legislative power is superior.

Locke's view was that the king, Lords, and Commons shared supreme legislative power. He saw this arrangement as desirable, and reflected the long-established view that what was done in Parliament through its representatives was done with the consent of the nation.

On the other hand, in terms of influence, Holdsworth argues that because Hobbes constructed a political theory on the basis of logic

148 Parliament

and expediency, his influence over his generation was small, and only in the beginning of the nineteenth century were his merits fully appreciated.[34] This fact disproves the allegation that the doctrine of parliamentary supremacy is of more recent vintage, or that the 'common law constitution' that supposedly controlled statutes was eroded by such theories, beginning with Hobbes'.

PARLIAMENTARY SUPREMACY DOUBTERS

General Discussion and Criticism Concerning McIlwain

In the development of parliamentary powers is found the origin of the peculiarly English combination of the doctrine of the rule of law with the doctrine of the legislative supremacy of Parliament. The doctrine that law should govern the state was held by lawyers and many other medieval thinkers. In England, it was given a more definite meaning and a larger practical effect. It was used as the premise to justify the control over taxation and legislation that Parliament acquired. The idea that law was supreme because the king could not change the laws or impose taxes without Parliament's consent became the chief article of political faith. At the close of the Middle Ages, this idea was coming to mean the supremacy of law which Parliament could change and modify.

McIlwain's view to the contrary is not persuasive. McIlwain's instances are taken from a case turning on the pre-Reformation view of the Church-State relationship, which is a special and a very intelligible exception to the ordinary rule.[35] Even more damaging to his claim is his attempt to explain the activist approach sometimes taken by the common law courts as being based on and justified by the fact that common law courts, Parliament, and Council had a common ancestry, and that these institutions often exercised several distinct governmental functions simultaneously, such as Parliament acting as both a court and a legislator.[36] As a legal and jurisdictional description, it is in error. As we have seen, while judges were members of Council, they could share in the power of the Curia. However, once the common law courts became completely separated, they no longer shared in these large and indefinite (sovereign) powers, and the judges themselves were well aware of it, which resulted in the common law becoming extremely technical and unchanging.

The court's jurisdiction is a strictly delegated one, with a very narrow range of inherent jurisdiction.

More importantly, it is surprising that McIlwain's book *The High Court of Parliament* is used as a leading source to cast doubt on parliamentary supremacy or to support judges declaring statutes void, because it provides no such authority for either of these propositions. In fact, even if we accept his argument that prior to the seventeenth century England possessed a medieval conception of law which acted in the way he describes it, McIlwain clearly admits that after the Revolution, the new doctrine of parliamentary supremacy was firmly established in the constitution, although he does not like this fact and wishes that constitutional changes would occur to limit it.[37] In this way, he is more of a parliamentary supremacy detractor, than a doubter of its existence. His views do not affect at all the legal inability of courts, in a system of parliamentary supremacy, to declare legislation void. He acknowledges that the courts have recognized this fact and have not struck down legislation or interpreted it as they might have at a time when, in his view, they were engaging in a freer approach. In fact, while admitting parliamentary supremacy, he does not examine, as should be done, the legal implications of what inferior bodies, and particularly courts, may legally do.

Another flaw in his approach is his faulty treatment of the legislative assembly and Parliament, which colours his analysis and leads to error. This error is illustrated by his statement that Parliament could not be a sovereign legislature until the people of the time distinguished clearly between the spheres of legislation and judicature, and Parliament became a pure legislature and nothing else.[38] He makes this claim even though he admits that distinctions were drawn between judicial and non-judicial business in Edward I's parliament and thereafter.[39] Because he does not look at the system of government, he is led astray. One of his fallacies is to use the way in which institutions were structured, or actually performed their tasks at a given time, to determine the extent of sovereign power they were *capable* of exercising. The fact that Parliament may have exercised various functions (that is, legislative and judicial powers), or that Council may also have had jurisdiction to legislate, does not mean that Parliament was not supreme in a legislative sense. Nor is the breakdown of time spent by Parliament on judicial or legislative functions at a given point in time relevant to determining whether or not it is sovereign, or its legislative jurisdiction supreme. Nor does the scope of use of legislative powers or actual legislative output at some point in the distant past limit or determine the full exercise of those powers. Even today, although Parliament is sovereign, other inferior bodies, particularly government bureaucracies, exercise an astonishing amount of legislative, judicial, and administrative functions. To state that cases determined by, and laws produced by, each institution are of equal force and status leads to confusion, because Parliament's jurisdiction to legislate is greater than, and its legal status superior to, all others.

As we have seen, the evidence supports Goldsworthy's rejecting the claim of parliamentary sovereignty critics, who say the doctrine was invented in the late eighteenth and nineteenth centuries by academic lawyers, such as Blackstone and Dicey, influenced by Hobbesian political theory, who persuaded judges to discard an older common law tradition in which Parliament's legislative authority was limited.[40]

Also, McIlwain exaggerates the importance in England of the conception of a fundamental law that even Parliament could not change. It is clear that Parliament made new law, as did the earlier Anglo-Saxon assemblies. McIlwain denies that the medieval ruler's law-making power was sovereign because it satisfied only Dicey's negative criterion – it was not limited by any law enforceable by courts or other legal organs, but was nonetheless limited by law.[41] It is, of course, true that the medieval mind would not have been attuned to postulating the absolute sovereignty of Parliament or the state because of the assumption that domestic law derived its force from divine law. As we have seen, parliamentary supremacy is compatible with a belief in higher law (for example, divine or natural), as long as it is not enforceable by courts or any human agency, nor set out in a formally enacted legal instrument.[42] Furthermore, Magna Carta, though in declaratory form, was enacted law; it both declared custom and made new law. It was amended and in part repealed even during the Middle Ages. When the king and Parliament spoke of fundamental laws in the seventeenth century, they were thinking of rights which, in their opinion, the existing law gave to them. These rights they deemed fundamental in the sense that they were the basis of the constitution, as the rulers conceived it, not in the sense that Parliament could not change them.[43] Furthermore, while there may be a feeling that some right or liberty, as for example arising from a longstanding custom or from legislation, is fundamental and unalterable, this is different from saying that there is a right or liberty which cannot be changed legally by Parliament. Gough's study of what the English meant when they spoke about fundamentals during the seventeenth century reveals that there was no single meaning to fundamental law. The phrase was very vague and ill-defined, and usually meant something of great importance to the speaker, while some doubted the concept altogether. The modern implication of judicial review was not, and never has been, part of English law.[44] Even this feeling of a fundamental law was lost with the growth of parliamentary power. Similarly, much confusion arose in England about calling an Act 'unconstitutional' legislation, when it was perfectly legal constitutionally.

Such a view about the purported invalidity of statute based on fundamental law contradicts the concept of custom, as discussed previously, growing out of social life as an inborn right, and not being under the control of any superior authority, but rather being determinable by the court of the people. If new laws were desired, the people had to adopt them in the Witan. In the Middle Ages, bodies of custom developed and adapted themselves to changing conditions. At a time when custom was a living system, there was less insistence on actual or fictitious antiquity; a ten-year-old custom was considered a long-standing one.[45] As Plucknett notes, custom was not just modified to meet changing conditions, but it was deliberately imported from one place to another, and it was common for groups of townspeople to examine the customs of more advanced communities, to choose the one they liked best, and to adopt it as their own. Custom in the Middle Ages could be made, changed, bought, sold, and developed rapidly as it proceeded from the people.[46] Therefore, there seems to have been no rule preventing people from changing their particular customs. Indeed, the fundamental customary rule appeared to be that the people could adopt what customs they pleased. Furthermore, in order to create one common law out of the patchwork of traditions that existed, the Curia necessarily had to change customs, and also did so when it thought a custom was unreasonable.

An idea of unchangeable fundamental law would have contradicted the concept of legislation even in Anglo-Saxon times. Jenks argues that legislation was known in the Middle Ages through

152   Parliament

Roman law, and that true legislation is the product of Roman ideas. Early Germanic laws were not really legislative, but were only official memoranda of tribal custom, until the tribes had become familiar with Roman political ideas and then began to legislate.[47] One striking function of the Roman Emperor was the power to legislate. However, as we have seen, Anglo-Saxon laws are truly legislative, and not merely declarations of custom, not only by the time of Egbert, but two hundred years before with radical legislation dealing with the new class of clergy.

According to Goldsworthy, McIlwain's thesis requires establishing that while medieval parliaments made new law, they did not do so in the full modern sense. Goldsworthy's statement is challengeable in that all depends on the system of government then existing, which is what determines the legal powers of state institutions or actors, and not the extent to which powers were actually exercised. The sixteenth century is not the most significant foundational point establishing that system of government, but rather 1688 is. Also, McIlwain's argument may confuse principle and substance and the meaning of a change in customary principle, or else he is unclear on the point. In any event, his argument is that, before the sixteenth century, law-making was attenuated; it was procedural and not substantive, concerned with proclaiming and enforcing customary principles, but not changing them. He believes wrongly that the medieval mind was not attuned to social change, and assumes these principles and practices were timeless and immutable. McIlwain concludes that Parliament could not change law.[48]

Goldsworthy argues that McIlwain exaggerates the difference between medieval and modern attitudes to law-making. Even today, there are principles and practices of the community that Parliament has the legal authority to change, but its doing so would not be regarded as legitimate. The differences between the medieval and modern attitudes is one of degree, not kind.[49]

We have already seen that substantive legislative changes had occurred. For example, *De Donis* created a fee tail allowing the creation of a virtually inalienable estate contrary to the common law, which lies at the foundation of the idea of legal estates in land.[50] Also of note is the fact that equity and other laws were outside the common law, and operated on different principles. These too were part of the law of England. Another example is the change from the principle of kindred to a breach of the king's peace as the basis of criminal law. Statute was at the basis of the action in trespass. Following the writ made by the king and Council in 1219 abolishing trial by ordeal, which was time-honoured and even regarded as a right, the Statute of Westminster I declared trial by jury to be the "common law of the land."[51] As Elton notes, if medieval parliaments did not legislate, much of the Rolls of Parliament become incomprehensible.[52] Furthermore, laws were regularly made in medieval England to bring about social and political change, and no fundamental laws were regarded as immutable.[53] The Reformation statutes, as we have seen, also refute McIlwain's claims. Other statutes deal with change in social and economic conditions, such as the poor laws, and the change in governing and economic statutes from medieval conceptions of the just price, just profits, and reasonable manufacture, to the focus on the power of the state, and later on mercantilism. Furthermore, during the Tudor period, the regulation of commercial and professional life by the crown replaced that of the guild and ecclesiastical authorities.

Finally, it is only very exceptionally[54] that one sees the idea of law which Parliament cannot change, and then only in the arguments of extreme prerogative lawyers. For example, it was asserted in *Godden v. Hales* that the king was the sovereign prince and had certain inherent prerogatives which could not be taken away even by Parliament. Even then, they avoided using this argument if they had any more solid reasons to advance.[55]

In Henry VIII's reign, it was realized that Acts of Parliament, whether public or private, were legislative in character, and the judges were obliged to admit that these Acts, however morally unjust, must be obeyed.[56] Furthermore, legislation deposing the Pope and making the Church part of the State made it clear that neither the morality of a law, nor the reasons inducing legislature to pass it, could not be considered by the courts. Some, such as Thomas More, argued that parliamentary legislation making the king head of the Church was void as contrary to divine law, as it would be if it legislated that there is no God. Furthermore, Henry VIII recognized that law could be changed by Parliament alone, and thus that England was a constitutional monarchy.[57]

A good illustration of this point is Bacon's argument in *Chudleigh's Case* to the effect that the law carries authority in itself. The argument was in respect of the preamble to the Statute of Uses. The preamble gives aim to the body of the statute, it sets the mark, and the body of law levels at it.[58]

Holdsworth argues that when an Act of Parliament acquired this authority, the last remnants of the idea that there might be fundamental laws that could not be changed necessarily disappeared.[59]

Common lawyers rarely showed any desire to question the power of Parliament to make, change, or modify law. The dominant legal opinion was that Parliament, not judges, had supreme power to interpret laws, and judges could not reverse their decision. That is, Parliament defined what was actually enforceable as law in courts, and only another parliament could reverse it.[60]

General Discussion and Legal Criticism Concerning Coke

Coke sometimes wrote as if he believed in the supremacy of law, which even Parliament could not change. The most prominent example is his dicta in *Dr. Bonham*, in which he stated, "In many cases the law will control acts of Parliament and sometimes adjudge them to be utterly void."[61] In *Calvin's Case*[62] there are some vague statements of the impossibility of altering a provision of natural law, even by Parliament. Holdsworth notes a number of errors or difficulties with this position.[63]

First, it is a mistake to place too much stress on isolated statements of this kind, as McIlwain does. Furthermore, although Coke relied on Bacon to the contrary, Bacon did not hold this view.[64]

Second, Coke is often inconsistent because he had the mind of an advocate, and often allowed himself to be carried away by the argument that he was urging at the moment.[65] As a crown lawyer he magnified prerogative. As head of the common law system he exalted law, and completely changed his attitude towards the crown. Furthermore, his advocacy tended to make him uncritical in the use of his authorities, and he misrepresented their effect in order to achieve the conclusion he wanted. When he became the leader of the parliamentary opposition, he reconsidered and recanted some of his previously declared opinions, which displays his political bias.

Other historians are less charitable and state that he sometimes carelessly and sometimes intentionally misrepresented historical facts. Compared to historians, such as Selden or Bacon, his historical

Parliamentary Sovereignty 155

work has been justifiably described as contemptible. One technique he used was to search back into the Record for writs, cases, or Rolls in support of one proposition, such as the denial that William created the institution of sheriffs, but to then attempt to prove another proposition which the precedent does not support. For example, he cites a pre-Conquest writ to a person acting as a sheriff to take security from the complainant and return the chattels allegedly stolen until the matter could be tried by judges, and to have twelve men view the tenament. From the twelve men returned by the sheriff mentioned, Coke then attempts to establish that trial by jury existed.[66] However, that conclusion goes well beyond what the writ established. Another example is Coke's claim that the Court of Common Pleas was not created after Magna Carta by statute in the ninth year of Henry III's reign. His basis was that Magna Carta mentions this court and uses the words 'justices of the bench.' He reasons that because justices of Common Pleas are justices of the bench (*de banco*), that court existed before Magna Carta. However, a logical fallacy is evident. Judges of Common Pleas are judges of the bench, but that does not mean that there are no other courts whose justices are justices of the bench, or that the Court of Common Pleas existed before Magna Carta. Coke also relies on the now discredited source *Mirrors of Justice*.

Plucknett argues that as lawyers voluntarily resigned to Coke their private judgment of the Year Books, by careful selection of material Coke was able to conceal the inconsistences and difficulties which were inherent in his position.[67] Still, his reports had a good reputation and his mastery of the English legal system was recognized, and allowed for the idea of the continuity of English law.

Third, Coke "was so thoroughly steeped in medieval law that he sometimes reproduced ideas which were obsolete or nearly obsolete, and that he himself would have admitted to be archaic."[68]

Fourth, Coke was often writing and thinking of the supremacy of the existing law, and not the question of whether Parliament was competent to change it. When Parliament was not sitting, it was the existing law as interpreted by judges which was in effect supreme, and when, as in the seventeenth century, the different component parts of Parliament could not act together, the same result occurred.

Fifth, in his *Fourth Institute*, when dealing specifically with the powers of Parliament, and in other passages, he admits its supremacy, including in the matter of law-making.[69] In the *Fourth Institute*, he recognizes that Parliament's law-making power is so transcendent and absolute that it cannot be confined within any bounds.[70] In the *Eighth Part of the Reports*, Coke describes Parliament as the ultimate and sacrosanct authority in laying down, confirming, abrogating, interpreting, and consolidating laws, in deciding the more difficult lawsuits between private people, and in all things whatsoever that may belong to the health of the state or to any private matter.[71] Coke gave examples of statutes that overrode basic laws of the land, such as the Statute of Attainder without trial, and even suggested the validity of statutes contrary to Magna Carta.[72] In the *Second Institute*, he said that the highest and most binding laws were parliamentary statutes, and a resolution of all the judges was next highest.[73] With respect to the effect of the Petition of Right, 1628, Coke stated that whatever the Lords and Commons agreed upon, no judge ever went against it, and when the judges in former times doubted of the law they went to the parliament, and there resolutions were given, to which they were bound.[74]

Furthermore, Coke clearly understood that Parliament was no mere court of justice, but a legislative body. He states of Parliament:

> This is not that Court that in *France* bear the Name of Parliaments, for they are but ordinary Courts of Justice ... But this is that which both *England* and *Scotland* agree in naming of it a Parliament, which the *French* doth term *Assemblee des Estats* or *les Estats* [assembly of the estates, or the estates], and the *German* a Dyet.[75]

In the *Eighth Part of the Reports* and the *Fourth Part of the Reports* Coke talks of two kinds of statutes enacted in the supreme court of Parliament: first, when an ancient pillar of the common law was taken out, which gave rise to dangers, and of which he gives examples when it was done and negative consequences arose; and, second, when new remedies were added to the common law.[76] Accordingly, Coke was very much aware that Parliament could both make new law and correct the old.

Coke's *Dr. Bonham* dicta, that the courts may declare Acts of Parliament void that are contrary to common right and reason or impossible to carry into effect, are founded on very little medieval authority, and on authorities which do not support such a suggestion.[77] In the Brownlow report, the proposition is illustrated by the case of the crown allowing a man to be the judge in his own case, which was assumed to be so legally or morally impossible that the grant was void, though it had been confirmed by Parliament. On the contrary, not only are there no medieval English cases holding that a statute is void because it contravenes some fundamental principle, but the Year Books constantly assert expressly that statutes were making new law and abrogating old law; therefore, the judges were conscious of the fact of radical legislation.[78]

It is true that Blackstone said that the law of nature, being coeval with mankind and dictated by God himself, was superior in obligation to any other. It was binding over all the globe and at all times. No human laws were valid if contrary.[79] However, this position must not be taken out of context. As discussed earlier, Blackstone says that such Acts were law and must be obeyed, but that there was a right to rebel. As such, there is no contradiction.

The view that any law contrary to the law of God, or to natural law, is void was ultimately derived from canon law doctrine prevailing on the Continent. This notion was employed, for instance, when the Church was not willing to allow state law to override its canons, and asserted that secular law must yield in cases of conflict. The principle was accepted by English churchmen, and set out in provincial canons. Becket lost his life maintaining it. So too did Thomas More, who refused to accept the First Succession Act of 1533, or to swear an oath under it which disparaged the power of the Pope and Henry VIII's marriage to Catherine of Aragon. More was executed for treason with the aid of perjured testimony.

Plucknett argues that in view of the coming conflict of crown and Parliament, Coke felt it necessary to attempt to curb what he saw to be the rising arrogance of both, and looked to legal history to do so. His attitude was expressed in his phrase "Let us now peruse our ancient authors, for out of old fields must come the new corne." Coke's solution lay in the idea of fundamental law limiting crown and Parliament indifferently.[80]

The issue did arise of whether statutes contrary to natural law were void as common law lawyers sometimes said. Even if so, it did not follow that they believed judges possessed authority to declare statutes invalid. Finch's *Law, a Discourse Thereof* (1627) was an

158   Parliament

exposition of the common law, the reputation of which was not superseded until Blackstone's *Commentaries*. He stated that positive laws against natural law lose their force and are not laws. Later in the book, he says Parliament had an absolute power in all causes, including making laws, and if Parliament erred it could not be reversed but by Parliament.

Elton notes that Parliament was the supreme legislator unhampered by other laws, though still obliged by piety and morality embodied in the unwritten laws of God and nature. Parliament's laws were dominant over the executors of the law – both crown and courts.[81] If Parliament erred it was legally unchallengeable. Divine or natural law were not enforceable by inferiors against superiors, and Parliament had no superior.

Natural law was compatible with parliamentary sovereignty. The important questions are which organ of government had ultimate legal authority to determine the requirements of God's law, and what the consequences were if Parliament errs. The orthodox answer to the first question is the king in Parliament, and to the second, if it erred, the only earthly remedy was repeal by statute.

It was generally agreed that subjects were not morally obligated to obey a statute manifestly contrary to God's laws, although disobedience was legally punishable and one had to submit to such punishment.[82] Thus, judges, like other subjects, might justifiably disobey such statutes, but it did not follow that judges had legal authority to declare them invalid any more than ordinary subjects had such authority. All were subordinate to Parliament. Therefore, the evidence leads to the conclusion that even lawyers accepting a common law theory had little support for judicial review of the validity of statutes.

The chief, and possibly only, clear instance of this doctrine of limits on Parliament's power actually stated in Parliament's Rolls is the Duke of York's argument against statutes entailing the crown on the Lancastrians.[83] However, it is clear that neither he nor anyone else attached much weight to it.[84]

Fortescue C.J. was reluctant to take the unusual step of deciding an Act of Parliament void, even assuming irregularities in its passage.[85] The king was not absolute. He needed the assent of the whole realm as represented in Parliament to legislate or tax. Parliament represented the collective wisdom, which was superior to that of the one or the few. Maitland doubted medieval judges considered themselves free to question the validity of statute on such grounds. The vigorous legislation of medieval parliaments rendered any theory of law above the king or the king and Parliament unworkable.[86] Subsequent historical research vindicates this conclusion.[87]

Such dicta by Coke were contrary to the principles of the common law as understood by Coke himself and other lawyers of the parliamentary party. The cases Coke cited only amount to the proposition that courts would interpret statutes *stricti juris*;[88] that is, the court would interpret in such a way as to give a meaning in accordance with established principle, and could not give effect to them if they were meaningless or impossible to apply. Blackstone correctly states that "[w]here some collateral matter arises out of the general words, and happens to be unreasonable, there the judges are in decency to conclude that this consequence was not foreseen by parliament, and therefore they are at liberty to expound the statute by equity, and only [to that extent] to disregard it ... But, if we could conceive it possible for the parliament to enact, that he should treat as well his own causes as those of their persons, there is no court that has power to defeat the intent of the legislature, when couched in such evident and express words as leave no doubt whether it was the intent of the legislature or no."[89] Such principles of interpretation would properly be accepted today. Furthermore, statutory provisions have at all times been criticized by judges and lawyers, and given a restrictive interpretation. The continued alliance between Parliament and lawyers prevented a general disposition among lawyers to question the omnipotence of Parliament.[90]

As we have seen, sometimes judges ruled that the truth of certain statements universally known to be untrue could not be questioned, which rendered ineffectual the clearly expressed will of Parliament. However, the use of fictions demonstrated that judges knew they had not the power to override legislation, and therefore acted illegally and dishonestly to achieve the result they wanted.

The evidence also implies, and most historians agree, that Coke did not even mean to say that courts could invalidate such a statute. In the case decided after *Dr. Bonham*, Coke held that diverse customs in London were permitted, despite being against common right and the rule of law, because they had the force of custom, supported and fortified by parliamentary authority.[91] From the examples cited, it seems clear that Parliament could sanction matters contrary to some of the dearest principles or reasons of common law. Thus, historians conclude that Coke only meant courts would interpret statutes *stricti juris*. Some suggest he was attempting to revive the medieval approach of judicial latitude in the application of statutes in sometimes declining to apply them, but without recognizing any judicial power of nullification. If so, this medieval approach was long obsolete given the development of constitutional practice and theory, and the separation of courts from Council.[92]

A few historians say that Coke intended to assert something like a power of judicial review. Boyer concedes that Coke was going well beyond the precedents he cited and broke new ground. Detmold says that Coke regarded Parliament as the final court of appeal, whose statutes were binding on lower courts only if and insofar as they settled disputes between particular named individuals. Otherwise, they were liable to be overruled just as common law doctrines could be overruled if judged to be erroneous. Goldsworthy cites two objections to these positions. First, they are based on McIlwain's erroneous account of Parliament's functions before the 1640s. Second, they implausibly attribute to Coke Detmold's own incorrect belief that an inferior court is entitled to overrule, as well as distinguish legal rules laid down by, a superior court.[93]

Even if in *Dr. Bonham* Coke advocated some power of judicial review, he soon later changed his mind.[94] By "common right and reason," Coke meant the common law, not natural law, and it was evident that Parliament could change the common law, even though Coke thought that ill-advised.[95]

Coke's *Bonham* dicta was largely ignored, and it was doubtful whether other judges sitting on the case endorsed it. There is strong evidence, based on a comparison of a newly discovered manuscript report of the case with Coke's official report of it, that it was an embellishment he added after judgment was delivered, when preparing his report of the case.[96]

Hobart C.J. made similar comments in *Day v. Savadge*, which also were interpreted as asserting a power of construction rather than nullification.[97]

The authority of Parliament was sometimes challenged in the 1640s when it was accused of trampling on traditional rights in the struggle with the king. Judge Jenking, a supporter of the king imprisoned by the Houses during the Civil War, argued that Parliament

Parliamentary Sovereignty

was bound by Magna Carta and relied on Coke's *Bonham* dicta to bolster his argument. This was the first appearance of that dictum as a matter of public, political, and constitutional importance.[98]

The dictum was cited by Dallison, who was punished for supporting the king. He denied that Parliament, or the Lords, was the highest court. He said that judges were the judges of the realm and people were bound to submit themselves to law. Fundamental law could override statute.[99] Also, Clevland in 1629 argued that if Parliament legislated against natural equity so as to constitute a person judge in his own case, the statute was void and controlled by the common law.

By the fifteenth century, legislation was much more clearly distinguished from adjudication. Chrimes studied the relation between statutes and common law. He concluded that the supremacy of statute was unquestioned. There is no case of nullification on the grounds of a law's being contrary to natural or divine law.[100] Doe states that legislators and judges at the time treated morally abhorrent statutes as valid law, and as operative until repealed by subsequent legislation. This was based on an incipient idea of parliamentary sovereignty. Judges invalidated local customs offending against reason or common right. They did not claim similar authority to invalidate statutes, and never did so during the fifteenth century.[101] Myres concludes that by the end of the fifteenth century, judicial opinion had established that statutes could override common law, were superior to ordinances, could bind all the king's domains and subjects, were upheld despite conflict with royal prerogative, could override the Law Merchant, and could define the limits of canon law.[102]

As stated earlier, Parliament was seen as representing the whole community and as infallible. In 1615 Ellesmere LC criticized Coke's *Bonham* dicta for advancing the reason of a particular court above the judgment of all the realm.[103] Coke asserts that Parliament possessed the highest wisdom of the realm, and could never be thought to act dishonourably or "against the truth."[104] English judges were bound by their oaths not to render judgments against the laws of the land even if commanded by the prince to the contrary.

Other Cases Implying that Courts Can Overrule Parliament

Rex v. Knollys (1695) involved an effort by the Lords to interfere with a decision of King's Bench. The court held that the defendant was a peer, ignoring the Lords' ruling to the contrary. Since he had been indicted as a commoner, the indictment could not stand. The court held that the matter had not been referred to the House by the crown, therefore the House had no jurisdiction to decide. Its allegation that it had such jurisdiction by the law and custom of Parliament was disregarded. The court stated that if there were any such law and custom of Parliament, then judges should decide on it when it came before them since they decided matters of as high nature every day; "for they construe and expound Acts of Parliament, and adjudge them to be void."[105] Holdsworth argues that Holt C.J.'s statement was an exaggeration.[106] Hamburger notes that this opinion of adjudging Acts void is curiously missing from Holt's surviving manuscript opinions, and indeed Holt rejected judicial review of parliamentary Acts, while justifying extra-judicial limitations based on natural law.[107]

During the eighteenth century, it was widely held that rules of international law were part of the law of England.[108] In *Heathfield v. Chilton*,[109] Mansfield J. made the same assertion and added that an Act of Parliament cannot alter the law of nations. Probably, he did not intend to assert that the English courts could disregard an Act of Parliament altering the law of nations, but only that the law of nations, being, as Blackstone said in his *Commentaries*, dependent on the principles of natural justice, could not be affected by an Act of Parliament. If he meant more than this, his dictum can be regarded, as Pound said, as "the last echo in England of Coke's doctrine in Bonham's Case."[110] Or some may say that Mansfield may have been guilty of the same confusion as above, of saying that no human laws contrary to the law of nature were of any validity while admitting the supremacy of Parliament, in which case these restrictions were only morally binding. However, this view is not a contradiction when properly understood as established historically.

Vaughan C.J.'s statement in *Thomas v. Sorrell* that a law making murder, stealing, perjury, or trespass lawful would be void in itself[111] is sometimes quoted as support for a judicial power to invalidate statutes. Goldsworthy argues correctly that much cannot be made of this statement because Vaughan C.J. said that such a law would be self-contradictory, as the very meaning of those words is that the acts they describe are unlawful. It would make the same thing lawful and unlawful, which is impossible, and a law which one cannot obey or act according to is void. Also, Vaughan conceded that killing or taking one's property are distinguishable, as a law can alter or transfer one's property in life, liberty, estate, or any interest. Thus, nothing unlawful is made lawful.[112]

Some dicta attributed to Holt C.J. in an unreliable report of *City of London v. Wood* suggest he may have believed Parliament's legislative authority to be limited by law.[113] Hamburger's analysis of two unpublished manuscripts of his judgment, one in his own handwriting, showed he held the opposite view.[114] The issue was whether Parliament could make someone a judge in a case in which he was also a party. Holt, influenced by recent natural law theory, saw this action as impossible. As the primary purpose of government was to end otherwise interminable private disputes by providing an independent arbiter, theorists such as Locke claimed it would be contrary to the essence of government for one party in a dispute to act as judge. Holt endorsed this view by stating that it was contrary to the principles and ends of commonwealths and civil societies for a man to be a judge in his own cause. A statute proposing to do this was an absolute contradiction because a judge and a party were in their nature and institution different and distinct; one excluded the other. It tried to do the impossible, like, De Lome says, turning a man into a woman. Thus, the Act must be interpreted in another way, such as designating someone other than the parties to adjudicate, or allowing one party to do whatever he wanted, in effect exempting him from legal judgment. In the latter case, both parties were returned to the state of nature, and government with respect to the matter is dissolved. There is no mention of statutes being void. Acts of inferior bodies not exercising sovereign power were subject to review, but an Act of Parliament bound absolutely without any question of its justice or equity.[115] Holt also says elsewhere that liberty and property could not be diminished or infringed by a lesser authority than the legislature.[116] Hamburger concludes that Holt's position was that the only power to defeat an act of a body with sovereign power lay, not in the judiciary, but presumably in those who had originally given that sovereign power, or else there was no obligation to obey.[117]

When the actual issue arose, the courts did not follow Holt's approach. *Parish of Great Charter v. Parish of Kennington* (1742) held that in some circumstances a statute could authorize someone

164   Parliament

to act as judge in a cause in which he had an interest, which was affirmed in *Grand Junction Canal Co. v. Dimes* (1849), despite *Dr. Bonham* cited to the contrary.[118]

Leiverman concludes that although eighteenth-century judges often criticized statutes for being poorly drafted or misconceived, and insisted courts were better qualified than Parliament to develop the law, they did not claim the courts could control Parliament's legislative will.[119]

VIEWS OF THE PERIOD

Whatever may be true of earlier periods, Holdsworth states that in the sixteenth century it is clear that the supremacy of law, taught by Bracton and the Year Books, had come to mean, not the supremacy of an unchangeable law, but the supremacy of a law which Parliament could change. The supremacy of law was coming to mean the supremacy of Parliament.

The lawyers did not obstruct this process. The supremacy of existing law, as long as Parliament did not alter it, was guaranteed by Parliament's powers, and to it could safely be left the political task of maintaining this position. There was no need for common law courts to be anything but useful servants of the crown. They thus continued to be the guardians and interpreters of the common law.

Holdsworth concludes that at the end of this period, the legislative supremacy of Parliament was fully recognized. Questions remained unsettled until the seventeenth century, such as the limits of crown and Council to issue binding proclamations or ordinances, and the reconciliation of the crown's dispensing and suspending powers over statutes with legislative supremacy. It was also clear that no medieval lawyer or statesman would have admitted that Parliament possessed theoretically unlimited powers of legislation.[120] Gough notes that in the seventeenth century, some thought that the legislative capacity of Parliament or other authority was limited by moral rights, and did not clearly distinguish these moral rights from legal rights or obligations.[121] Today, there is no difficulty in distinguishing between law and morals. Although at the end of this period, the modern territorial state was practically formed, a political theory based on the new conditions had not yet been developed. Medieval lawyers and statesmen would have conceded that Parliament was the supreme law-making authority in the state, but would deny that this constituted legislative omnipotence, as the law made by Parliament was one among many kinds of state law. For example, they would have denied Parliament's competence to pass laws against fundamental moral rules, those being part of the law of nature which natural reason taught all mankind. Also, the Church and State were still separate, and a large part of the nation in the religious orders would have denied that Parliament could freely legislate within the ecclesiastical sphere.

Respect for fundamental laws, however, did not mean that Parliament recognized any legal limit to its legislative capacity.[122] For example, the Act to Preserve the King (1661)[123] recognized fundamental laws and liberties, but another clause provided that it should not deprive Parliament of its just and ancient freedom and privilege of debating matters touching the repeal or alteration of any old laws, or preparing any new ones. Parliament knew it could enact and make into law whatever it chose, but its laws might be wrong. The Act Restoring the Temporal Authority of Ecclesiastical Persons (1661)[124] allowed the bishops to regain their seats in the House of Lords. Parliament did not pretend that the Act of the Long Parliament depriving the bishops of their ancient right was invalid. It stated that this Act "made several alterations prejudicial to the constitution and ancient rights of parliament, and contrary to the laws of the land."

These *ethical* limitations on the legislative supremacy of Parliament gradually disappeared during the sixteenth and seventeenth centuries with the change in Church-State relations, the constitutional changes with the Reformation, the rise of the modern territorial state, the growth of the modern doctrine of sovereignty, the Civil War, and the Revolution.

Post-Revolution, Eighteenth Century – The Meaning of Parliamentary Sovereignty

The accepted theory is that the king, Lords, and Commons in Parliament together make up the sovereign power in the state. Blackstone describes Parliament as the sovereign, uncontrollable authority to make, repeal, modify, and expound laws on all possible matters. This is the place where absolute despotic power resides as entrusted by the constitution, which must in all governments reside somewhere. "It can, in short, do every thing that is not naturally impossible."[125] Thus, an Act of Parliament is the exercise of the highest authority Britain acknowledges on earth. It has the power to bind every subject, even the king. It cannot be altered, amended, dispensed, suspended, or repealed, other than by the same form and authority of Parliament. The basic maxim in law is that it requires the same strength to dissolve as to create an obligation.[126]

The doctrine holds that there are no fundamental constitutional laws Parliament cannot change, other than parliamentary supremacy.

Dicey states that the positive criterion of sovereignty is that Parliament has the right to make or unmake any law whatsoever.[127] Its negative meaning under English law is that no person or body has a right to override or set aside Parliament's legislation. This is a legal (not moral) right. He defines law as any rule which will be enforced by courts. In his restatement, he says that from the positive side any Act of Parliament making law or repealing or modifying existing law will be obeyed by the courts. On the negative side, no person or body can override or derogate from an Act of Parliament, and no court can enforce an action in contravention to the Act. Goldsworthy states that this clarification is to address the distinction between legal and moral duty, and that only Parliament has the legal authority to override its own statute, and courts must obey statute (even if in an extraordinary situation they might disobey on the grounds that their legal duty to obey is overridden by a moral duty to disobey).[128]

Goldsworthy wants to qualify Dicey in two ways.[129] First, the final appellate court is not sovereign. It is bound by law, even if its mistakes in applying law are not subject to correction, and its decisions are therefore legally conclusive. It is generally regarded as bound by, and in fact generally obeys, laws that are written or incorporated in formally enacted legal instruments, and that are relatively clear. While courts are widely believed today to exercise a discretionary, law-making power to change the common law in the interests of justice, they do not possess a sovereign law-making power. They cannot repeal statutes, and can only decide particular disputes brought to them, rather than acting on their own motion and enacting whatever laws of general application they please. The law-making power of the 'high court' of Parliament is not so limited.

The second qualification follows from Hart's criticism of Hobbesian theories of law. Legal rules, especially rules of recognition, constitute the foundations of the legal system, and their existence is explained by their being accepted as binding, at least by senior legal officials, rather than the commands of a legally transcendent sovereign. The sovereign law-maker is created by fundamental laws that allow it to legislate. Thus, Goldsworthy states that a legislature is the sovereign law-making power if its ability to change the law is not limited by any norms concerning the substance of legislation that are judicially enforceable, are relatively clear, and are set out in formally enacted legal instruments. That is so even if this legislature is governed by judicially enforceable norms that determine its composition, its procedure, and the form by which it must legislate. Its sovereign power is a continuing one even if it includes the power to change the norms that govern its own composition, procedure, and form of legislation, provided only that it cannot use that power to unduly inhibit its own ability to change the substance of the law however and whenever it chooses.

However, part of Goldsworthy's argument may also show some confusion between sovereignty itself (a legal conception) and the effective exercise of sovereignty, a confusion shared by Holdsworth. These questions are separate. Thus, it is difficult to disagree, as Goldsworthy does, with the Judicial Committee of the Privy Council's *Ranasinghe* decision,[130] which held that no question of sovereignty arises from the fact that the Constitution of Ceylon is amendable by a two-thirds majority of Parliament and remains sovereign if the requisite majority is not obtained.

Much confusion can be avoided if a clearer and more precise description of the system of government is made, rather than a more philosophical and abstract analysis of the nature of law, or a description of what senior legal officials at any point in time generally agree upon, except for events directly related to the creation or modification of the law of the constitution or the system of government.

Medieval Ideas of Limitation on a Ruler's Power

The above-mentioned limitations on a ruler's powers, in terms of both divine and natural law, which were important in medieval thought, were ethical and not legal limitations on such powers. Even

168 Parliament

common law lawyers who supported the supremacy of law, such as Hale, stated that the king was bound by natural justice and equity, but could not be called to account by the subject:

> And as the obligation of Naturall Justice bindes Princes and Governors as well as others to stand to their Pacts and agreements with their People, So there is Superadded to that obligation the greate Solemnitie of the Oath which he takes at his Coronation to observe & keepe those Laws and Liberties. And tho' it is true that the Kinges Person is Sacred, and not under any Externall Coertion, nor to be arraigned by his Subjects for the violation of that Sacred Oath yett no man can made a Question whether he not in the Sight of God and by the bond of Naturall Justice oblidged to keepe itt.[131]

Nevertheless these ideas of the ethical limitation on Parliament's legislative supremacy had a great part to play in political controversies, giving rise to a belief in the existence of indefeasible rights superior to state authority, to the advocating of a right of resistance to tyranny, and to popular encroachments on royal rights. It was used by Locke to defend the 1688 Revolution. It was also used by royalists regarding the extent of prerogative in the Middle Ages, and in the seventeenth century when the king thought statutory or common law rules restricted prerogative too much, and made appeals to the doctrine of indefeasible prerogative.[132]

Some Fallacies and Myths

Another incorrect claim sometimes made is that an authoritarian, legal positivist dogma misconceives the 'real' foundations of the British constitution.[133] These writers attempt to reject the argument that Parliament has the ultimate authority to determine what the law shall be. They reject the generally accepted view that judges have the legal authority to declare what the law is and to change the common law, but are bound to accept parliamentary law as valid law, and that their decisions can be overturned by Parliament. These critics claim a logical relationship necessarily exists between statutory and common law. First, it is the responsibility of judges to declare what the law is. Second, therefore, the extent of Parliament's lawful authority to legislate is a matter for judges to determine. Specifically, it is necessarily a matter of common law (which is defined as a body of judicial decisions based on fundamental principles, such as justice and the rule of law). Third, therefore, Parliament is entitled to override much of the common law, but not its most fundamental principles, because they are the ultimate source of its own authority.

This argument is mistaken on different levels. First, even accepting the premises, which are in fact incorrect or misleading, the conclusions do not necessarily or even logically follow, and certainly ignore the relevant historical facts. This court-centric view is misleading as judicial powers cannot be evaluated without a full understanding of the system of government, including the legal framework of governmental powers. Court powers are only one part of that overall system. For example, this view says nothing about the ability of other state organs to declare the law, nor about the hierarchy of elements within that system of government, nor the relative authority of those organs in their pronouncements on what the law is or shall be. It ignores the fact that judicial authority itself is a matter of law, and therefore limited. For example, while judges have the power to declare what the law is, this is only a power to faithfully propound the law as it exists, and not a license to substitute their own preferences, values, purposes, or principles. Courts' jurisdiction may be limited by Parliament, and courts may be eliminated by Parliament. History has demonstrated that courts are to remain silent on matters of high politics, such as sovereignty, succession, and the like. A judicial responsibility to declare the substance of the law does not mean that judges can determine Parliament's legislative jurisdiction. In fact, some versions of 'administrative' law on the Continent make it clear that courts are to remain silent on a vast range of matters concerning government.

It is hard to find any evidence in the British system of government of the courts' legal ability to determine Parliament's authority. Rather, the opposite is true. Courts are bound to apply the laws duly passed by Parliament, a state of affairs going back to the Witan. The movement to accept the view that courts have the authority to change the common law (the portion based on judicial decisions), and the courts' appropriation of such a power, comes relatively later. This movement is to be distinguished from the power that judges held when they were part of Curia or Council. The customary portion of the law was the law because it came from the established practices of the people viewed as binding, not from judicial or any other authority, which judges were thought incapable of changing. Blackstone states that law and a judge's opinion are not the same, as the judge may mistake law. The general rule is that court decisions are only evidence of what is common law, though they are held in high regard.[134] In fact, pre-Conquest, the people were thought to have an inalienable right in custom which judges were incapable of changing.

The next step in the argument contains even more difficulties. It states that the law determining Parliament's legislative jurisdiction is necessarily a matter of common law, which is a body of judicial decisions based on fundamental principles, such as justice and the rule of law. First, as we have seen, the definition of common law used is patently incorrect. Common law is a mixture of statute and the custom of the royal court to the extent that said custom was not overruled or modified by legislation. Even Hale recognized this fact. The most foundational events legally establishing the system of parliamentary sovereignty were the Reformation, the Rebellion, and the Revolution. The principles underlying this system of government were not created by courts and judges, nor did courts and judges have either the power or the legal authority to do so. Furthermore, the history of the common law reveals that the common law is not even based on 'fundamental' principles, such as justice and the rule of law. Custom or the common law can be said to be based on principles, in the sense that it characterized the goals and rules of the system of law (or a particular area of it, such as kinship and *wergeld* paid in order to avoid blood feud). Any such principles are not superior to legislation, however, and legislation can overrule or modify judicial decisions. Judges are required to follow legislation, and are not at liberty to develop their own notions of principles in this respect. Furthermore, much of the common law in the hands of judges was actually quite unjust – for example, in the working of its technical procedures (which incidentally required prerogative and especially statute to overcome), and substantively in denying the rights of tenants who made arrangements with their lords to beneficially own the property they worked on. The argument of the rule of law actually tends to disprove the critics' argument given that the rule of law is upheld when judges obey the law in arriving at their own decisions, including laws with which they do not personally agree, as no one is above the law. Activist judges injecting their own values into their decisions means the law is not being applied, but rather their own values and personal opinions. This is the logical opposite to the rule of law; in other words, it is the arbitrary rule of judges. There is no necessary logical link between the existence of a system of government, as well as all the 'principles' or rules that it reflects, and judicial recognition.

Finally, the first two premises actually undermine the critics' argument. Even accepting the erroneous argument that judges are to determine Parliament's lawful authority to legislate, judges are to declare what the law is, and at least since 1688, the one pre-eminent fundamental rule of the law of the British constitution has been parliamentary sovereignty.[135] The critics' argument is absurd to the extent that it holds judges to be the sovereign power in Britain because of their ability to 'legislate' or veto parliamentary legislation on the basis of unwritten constitutional principles.

DID THE COMMON LAW GIVE PARLIAMENT ITS POWER?

It is recognized, by Hart and others, that parliamentary sovereignty is established by fundamental law. However, some argue that this fundamental law must be common law, which was made by judges, and therefore may be legitimately modified or overruled by them.[136] Goldsworthy notes that the argument usually proceeds by a process of elimination.[137] First, the doctrine of parliamentary sovereignty was not, and logically could not have been, originally established by statute; that proposition is circular. Second, if it does not come from statute, it must come from the common law, as the legal system knows no other sources of law. Third, therefore, the common law is the ultimate constitutional foundation, and Britain has a 'common law constitution.' Fourth, judges have always had a power to decide what the common law is, and are now generally believed to be able to change it or to overrule settled doctrines of common law, even constitutional ones, if persuaded that they are unjust or incompatible with contemporary circumstances or values. Some say that Parliament is sovereign because judges acknowledge its legal and political supremacy, or that the doctrine was never firmly established in common law.

The problem with this argument is that it does not accord with reality. Parliamentary supremacy was established by the actions of relevant political actors, particularly during the Reformation, the Rebellion, and the Revolution. Judges did not, nor could they have, accomplished this establishment, as they lacked the physical or legal power to do so. At best, they acquiesced to the parliamentary sovereignty which was already established elsewhere, nor did they dare or have the ability to challenge it or otherwise rebel. This objection is a complete answer.

There are also theoretical difficulties with the argument. If Parliament could not confer sovereign authority on itself by statute, for similar reasons the doctrine of parliamentary sovereignty cannot be a product of judicial law-making. The argument fails as it states or assumes that all law in Britain has been deliberately made according to a certain established law-making process, either by Parliament, or by judges. If that were so, what would be the legal source of the judges' authority to make common law? By this argument, it could not be statute, as that is circular, given that the point of the argument is that Parliament's authority to enact statutes was conferred by judges. The only consistent alternative is that judges conferred authority on themselves, which is circular.

There is no logical or practical necessity that judges should have authority to determine and enforce limits on the authority of the other branches of government. Hart states that they may have it, but only if other senior legal officials agree that they do.[138] However, he omits the possibility that, while the judge may not have the power to make the decision and other officials do not agree to it, the officials may nonetheless not oppose this illegal judicial law-making for various reasons, including self-interest, a desire to avoid controversy, a fear of public controversy, and so on. Such fears are what is behind Canadian governments' failure to rebuke the courts for a number of their decisions, such as the Judicial *Remuneration Reference* decision.[139] In this case, judges illegally resorted to 'unwritten constitutional principles' to override legislation and the Constitution itself in order to constitutionalize their salaries through the invention of judicial compensation committees, resulting in tremendous increases to judicial salaries. The lack of rebuke was not an indication that the decision was legally proper. Therefore, Hart confuses the actual system of government of sovereignty (legal concepts) with political considerations which are irrelevant to the actual legal powers within the system (but may be relevant to the practicalities of exercising those powers).

Goldsworthy sees the source of the logical difficulties featured in the critics' argument in the Hobbesian assumption that every law, including those conferring authority on Parliament, and on judges, must originally have been deliberately made by someone, and if that someone was not Parliament, it must have been judges. Goldsworthy seeks to overcome this difficulty by a modification of Hart's argument, namely, that the necessary condition for fundamental rules is a consensus among the (most senior) officials of the legal system in all three branches of government, and not among judges alone.

The argument is problematic. First, it is more historically and legally accurate to argue that the common law was not made by judges, at the very least in respect of sovereignty or the most fundamental aspects of the system of government. The usage of the term 'common law' is ambiguous. It is plainly wrong to say the doctrine of parliamentary sovereignty is a matter of common law in the modern sense of judge made law. Secondly, the critics' argument would make nonsense of Hobbes in that, for him, all law was not just made by someone, it was made by the sovereign, which he equated with the king (as opposed to Parliament). In fact, Hobbes' *Dialogue of the Common Laws* was an effort to refute Coke's two contentions that most law was law because of immemorial custom, and that law of this kind constitutes 'artificial reason' comprising the accumulated and refined wisdom of many generations, which only professionals (judges) could comprehend and no individual intellect could have produced. Rather, for Hobbes, law was the dictate of a simple and universal 'natural reason,' which commands that which is good for our self-preservation; and, it was made law by the command of the sovereign, not because he possessed more or less natural reason, but because he had been instituted by men in the state of nature to enforce a certain mode of living which 'natural reason' enjoined. It is plain that Hobbes would never have considered judges the sovereign. Furthermore, he agreed with Filmer that law may be custom, but custom alone had no binding force unless there was an authority capable of making law that recognized it. Finally, even the most cursory look at English history or the British system of government would show the absurdity of considering inferior courts to be sovereign, and sovereign parliaments to be inferior.

Goldsworthy says parliamentary sovereignty is a creature of custom (at least custom among senior legal officials) that gradually

174 Parliament

evolved from the sovereignty of the medieval king. It is *sui generis*, a unique hybrid of law and political fact deriving its authority from acceptance by the people and the principal institutions of the state, especially Parliament and the judiciary.[140] Even those arguing that parliamentary sovereignty is a common law doctrine might agree it is *sui generis*; however, the typical parliamentarian argument based on the common law was that Parliament existed from time immemorial, from which antiquity it derived its authority. As long as parliamentary sovereignty continues to be law, Parliament can change, repeal, or codify the rest of the common law. It can abolish or modify ordinary doctrines from common law, and remove it from further judicial decision-making. Since judges could not have established parliamentary sovereignty in the first place, it must be equally true they have no authority to unilaterally change or reject it.

As discussed earlier, the matter is not just a question of logic, but also a historical fact. The real question is how British sovereignty and its system of government were actually established, and what was actually established. Furthermore, any rudimentary understanding of that system of government, and the legal framework for judicial review, reveals that judges had no legal authority to create sovereignty, the British system of government, or parliamentary supremacy.

Courts only had authority as delegated by the king, and later Parliament, to decide disputes among subjects brought before them. Courts applied the common law (the custom of the people, and statute). They could not deal with matters relating to higher authorities themselves, matters of sovereignty, or the governance of these higher bodies. To that extent only could it even be figuratively said that sovereignty was established by custom; it was not the sort of custom which courts had any jurisdiction to consider and apply. But it is best not to speak of custom in these terms. Sovereignty is a legal term. A system of government is a legal system. It is different from custom. Custom can change, but not sovereignty without a change in the sovereign, or a system of government without an actual legal change occurring.

Custom in the proper sense constitutes the actions of people and the way they settled their disputes. It is external to them, but created by their decisions. Sovereignty is an internal concept. Once established, it has certain rules, which can be changed legally in the manner set out by the sovereign. The only relevant role of custom here (an external consideration) is constitutional convention. Such conventions can never amount to legal changes in the system of government or sovereignty, but can modify practices within the system which can even contradict the law or nullify it in practice. However, these practices can never be the law itself, unless such changes are legally enacted, or the sovereign is replaced and those practices are then made part of the legal system of government.

The only way courts can consider law as fundamental or pre-eminent law is if statute gives them that power, for example through an entrenched bill of rights.

Significance of Common Law Court Recognition

The fact that common law courts recognize Parliament or its laws does not mean that they are not legally obliged to do so. It is a fallacy to say that it is so because the courts said so. To say that Britain's sovereign system of government was based on judicial recognition is a view wholly at odds with reality. Judges were the least important political figures in establishing parliamentary sovereignty, and in fact were more of an obstacle than a help in establishing it, especially as a result of their support of royal prerogative during the Restoration.

Furthermore, at least in modern times, a major factor in the establishment of state sovereignty is recognition by other states. Judicial recognition is nowhere in the world recognized as a condition or even a factor in establishing legal sovereignty, and it would be absurd to require it.

PART THREE

The Executive, and Further Public Law Developments

6

The Executive and Parliament's Relation to It

A full detailing of the executive branch of government is generally not necessary to understand the British system of government. This system of government is a legal concept, and includes parliamentary sovereignty as well as the jurisdiction of courts. Executive government initially derived from royal prerogative, but has been overtaken by statute. This examination, however, is important to understand the way in which the British system of government actually operates on the most fundamental or constitutional level; that is, the manner in which sovereign powers are actually exercised. Chapters 6 and 7 also provide important background information for studying the former Dominion governments, such as Canada, particularly the constitutional conventions that were incorporated. These chapters provide a fruitful reminder of what it took to achieve the system of government and its operation that we may too easily take for granted today.

This chapter examines the executive with a particular focus on its relation to Parliament. It examines the various events or means by which, over a very long period of time, the House of Commons was able to put a check on the influences of the king or Council, and on their activities. As well, it examines how the Commons obtained ultimate control over the executive through the use of legislation, the Commons' legal powers, constitutional conventions, and other methods. The development of parliamentary procedure and privilege were important elements in giving Parliament, and especially the Commons, an independent and authoritative position.

The previous discussion on the king and Curia, and the division which occurred in the Curia, is the starting point to understanding government in all its functions. During the early period, there was no clear division in the branches of government; the Curia performed all of the functions. As differentiation in government increased, separate departments grew, including a separate judicial branch, and differentiation also occurred within the legislative function, especially with the development of Parliament. Much constitutional history attempts to solve the problem raised by Magna Carta of combining an efficient executive with some sort of national control over it.

Early on, important political acts and legislation required the counsel and consent of the deliberative body of the nation. Still, the king possessed large discretion in carrying on centralized government. It is not until the final form of the constitution was fixed under Edward I (1272–1307) that there is firsthand evidence of the doings of Parliament.[1]

The common law courts' role in establishing the supremacy of law, which supremacy was aided and guaranteed by the growth of parliamentary power, helped to play a significant role in developing the Commons' control over the executive. Also, common lawyers played an important role in aiding the Commons to become a more efficient body, with its own procedures and privileges, which in turn aided the capacity of the Commons to assert growing control over the government, or more specifically the executive.

At the end of the medieval period, Parliament acquired large powers over legislation and finance. Through its control over finance, it obtained the ability to criticize and control the conduct of the executive. By impeachment it was able to try and punish royal officials who broke the law. It would, however, take quite some time before the Commons could shake off the power and influence exercised over it by the crown and Council.

COUNCIL

During the twelfth century, the Curia was not an organized or stable body. Meetings were sometimes composed of a few officials, and sometimes a larger body of officials and magnates attended. Disputes arose during Henry III's reign between the king and his barons, which later led to Council becoming a more defined body. The barons' demands included high offices of state and summonses to Council. During the fourteenth century, Council gradually became a distinct body, with a clearer definition of which nobles formed

The Executive

181

part of it, and a distinction of those nobles from officials such as judges who became merely assistants. Parliament was suspicious of the vague and indefinite jurisdiction of Council, viewing Council as an executive body identified with the crown and royal prerogative, which Parliament wanted to control. Council exercised a rival jurisdiction outside the common law and operated according to a different procedure. Its powers were often not used impartially to enforce the law, but to pervert it in favour of powerful individuals. Thus, general feelings arose against the exercise of arbitrary power. The Commons was anxious to secure the enforcement of statutes and other limits to Council's activities.[2]

After the deposition of Richard II, the use of Parliament's powers increased, and it exercised constant control over the composition of Council and its conduct of government. The result was a recognition of Council's jurisdiction. This victory of Parliament was not a victory of law, but of great nobles. The failure of such government by nobles was demonstrated by the War of the Roses, paralysis of government, breakdown of Council, and Council acting in a self-interested manner, applying law not impartially but for its own benefit.[3]

Nobles were running the country for selfish ends at all levels. Many judges were in the retinues of great lords. Despotism was followed by anarchy. Then, the nation turned to the king for protection.

Statutory control over the executive attempted to deal with various matters, such as improvident gifts by kings, abolishing unlawful customs, indiscriminate pardons and protections being granted, demanding ministers the nation could trust, and illegal practices by royal officers. Some of the provisions were too general at this time to be really effective.

One effectual tool was the growth of the common law principle that executive officers acting beyond their powers were personally liable. While the principle was not applied to all royal officers in the thirteenth century, the Year Books show it was constantly applied to officials, such as sheriffs, franchise holders, and collectors of subsidies.[4] These notions came partly from statute and partly from the growing idea that, as wrongs could not be imputed to the king, they must be imputed to his servants who did the action. Once the principle was applied to all officials, the constitutional doctrine of ministerial responsibility became established. Until that time, control over ministers was limited to rare cases of impeachment.

Some statutes were directed at officers of justice perverting the law, including by imposing penalties on judges and clerks who deliberately made false entries on the rolls.[5]

During the Tudor Period, there was a revival of Council acting as an executive and judicial body in order to establish a stronger and more efficient government, and to overcome the lawlessness of the period. Henry VII established a council of professional advisors. He began to create an efficient executive, and a secret service. He used and abused the law to obtain these goals. During Henry VIII's reign, the chief organs of government were Council and its various branches, such as Star Chamber, Chancery, and Court of Requests. Parliament was held infrequently during this period.

Council organization tended to the further elaboration of government. A division of committees became necessary to address business. Also, there was a committee of more important councillors to settle the main lines of policy. There was variety in the kind and permanence of these committees. In them, we see the germs of the political and legal institutions of the modern state. All routine government work passed through Council's hands. One aspect of its work was to supervise the working of all organs of government, both central and local. Much of this supervision was done by common law judges, including supervising the judicial machinery of the state. This situation tended to give rise to the ideas that the crown and its servants were outside ordinary law, that crown servants were governed by special courts and law, and that their dealings with the king's subjects need not necessarily be according to common law. The executive tended to rely on its 'high and pre-eminent power' in matters of state interest, assigning reasons of state for arrests and for other government orders.[6]

Lawyers began to question the legality of these commissions. They feared that the extensive powers given were endangering the supremacy of law and the liberty of the subject.[7] In the following period, lawyers limited the sphere of action of these commissions, and with the victory of Parliament and common law, these limitations became part of modern constitutional law.[8]

Council prevented both the common law and Parliament from being as effective a security for the liberty of the subject as they later became.

As a judicial court, Star Chamber, which was a committee of Council, was an instrument to restore good government to the country. Under the Stuarts, it was used for prerogative government. During this period, the tyrannical proceedings of the political cases held before Star Chamber aroused popular hostility. By legislation, Parliament abolished the jurisdiction of Council in 1641 within England, and abolished Star Chamber entirely. As a result, English law now follows a theory of ministerial responsibility and not a system of administrative law such as that known on the Continent.

Council exercised great control over Parliament, which increased its efficiency in obtaining the measures it wanted. During the Middle Ages and continuing in the sixteenth century, service in Parliament, like other public service, was seen as burdensome.[9] The crown and Council used this fact to gain large influence over Parliament's composition by influencing elections. For example, burgesses were told that if the persons the crown wanted were elected, they would not have to pay for their representative's wages; the crown also granted leaves of absence to opposition members. The greatest influence exerted in favour of crown candidates and royal servants was through the crown's instructions to sheriffs in the conduct of the elections, telling them which candidates it wanted to win, and interfering with the elections themselves. When the value of holding a seat in Parliament grew, crown and Council could still use their influence over the nobility, and gain seats through the creation of "rotten" boroughs. In this way, they were generally able to secure a sufficiently large majority to control government business.

Some ways of executive control over the business of the House of Commons included the fact that initiative was with the crown; later, Council appointed, before Parliament met, committees to consider legislative proposals; Council appointed the Speaker of the House (until 1679); and, a certain number of privy councillors were always members of the Commons, who were in a position to explain or justify government measures, make necessary concessions, or avert defeat by withdrawing measures.

THE GROWING AUTONOMY AND INFLUENCE OF THE COMMONS

Part of the solution to the problem of the king or Council's influence over the business of the Commons was the use of impeachment. It is a criminal proceeding initiated by the House of Commons against any person. Impeachment is tried before the whole House of Lords based on majority vote, and sentence is passed there.

184 The Executive and Public Law

The practice originated in the prevalent political ideas and conditions of the period.[10] First, it reflected an ideal, pertaining to rulers and their officials, that government be in accordance with law. Second, the Commons and Lords were united in desiring to limit the activities of royal officials or favourites and to prevent them from breaking the law. Third, the limits of the Lords' jurisdiction were ill defined. Essentially, the Lords was a court for great men and great causes, and occasionally that House thought it could do justice when the ordinary law failed. Thus, when the Commons discovered that royal officials or others had broken the law, it was natural for it to make a complaint to the Lords in the form of an accusation.

Charles I complained about the rule and supremacy of law. While the king was not subject to the law as he could do no wrong, his subjects could and would be legally liable. The king's command or protection was no defence. The fiction was created that the king was deemed to have been deceived. Otherwise, if the king and his servants were immune, no public servant could be brought to account and judgment. As the servants were subject to the law, however, the House could censure and impeach them. With standing committees and the absolute privilege of freedom of speech, they could easily and quickly collect evidence. With the alliance between Parliament and common lawyers, the medieval principle of liability to law was resuscitated, pushed to its logical conclusions, and applied to even the highest ministers of state.

During the War of the Roses, impeachment was used by rival factions by Acts of Attainder. During the Tudors, Attainder was used by the king to get rid of ministers he ceased to trust, or persons considered dangerous to the state. It was revived again between 1620 and 1715.

The constitutional importance of impeachments was evident during the Rebellion and Revolution. Parliamentary opposition to the Stuarts was essentially a legal opposition based on precedents drawn from the records of medieval parliaments, and the medieval ideal of maintaining the common law. By impeachment, the greatest ministers of state and lower official could be made responsible to the law. Its greatest service to constitutional government was that it established the doctrine of ministerial responsibility to law; it applied even to crown ministers; and, consequently, it led to the maintenance

The Executive

of the supremacy of law over all. Buckingham's impeachment negated Charles I's contentions that he was personally above the law, as were his ministers acting under his orders. Danby's impeachment decided that the king could not use a pardon to stop impeachment, which was a proceeding taken in the name of the Commons. For its own safety, the Long Parliament impeached Strafford and other agents of prerogative rule, as well as some judges. This action settled the parliamentary doctrine that all ministers were answerable to law for their illegal acts, including judges. It also introduced the practice that all royal acts must be countersigned by the secretary of state to ensure there was always a minister who could be made responsible for them. Although the trial for impeachment formally takes place before the king in Parliament, the king plays no active part.

Because impeachment was limited to prosecuting offenders against the law, its utility became limited during the eighteenth century and fell into disuse. The Commons wished the king's ministers to observe the law and the policy they approved. The weakness of impeachment was evident during the proceedings against the Earl of Strafford because his actions could not be proven to be treasonable even though they would have been fatal to constitutional government. However, until the growth of cabinet government, impeachment was the only remedy. The king chose his ministers and there was no way for the Commons to get rid of them unless they could be convicted of a crime. This explains why charges against unpopular ministers in the later seventeenth century were often supported by little evidence, or why ministers were sometimes put on trial for offences created for that purpose by Parliament. Impeachment is not necessary when ministers can be dismissed by a vote of the Commons.

Interestingly, Holdsworth argues that with suitable modifications in procedure, impeachment may still be a useful weapon against ministers and officials, who should be made criminally liable for corruption, gross negligence, or other misfeasance in the conduct of affairs. Presumably that principle would include judges who act illegally in making decisions to secure a result they desire or otherwise disregarding the rule of law. For Holdsworth, such a rule would provide balance with the principle of security of tenure of higher permanent officials, which is held more important than the need to punish their mere negligence or ignorance.

186 The Executive and Public Law

During the eighteenth century, the Commons gained the power to choose ministers, and in this way its power to supervise the executive took on an executive character.

The system for settling national finances gave the Commons the power to supervise and criticize all activities of the executive. The procedure of the House provided opportunities for scrutiny, debate, and supervision. It effectively prevented ministers from pursuing undefendable courses of action, or courses to which the Commons was in definite opposition. The debates both required ministers to defend their decisions and educated the members of Parliament in the theory and practice of government.

Statute was necessary to deal with the problem of the crown and Council gaining large influence over Parliament's composition by influencing elections. Rules with respect to elections, such as actions against a sheriff for making a false or double return, were put into effect, and it was made illegal for an officer to make a return conflicting with the last determination in the Commons. Legislation was passed with respect to the procedure of elections, and there was an attempt to suppress bribery and treating by candidates.

The *Statute of Proclamations*[11] was an attempt to deal with the problem of the use and scope of prerogative, and its vague limits. Larger authority to make proclamations was claimed after Henry VIII's reign, when the crown could not so easily induce Parliament to pass its legislation. The statute gave proclamations the status of an Act of Parliament, but limited them in several ways, including by safeguarding the common law, by upholding the supremacy of existing Acts of Parliament, by confirming rights of property, and by prohibiting the death penalty for violating a proclamation. The Act was repealed, leaving the matter unresolved.

The use and extent of proclamations increased significantly in respect of commerce and industry. The medieval ideal was a moral ideal of honest manufacture, just price, fair wage, and reasonable profit. With changed commercial conditions, changed moral outlook, and competition between nation states, the guiding principle of the mercantile system developed. The idea was that the state must protect itself against rivals. The state regulated all branches of industry not as matters of right and wrong, but for political expediency and in the interests of the power of the state, both domestically and relative to other states. One aspect was in relation to foreign trade. The crown held large powers over foreign affairs, which was thought to include trade. Legislation was also passed in relation to foreign affairs and trade. Crown demands for more power were in substance recognized by legislatures during the reigns of Henry VII and VIII. The crown claimed prerogative to set impositions to regulate the balance of trade. It was recognized that for the purposes of raising revenue, these customs duties could not be increased without a parliamentary grant.[12] Thus, a tension arose between the prerogative over trade and Parliament's right to control revenue, which became a live issue after the Tudors.

Monopolies given by crown patents were abused, and in 1601 the Commons again took up this issue. Debates arose on questions of crown power to make these grants and to grant dispensations from statute, on the granting of privileges to trading companies, and even concerning the nature of prerogative and its relation to law. The complaint was that the common law did not warrant these infringements of liberty to trade, which actually damaged the public interest. Elizabeth I evaded the question when she promised to leave the validity of the patents to the common law, which shifted the criticism from prerogative to the patentees, and as court discussions turn largely on the facts of individual cases, more comprehensive parliamentary discussions on prerogative were avoided. The court, not surprisingly, found that the monopoly was *prima facie* against the common law, statute, and the liberty of the subject, and was damaging.[13] The court followed the principles of medieval common law that trade must be free and only curtailed by definite restrictions in the common law. That is, there was a freedom from arbitrary restraints not recognized by the law.

These legal rules with respect to the limits of prerogatives to grant monopolies were breached by James I, who resorted to illegal grants to raise money. However, the rules were put into statute in 1624, which largely formed the basis of modern patent law and which provided for common law court jurisdiction over disputes about grants, but otherwise reproduced the existing law.

The question of the relation of crown and Parliament was closely bound with fiscal and economic questions. In short, the crown needed money. The regular revenue of the crown, and the subsidies

188   The Executive and Public Law

tenths and fifteenths granted by Parliament, were decreasing in value when the influx of precious metals from the New World caused inflation. For example, Elizabeth I died in debt.

It was clear from medieval authority and the Petition of Right that the crown had no right to impose direct taxation without Parliament's consent. This proposition was admitted by the pro-crown judges in the *Case of Ship Money*, even though they tried to minimize medieval precedents and argued that the Petition of Right merely declared old rights and did not make new law.[14]

During the Tudor period, the crown or Council did not dare to impose a general tax, but assumed considerable powers over raising money, such as giving directions about raising contributions by local authorities, compelling its more wealthy subjects to contribute benevolences or loans, levying ship money in emergencies, overseeing customs, and so on. Parliament maintained its absolute and exclusive control over all taxation, which was supported by medieval precedents.

Even under James I's 'divine right of kings' theory the king did not hold the power to tax, and he acknowledged this position.[15]

In *Darnel's Case*,[16] the crown used its supposed power to commit a person to prison without cause against someone who refused to give the king a loan, because the king lacked the power to exact a loan directly. The Tudors' financial extractions were not as frequent or severe as those of the Stuarts. They exacted loans from richer subjects, and compelled them to pay the sums promised by summoning them before Council; imposed tariffs for promoting English trade; and, levied ships and ship money for defence. The Stuarts used these precedents and tried to develop them in a manner that raised greater criticism.

In terms of fiscal extractions, *Oliver St. John* held that the crown was at liberty to persuade its subjects to lend their money, and a letter stating that this act was contrary to law and otherwise reflecting on the king was seditious libel.[17] However, in 1626, Charles attempted to compel loans, which was clearly contrary to statute,[18] and was declared illegal. The Tudors had made similar illegal demands, but never did so when there was strong disapproval in the country of government policy.

With respect to tariffs and customs, as a result of medieval statutes or precedents, the king lost any power he might have had to impose

The Executive   189

new customs duties without Parliament's consent.[19] Instead, certain duties were fixed to the crown in perpetuity,[20] and from the end of Edward II's reign any increases required Parliament's sanction. Since 1453, tunnage and poundage was voted by Parliament to each king at the beginning of his reign for his life. However, the king had large powers of rearranging tariffs to further the commercial interests of his subjects. These principles conflicted. *Bates's Case* held that the king's imposing a poundage on currants in addition to that imposed by statute was legal on the basis that it was in respect of the regulation of foreign trade, which was a branch of foreign affairs, and therefore within the king's absolute power.[21]

Acting under the prerogative over trade for fiscal purposes, James issued new rates and placed impositions on articles produced and sold within the kingdom. The court in *Bates* stated in *obiter dictum* that the crown had a similar power on commodities produced in England. The king claimed that the power of impositions belonged to kings to maintain their crown and dignity. The result was the great House of Commons debate of 1610, which resulted in the crown abandoning impositions on domestic products, which Bacon admitted to be illegal. The crown continued to levy such impositions under the prerogative to regulate trade. The Petition of Right did not deal with this situation as it dealt only with direct taxation. A statute of the Long Parliament and the Bill of Rights stated that if prerogative imposed any new charge on the subject, it must have the sanction of Parliament.[22]

Medieval precedents were clear that the king was entrusted with defence and had wide powers to take necessary measures, including to take ships, money, and men. Such power was rarely if ever contested by medieval parliaments,[23] and was recognized by later lawyers.[24] The obligation to provide ships developed into an obligation to pay money, and this obligation was extended to the whole country. Then, the idea arose to use it for fiscal purposes. The first step was to extend old precedents to make this demand not on actual but on apprehended danger, on the basis that prevention was better than cure. Second, it was extended to the entire country based on the principle that the whole country was equally interested in repelling invasion.

Accordingly, prior to the Rebellion, the courts recognized for the king large discretionary powers to imprison dangerous persons,

190 The Executive and Public Law

to regulate trade, and to act as he pleased to secure the safety of the country. The courts gratuitously introduced into their decisions much dogma on divine right. Popular resentment was aroused. The king lacked a military force and civil service which could enable him to ignore this resentment and rule by prerogative.

As outlined previously, the first half of the seventeenth century was a turning point in English constitutional history. It established firmly the system of government by the king and Parliament, and not by the king alone as in most Continental countries. This result was achieved by parliamentary opposition. As a practical matter this opposition compelled the crown to modify its prerogative to give greater practical effect for Parliament to exercise its sovereignty.

During the reign of Charles II, the Commons occasionally asserted its right to appropriate supplies for specific purposes of executive government, and to examine the accounts to determine if the money was properly spent. It could not do so with respect to hereditary revenue, or revenue granted at the beginning of the king's reign for his life, and did not pursue this right with respect to supplies granted by James II's parliament of 1685. In order for the Commons to wrest effective control over finance from the king, two changes were made.[25] First, the revenue granted to the king in perpetuity decreased, and the annual grants for limited term increased. Short-term revenue was the best security for frequent parliaments. Second, there was a rule of strict appropriation to the specific purpose granted which was applied to annual or limited grants, resulting in the House securing control over the amount and kind of expenditure which the crown could incur. This arrangement not only permitted criticism, but also allowed some measure of control over the conduct of government. The Commons also assumed a right to inquire into the workings of all government. Additionally, from time to time, Acts for audits were passed.

By the close of the seventeenth century, the Commons had gained control over the king, and, as we will see later, over the Lords as well. After the Revolution, the king was voted a civil list for his life to meet the ordinary expenses of his household and the civil service. This system was maintained until the eighteenth century. The crown was dependent on the House for sums exceeding this annual sum. Hereditary revenues were nearly all surrendered in exchange for an annual sum for the life of the king. Accordingly, the king had

The Executive 191

to come to Parliament for money, and to prove the necessity for his expenditures. Supplies were appropriated, which meant that they had to be used for the purposes voted, and the king's accounts could be audited.

PARLIAMENTARY PROCEDURE AND PARLIAMENTARY PRIVILEGE

Parliamentary procedural rules can be traced back to the fourteenth century, but in the sixteenth century they obtained their first clear and authoritative statements and attained almost their final form.[26] Such procedural rules include the opening and closing of Parliament, the rules of debate, the duties of the Speaker, the system of three readings, the forms of legislation, and the development of the committee system. Parliamentary procedure is regarded as a special law governing Parliament. It is customary law, ascertained mainly from the precedents in the records of Parliament,[27] and is a permanent and independent body of customary law like the common law itself.[28] This conception gave to Parliament a position as independent and authoritative as that of the king.

The origin of this body of laws is the recognition that, as every court of justice has laws and customs for its direction, so too does the high court of Parliament. Privileges of Parliament confer on each House the rights and powers essential to its efficiency. During the time of the Tudors, privileges necessary to the efficiency of the House of Commons were maintained and strengthened, and it gained as well the privilege of deciding disputed elections. In the seventeenth century, each House asserted and guarded these privileges. The main controversies surrounded the privilege of freedom of speech, and the Commons successfully asserted control of its order of business, which is both a procedure and a privilege of Parliament. Restrictions were imposed in favour of the crown so as to prevent its embarrassment or the taking away of its power to initiate legislation. Charles I's attempt to curtail speech and to deny the Commons' right to decide the order of business would have prevented the Commons from criticizing government or its agents effectively. It would also have removed the Commons' ability to force government to take notice of its concerns through obstruction, including by refusing to vote supplies before other measures the Commons wanted were taken.[29]

Controversies surrounding parliamentary privilege were at the forefront of the constitutional controversies of the period. In James I's first parliament, the Commons asserted that the privileges of Parliament were their undoubted right, that the Commons was a court of record and the highest court of the land, and that these privileges were necessary for the conduct of the House's business, which could not be denied or impaired.[30] James I and Charles I would not admit these statements.[31] Instead, the royalist position was that kingship was primeval, and that Parliament did not have an inherent but a granted right.[32] The Commons made its Famous Protestation of 1621 that the privileges and jurisdictions of Parliament were ancient and the undoubted birthright and inheritance of the English subjects. It declared that affairs of state, matters of the Church, laws, and the redress of mischief or grievances were proper subjects for Parliament; that Members had freedom of speech; that the Commons had to deal with such matters as it considers best; and, that Members had freedom from impeachment and molestation except by censure of the House for any matter of expression or matter within Parliament's jurisdiction. James was enraged because the acceptance of these propositions would have made his theory of ultimate sovereignty in himself and prerogative unworkable as parliamentary privilege would have been placed on a level with prerogative.

Precedents drawn from parliamentary rolls (the record of proceedings of Parliament, which were later replaced by Journals of the House of Lords and the House of Commons); and parliamentary writs (on which petitions and answers were entered) were the principal sources for the *lex et consuetudo Parliamenti*. As a superior court, indeed the highest court, its rolls were conclusive evidence of its proceedings.[33]

As Parliament is above all other courts, it has privilege above all other courts; and, as it has privilege and jurisdiction, so too does it have the power of coercion and compulsion.

The conflicts of the seventeenth century gave rise to new developments in defining or amplifying procedural rules with respect to concrete cases. These were entered on the journals, or met with new orders in the form of decisions of the House regarding the conduct of its business.

The Speaker's relation to this law was similar to the relation of a judge to the common law, and the Speaker had large control over the

The Executive 193

business of the House. The Speaker's position under the Tudors was that of the representative and chair of the House, a royal nominee, and a messenger between House and king. Over time, the Speaker became less the king's representative and more the representative of the House. This transformation was complete by the later seventeenth century. Thus, the function tended to become more judicial, and the Speaker more of an impartial and independent interpreter of the *lex et consuetudo Parliamenti*, subject only to House control.

This process was established by precedents. In 1679, the Commons elected Seymour. The king objected and ordered the House to choose Meres. The House refused and elected Seymour. The king refused; the Commons insisted. Parliament was prorogued. Eventually, the Commons chose Gregory, whom Charles accepted. While the king achieved his goal of preventing Danby's enemy being installed, the permanent gain was with the Commons. No king would again issue a direct order for the Commons to choose a certain person as Speaker. In 1694, when the crown nominee was proposed, the House passed a resolution that it was contrary to the undoubted right of the House for the king to choose its Speaker or to have any person bring a message from the king to nominate a Speaker.

The Commons also successfully made out its claim that it could only be adjourned by its own act. The king could end the session by prorogation, or Parliament by dissolution, in which case all business before the House must begin again from the start. If the House adjourned, it could recommence business from that point. On several occasions, the Stuart kings assumed the power to adjourn, but it was generally recognized that adjournments are the act of the House. This proposition was always accepted as the rule since the Revolution.[34]

The Commons' privilege to determine contested elections was gained in 1604 with the case of *Goodwin v. Fortescue*. In the eighteenth century, electoral jurisdiction was exercised generally by the House. Disputes were persistently regarded as trials of party strength. In 1770, the Grenville Act turned the matter over to a committee, which was defective but a significant improvement in procedure. The Act was passed and continued despite George III's opposition, which also shows that the House was becoming more able to be responsive to public opinion, and that the king was obliged to pass statute with which he personally disagreed. The Act was made perpetual in

1774, and though amended, was the basis of the law until the House by statute in 1868 abandoned this privilege and delegated the power to the courts to determine contested elections.[35]

From the Revolution to 1832 there were few procedural changes of great importance. The most important was the Grenville Act's changes to the machinery for trying election disputes; also significant were two Standing Orders of 1707 and 1713 with respect to financial measures and to discussion of petitions.[36] The principles established in the seventeenth century were accepted and elaborated. By statute of 1790, the Speaker was to have no office of profit under the crown tenable at the crown's pleasure. Public opinion demanded the Speaker be nonpartisan, which became the standard. The procedure developed was designed to protect a minority, and prevent the danger that government business could be held up as a result. In this way, the procedure helped the Commons to be representative of politically conscious classes and kept it in touch with public opinion.

After 1688 when the battle for the constitution had been won, some believe that Parliament showed a tendency to extend and to use its privileges almost as arbitrarily as the king used prerogative.[37] The Long Parliament claimed authority to sanction practically anything the House wished, or to punish any conduct of which it disapproved. The courts had few precedents on which they could rely. During the Middle Ages, judges declined to give opinions on questions of privilege, as in *Thorpe's Case*, thus establishing the rule that Parliament was the proper judge with respect to the mode and use of its privileges.[38] However, now they were willing to be bold. In *R. v. Knollys*,[39] Holt C.J. rejected a claim of the Lords to extend its own privileges at its will and pleasure. In *Ashby v. White*,[40] Holt C.J. opposed a similar claim by the Commons. It was held that if the issue was the existence of privilege, the courts must decide the question, as it was a matter of law. Parliamentary privilege was part of the law, and a Resolution of the House that it was privileged to determine the matter was not relevant. The court seemed to imply that if a matter was within the court's jurisdiction, judges were bound by their oaths to judge it, and that they 'must exert the Queen's jurisdiction.' In *Paty's Case*,[41] Holt C.J. held that if the House committed a person to prison and specified the ground, the court could decide its sufficiency, and if insufficient, the prisoner must be discharged. A person doing a legal act could not be made illegal by vote of the Commons

The Executive   195

or Lords, nor both jointly. The person's liberty or property could be disposed of, but the queen must join in.[42]

May argues that the precedents of Parliament were contradictory, judicial opinions and decisions differed, and general agreement was lacking.[43] The two maxims or principles were: parliamentary privilege is part of the law of the land, and each House is the judge of its own privileges. The apparent contradiction can be resolved. The first maxim applies to cases such as *Ashby v. White* and *Stockdale v. Hansard*,[44] in which the existence of a privilege claimed by the House is a question of law which courts decide. The second applies to cases such as *Sheriff of Middlesex*[45] and *Bradlaugh v. Gosset*,[46] which do not question the existence, but rather the mode of use, of an undoubted privilege. Courts will not interfere with the latter as each House is the sole judge of whether, when, and how it will use one of its undoubted privileges. The cases show that courts are subject to the enactments of Parliament (king, Lords, and Commons) on the basis that they are law, but not to mere resolutions of a House.

Thus, the rule was established that the exercise of the established privilege of a House is a question for it alone, but the question of whether a privilege exists is a question of law for the courts to decide, and not by House resolution. The Commons never acquiesced to these decisions, particularly *Ashby v. White* and *Paty's Case*. As a practical matter, this proposition became the settled view or acquiesced to with nineteenth-century decisions, such as *Stockdale v. Hansard*. It further meant that any improvement to the law must come from legislation; it could not be done under the name of privilege. However, controversy about the legality of the decisions remains.

DEVELOPMENTS OF THE COMMITTEE SYSTEM

The desire of the opposition to criticize government policy, and to prevent actions it disliked, led to extensions of the committee system. By later Elizabethan times, the committee system was well developed. There were further developments in the seventeenth century. Money bills and other bills of great public importance were referred to committees of the whole House. The practice of creating committees to deal with certain subjects gave rise to the appointment of certain grand or standing committees, which by 1628 became committees of the whole House. Their numbers and the subjects referred to them

The Executive and Public Law

differed from parliament to parliament. Three topics were important: religion, grievances, and courts of justice, including all corruptions and injustices coming from the courts. The committee on parliamentary privileges became a standing select committee and a most important one at this time.

The growth of the committee system made criticism of government policy and its agents more effective. For example, Charles I's charge against the Commons in his 1629 declaration complained about the extension of their privileges by standing committees. Charles also complained that they sent for and examined the Attorney General, the Treasurer, the Chancellor, Barons of Exchequer, some judges, and other officials for matters done in the course of their duties, although these persons were not accountable legally to the Commons. Many enquiries and complaints were entertained, such as the unsufferable disturbance and scandal of justice and government: "insomuch that young lawyers sitting there take upon them to decry the opinions of the Judges; and some have not doubted to maintain that the resolutions of that House must bind the Judges, a thing never heard of in ages past."[47] He complained that they were "breaking the ligaments of government" and creating an overswaying power to themselves, which properly belongs to the king.

CONSTITUTIONAL CONVENTIONS

Burke said that "the constituent parts of a state are obliged to hold their public faith with each other ... as much as the whole state is bound to keep its faith with separate communities" and this obligation naturally gives rise to the "customs, practices, maxims, or precepts" which create conventions.[48]

Conventions are important for two reasons. First, conventions show the manner in which the constitution works in practice. They determine the manner in which the rules of law, which they presuppose, are to be applied. Conventions can and do differ from the law itself. As political practices, they are not enforceable by courts. Second, conventions arise in order to ensure that the constitution works in practice in accordance with the prevailing constitutional theory of the time. Perhaps, at an even more basic level, constitutional conventions were and are necessary to ensure the continual working of a constitution in which government powers are divided between different persons and bodies. Put in the negative, conventions prevent a breakdown in the government's workings. The exact content of these conventions varies from age to age in order to address particular situations.

A general discussion on conventions or the debates surrounding them is not possible here. A full discussion could justify a study in itself, and several have been written.[49] However, a more precise understanding of the system of government is helpful to clarify matters related to conventions also.

Various authors have recognized and explained the existence of these conventional rules. For example, Dicey sees constitutional conventions as customs, practices, maxims, or precepts (constitutional obligations) obeyed although not enforced or recognized by courts.[50] However, he believes that a breach of convention ultimately leads to illegal conduct or a breach of the law. He defines convention as the rules for determining the mode in which the discretionary powers of the crown – or of its servants, such as ministers – ought to be exercised. He argues that conventions are intended to secure the ultimate supremacy of the electorate as the true political sovereign of the state.

Jennings is more doubtful that conventions rest ultimately on law, and thinks there is not much difference between conventions and positive law. Heard agrees that there is no clear boundary between law and convention.[51] Jennings also sees conventions as putting flesh on the bones of the law, and keeping the legal constitution in touch with the growth of ideas. His view of conventions is broader than Dicey's view. Jennings' test for determining if a constitutional convention exists is: (1) What are the precedents? (2) Did the actors in the precedents believe they were bound by a rule? (3) What is the reason for the rule? A single precedent with a good reason may be enough to establish a rule. A whole string of precedents without such a reason is not enough, unless it is perfectly certain that the persons concerned regarded themselves as bound by it.[52]

Marshall sees conventions in the UK as playing a central part in the theory of British government. Precedents, for him, are an important factor in establishing a convention's existence. Also, externally, they regulate the relation of UK political processes to member nations, focusing responsibility at appropriate points regardless of legal forms. Marshall agrees with Dicey that conventions provide

198 The Executive and Public Law

the framework for cabinet government and political accountability and often modify rules of law. He argues, however, that they are wider in scope than Dicey describes, and disagrees that violation of convention will necessarily bring its violators into conflict with the law of the land.[53] In some ways Marshall's conclusion is similar to Jennings' on the latter point, but Jennings holds other points of difference with Dicey. However, Marshall does state that the main general aim of convention is the "effective working" of the machinery of political accountability, which may signal a difference in degree, but not of kind, with Dicey. Marshall also believes that sometimes the application of some conventions to a particular circumstance can be unclear.

This book focuses upon the development of the main conventions up to approximately the mid-1850s, which were of direct relevance to the conventions established in other countries inheriting the parliamentary model of government. The conventions to be discussed will reflect the following elements. First, there is consensus among the relevant political actors creating the convention that it exists and that it ought to be followed; and, the convention generally is observed, or, at the very least, is not seriously challenged over the long term. Second, the convention as a kind of political agreement, although not usually an express one, deals with the appropriate conduct of state actors relating to most basic rules of the system of government pertaining to the exercise of sovereign state powers; that is, the exercise of their highest functions or constitutional aspects.

The most obvious example of constitutional conventions involves practices that deal with the relevant political actors in relation to their sovereign act of legislating. In the British case, the relevant actors are the monarch and the two Houses comprising Parliament. Another example involves the practices surrounding the exercise of crown prerogatives concerning executive government, including in relation to its ministers. Conventions also deal with the ability of a party or individuals to form the government, and to remain in power.

The most important conventions to be examined are those that form the constitutional convention of responsible government. Responsible government is the most important convention for countries following the parliamentary supremacy model of government.

The historical evidence disproves some modern theories that conventions are simply principles, the meaning of which the actors in the events or precedents may not have known or understood, and that conventions are only binding on contemporary politicians if there is some generally supported principle to be respected.[54] This position leads to the unsupportable assumptions that, first, present-day people can understand the convention better than those who actually created it; and, second, that the consensus supporting the principle behind a convention and its details should not be restricted to what the political actors directly involved intended to establish, but also involves the consensus of the academic community, judges, and the concerned public. This approach inappropriately devalues the historical precedents. The fallacy of paradox is also evident. Constitutional conventions were clearly established by what the relevant political actors actually established as practices or customs, by what they thought they were achieving, and their reason for it. However, the unprincipled 'principled' approach asserts that precedents are about consensus of opinion on a particular behaviour in a given circumstance. We are not told how that is to be measured, nor who is to decide. Thus, what political actors thought and actually established is really deemed to be the principle created or thought up by latter-day academics or judges looking at the precedents, and also by their reaction to the behaviour or practice. The theory can even become more farfetched in asserting that precedents are not necessary to the existence of constitutional convention, but only serve as a useful gauge to the consensus of opinion that actually creates a rule. However, since a convention is necessarily a practice, it must actually exist in the first place for a convention to come about. Taken to its logical conclusion, paradox or absurdity arises, as there can be a general consensus about the desirability or ethics of a certain practice among the community in general, but that practice may never have been adopted by the relevant political actors. As a result, for such authors a convention must be said to exist, even though it does not exist.

A historical examination makes it clear that the actors in the precedents or in the events establishing the convention knew that they were establishing a rule of conduct, and understood the reason for it.

Some say that conventions existed in the sixteenth century during the reign of the Tudors, which gave them political predominance.[55] However, there may be some underlying confusion in terms of conventions and the law or legal issues. For example, some may confuse conventions with the scope of prerogative or parliamentary privilege. Furthermore an illegal exercise of power such as forced loans, even if successfully carried out, cannot result in a convention, as such actions lack the requisite element of agreement that a particular convention exists. Arguments about sovereignty, such as the divine right of kings, are legal arguments and not mere political practices.

Furthermore, given that Parliament was ultimately victorious and the modern constitutional conventions we know today arise from its efforts, these developments will be focused upon, rather than on conventions doubtfully in existence or which do not meet the criteria of conventions as outlined, and which have been superseded in any event.

Whitelocke's theory became the accepted theory of the constitution, and in the eighteenth century the growth of constitutional conventions made it workable. From the supremacy and rule of law, including the use of impeachment, developed a theory of ministerial responsibility to law, which is distinguishable from systems of administrative law that exist on the Continent, such as in France.

Parliament also sought to guide state policy by controlling the appointment of ministers, which was legally the prerogative of the king. Leaders of the Commons lived in fear and suspicion, and concluded that they would not be safe unless they could obtain large control over government conduct. The only effective means to do so was to restrict the king's choice of ministers. This control was an important aspect of the fight for responsible government, wherein ministers had to be responsible to the king and Commons, and ministers who lacked the confidence of the Commons had to be dismissed.

There were a number of precedents establishing this convention. First, in 1629, Coryton asked for the removal of a minister. Another important precedent was the Ten Propositions of June 1641 of the Lords and Commons. One demand therein was that the king should remove from his council some chancellors, and that he should take into his council such officers and chancellors in whom his people and Parliament might have confidence. The king refused. When the English and Scotch parliaments were asked to suppress the Irish rebellion, Pym moved that the House refuse unless the king removed his evil councillors, and accepted those of whom the House approved. The position was opposed and ultimately rejected. However, the House did succeed in a similar motion, namely, that if the king did not appoint ministers approved by Parliament, the House would be forced to adopt a method of defending Ireland and entrust the duty to persons upon whom it could rely. The Grand Remonstrance lists illegal and arbitrary actions of Charles I, and states the policy that Parliament intended to pursue, including its intention that the king was to employ ministers holding the confidence of Parliament. The measure was strenuously opposed on the ground that the Commons was no longer seeking the observance of law, but was obtaining control over state policy. It passed by eleven votes.

At the outbreak of the Civil War, the Commons took a leading position in defending constitutional liberty and magnifying itself at the expense of the Lords, as it was the representative House. The Lords found it impossible to work with the king, and the circumstances made it necessary for Pym and the Commons majority to insist on the subjection of the king to the will of Parliament.

Further developments in constitutional conventions are discussed in the next chapter, along with developments in public law in the eighteenth and nineteenth centuries.

7

Public Law in the Eighteenth and Nineteenth Centuries

The eighteenth century marks the progression in English economic life from medieval times, when the economy was based primarily on land, to modern times, which changed life and the sources of wealth. It was the time of the industrial revolution.

This chapter is divided into two parts. The first part begins with a discussion on the separation of powers and checks and balances. It then examines the further reform of parliamentary government and the overcoming of executive influences on the Commons. It also deals with the main constitutional conventions that arose at this time.

The second part completes the picture on courts by examining judicature reforms, and by examining the question of whether courts exercise any inherent powers.

REFORM — PARLIAMENTARY GOVERNMENT

Separation of Powers and Checks and Balances

The constitutional position that Parliament won with the Revolution resulted in a new position for the king and central government, which led to new constitutional practices. Parliament's restriction of central government power emphasized the traditional independence of local government, the constitutional rights of the subject, and the supremacy of law. These salient features of public law united to create the constitution of separated powers and checks and balances, as eulogized by Blackstone and Burke. There was a division of state powers between the king, Parliament, and courts. There was also the division of legislative power between the king, Lords, and Commons. In short, there was a separation of power between separate organs of government, checking and balancing one another.

The king was a check on Parliament and Parliament was a check on the king. The Lords and Commons were a check on each other. The courts, presided over by judges with security of tenure, were a check on the executive and an important safeguard for liberty. As Blackstone noted, this separation was necessary for public liberty.[1] This separation also implies that courts were to stay within their role and jurisdiction strictly, and not act as if they were part of the legislature or the executive. If judicial power were not separated from legislative and executive powers, there would be no liberty. If it were joined to legislative power, the power over the citizen's life or liberty would be arbitrary; the judge would be a legislator. The life, liberty, and property of the subject would be in the hands of arbitrary judges, whose decisions would then be regulated only by their own opinions, and not by any fundamental principles of law, which, though legislatures may depart from them, judges are bound to observe.

If judicial power were joined with executive power, the judge would have the strength of an oppressor. The judiciary might become an overbalance for the legislature. Thus, statute abolished Star Chamber, and judicial power was removed from the privy council, whose members showed they were inclined to pronounce as law that which was most agreeable to the prince or his officers. The uniting of judge and minister of the state must be avoided in a free constitution.

Indeed, contrary to the writings and criticisms of socialist writers, experiences with the 'people's courts' under marxist/communist regimes demonstrate the tyranny and mock trials that may occur when a judicature is subordinated to government policy.

Montesquieu[2] observed that if legislative power is combined with executive power in the same person or body, then there will be no liberty, as it is to be feared that the same person or body making tyrannical laws will enforce them tyrannically. All would be lost if the same person or body exercised these three powers.

Locke also advocated the separation of legislative and executive powers to avoid tyranny. His suggestions on the separation of powers were derived from his observation of contemporary English practice. His work was used as a basis for Montesquieu's rediscovery of a general theoretical doctrine of the separation of powers, as

204 The Executive and Public Law

Aristotle and Marsiglio had suggested in ancient and medieval times respectively.

Plucknett argues that the separation of legislative and executive powers was achievable by the Act of Settlement, which excluded ministers from the House of Commons.[3] For example, no person who had an office or profit under the king, or received a pension from the crown, could be a member of the Commons. The Act was subsequently amended by statute to permit crown ministers to sit by allowing them to seek re-election after appointment to salaried office. This provision lasted until 1926, when the need for re-election was abolished.

THE COMPONENT PARTS

The Succession of the House of Hanover, and the Whig victory and its hold on power for half a century, had a direct influence on the development of eighteenth- and nineteenth-century public law. The salient features include the development of a system of parliamentary government in which the king, Lords, and Commons were partners though unequal in government; the development of party government; and, the beginning of cabinet government.

During the eighteenth century, sovereign power in the state was exercised by the crown, Lords, and Commons, acting independently, which gave rise to a system of checks and balances. The queen could effectively command a body of persons in both Houses through a kind of bribery, and a conviction that the queen's government must be carried on. In this way, the crown had considerable influence on or control of Parliament and a considerable hand in shaping state policy.

The Lords was in theory the upper House, but in reality became less powerful than the Commons. At this time, the Lords played an important and independent part in the constitution. Except for finance, it enjoyed co-ordinate legislative powers. It was also a council of the crown and the final court of appeal, it held a large portion of great state offices, and it held many privileges.

The Commons was the strongest of the three partners. In spite of the defects in the representative system, it gave a representation of the governing classes in town and country. Its control over finance allowed it to assert its power to scrutinize administration and the conduct of ministers, and even to influence legislation. Its power of impeachment could be used to ensure that the king's ministers obeyed the law, and could even be used to attempt to get rid of ministers whose policy the Commons disliked.

Government was difficult, and more so in light of the supremacy of law and judicial independence providing a barrier to illegal actions. This separation of powers and supremacy of law also made the executive weaker.

Separation of Powers and Local Government

Part of the notion of separation of powers involved local government. Local government organization in the sixteenth century affected public law in England. Local government was the stronghold of feudal ideas, which had to be mastered for strong centralized government to grow. The mere existence of centralized institutions was not enough. In England, there was not the same degree of central control as on the Continent. Rather, there was a blending with the old, which resulted in complex and unsystematic institutions.

Communal officials and franchises that survived in the country or in the boroughs retained many legal ideas and institutions of the earlier medieval period. The effect was that they kept alive the idea of a community that governed itself under judicial forms, subject only to the law.

Justices of the peace began to supersede the communal courts and to control communal officials. Their growing duties made them rulers of the county by the end of the fifteenth century. Their role was not so much to enforce the law, but to punish breaches of it. The procedure was judicial. Thus, the old idea of local self-government subject to law was retained.

Because justices of the peace had such a large scope of duties given by statute, the judicial and administrative functions of that office began to separate. Also important was the Tudors' use of the parish as the unit of local government, under the control of the JPs. The parish was originally an ecclesiastical, self-sufficient unit of self-government, which only gradually became a unit of secular government in the second half of the sixteenth century due to the Reformation.[4] A statute passed in 1535 was the first to give the parish extensive functions with respect to the poor. Later, it was given an organized machinery, taxing powers, and other duties.

The system of local government was in full working order during the time of the first two Stuart kings. It successfully administered the poor law, and the economic policy of the state. It kept local government running smoothly and efficiently. The system was supervised by justices of the peace, assisted by sheriffs who executed writs and orders, and by the lord lieutenant and his deputies who superintended the military forces. Below them were a number of other officials, such as constables and churchwardens. The smooth running of that machinery depended on the king's policy being approved of by the officials and bodies entrusted with local government, and their willingness to co-operate.[5] These officials were inspired by the ideals of the common law, which they applied through the judicial machinery, and not ideas of a department of the central government in spite of supervision by Council or Star Chamber. Statutes and common law rules defined their powers and duties, but left much to their initiative. By the seventeenth century, opposition to crown policy increased, including to the crown's attempt to substitute supremacy of prerogative for supremacy of common law, and to its raising of taxes without Parliament's approval. These self-governing officials and communities, educated by their unpaid service, resented a strengthening of central control that threatened their independence. The Rebellion and Revolution abolished administrative control, and left only the system of judicial control. For the most part, from the eighteenth century onward, central government in effect lost much of its control over local government and the justices of the peace. Private citizens could use procedures open to the crown, and initiate a civil action if they were injured as a result of negligence or wilful breaches of law. This ability to sue government became an effective control and safeguard of liberty, and a security for the maintenance of the supremacy of law. In the second half of the century, the legislature created many ad hoc authorities to perform functions that existing authorities were unable to do. Much discretion was left to justices and other responsible officials. In exercising discretion, these bureaucrats created machinery which was often new, extra-legal, and sometimes even illegal. Thus, much of the machinery of local government was based on practices and techniques that developed organically. It was not until the Municipal Corporations Act, 1835, that a uniform pattern of town government was substituted for the old survivals of the Middle Ages.

Constitutional Developments and Beginnings of Reform

The post-Revolution phase of history established parliamentary sovereignty and Parliament as the major driving force for legislation and government. These results were achieved primarily by legislation being vindicated over prerogative, but there were also various other ways by which Parliament gained control over the executive or decreased the executive's influence on the Commons, including the ways in which the executive perverted elections through electoral rules.

Anomalies in the representative system itself had to be remedied. As with previous kings, William also corrupted the Commons in order to manage it. Neither the king nor larger landowners were willing to give up the opportunities for exercising influence, for example through nomination by patrons. Furthermore, the power to dispose of or sell a seat in Parliament became valuable, and a kind of market developed. Reform of this process did not occur until 1832.

Tensions existed after the Revolution between Whigs and Tories, which made it increasingly impossible to retain a mixed ministry. Tories came from the country and represented the landed gentry. Whigs came from the towns and represented trade and finance, large landowners, and dissenters from the national Church. A split in the Tory party resulted in the Whigs being in power for nearly half a century. George I and George II were convinced of Whig loyalty and the disloyalty of the Tories. They supported the Whigs with prerogative, and gave them a majority in all parliaments. The result was the development of a system of parliamentary government in which the king, Lords, and Commons were partners, though unequal, in government; it led also to the development of party government, and the beginnings of cabinet government. The king was still regarded as a chief magistrate. The government was his government, and a formed opposition was regarded as factious.

Walpole's long ministry began in 1721. He created a disciplined party, and used unsavory methods. Politics was venal at that time. There was nothing in the constitutional ethics of the time requiring a politician to resign so long as his party maintained a majority in the Commons.

Later, George III was able to overthrow the Whig electoral dominance. Pitt sought to entrust government to the most able, loyal, and honest. George III's goal was to secure crown independence. As a result, he broke up Pitt's ministry, removed Pitt, and made peace with France. The king was gathering a party and a department around him by using the unsavoury methods that Walpole and Newcastle employed, but in exaggerated form. His government roused public hatred. His party was supreme in both Houses through patronage and corruption, and North was an able prime minister under his control. Burke complained that the power of the crown, almost dead as prerogative, had grown with more strength and less odium under the name of influence. Furthermore, the king and ministers were using the sovereignty of Parliament to cover their misdeeds in perfect safety.[6] Thus, this control over the legislature tended to weaken one of the principal checks or balances in the eighteenth-century constitution. On the other hand, the power of the crown did not affect the other principal check or balance against arbitrary power, which was safeguarded by judicial independence as set out in the Act of Settlement and helped to prevent an undue encroachment on liberty. Some perceptive commentators saw the real danger of the 'new despotism' of executive officials, in which a ministry with crown prerogatives, backed by a vast bureaucracy, was able to get what powers it wanted from the Commons.[7]

Now the practical danger to the constitution was manifest, and agitation widespread. The root of the evil was the degradation of Parliament due to corruption and the anomalous state of the representation. These circumstances gave rise to the impetus for parliamentary reform to address the various methods of corruption. They also produced a reformed Whig party, which was the first 'formed opposition' to the crown in that century. This development was the condition precedent to the growth of the modern system of cabinet government.[8]

The opposition gained strength, and various defeats compelled North's government to resign in 1782. Although the king and his friends were still able to exercise considerable influence for many years, North's resignation marked an end to their reign.

The Whig ministry diminished the crown's power to exercise a corrupt influence over Parliament. Statutes were passed to exclude contractors from the Commons,[9] and to disenfranchise revenue officers.[10] The government also passed a measure for economic reform resulting in considerable savings, despite the king's opposition, which also was a precedent supporting the constitutional convention that the crown must give royal assent to and pass into law any bill passed by the two Houses of Parliament.

The Fox-North coalition drove Shelburne to resign, even though the king had called him. The king was furious, but was obliged to yield, while seeking the coalition's downfall. This episode is a firm precedent supporting the constitutional convention that the king is obliged to call only ministers in whom the Commons has confidence, and to dismiss ministers who lack that confidence.

The king knew the India Bill would pass the Commons. Therefore, instead of attempting to influence the Commons, he used royal influence in the Lords to defeat the bill. Its rejection was used as an excuse to get rid of his ministers.

The king called on Pitt. Though it was ostensibly a victory for the king, it was also the final defeat of his system of personal government. He could not get rid of Pitt, who was the only alternative to the hated coalition, and Pitt was too great and able a statesman to be a servant of the king as North was. During Pitt's ministry, the Commons increased its power at the expense of the Lords and king. This marked the beginning of the disappearance of the separation of powers constitution that gave rise to checks and balances. Despite other differences, both Tories and Whigs agreed that it was undesirable to change the fundamental principles of the constitution, but that obvious abuses should be corrected. Both Burke and Blackstone agreed with this position.

The Revolution settlement and its theory as expounded by Locke were accepted. That settlement divided the powers of the state between the king, the Lords, and the Commons, as well as the courts. This settlement structured the conflicts between the king, Lords, and Commons in the contest to become the managing power of the state.

PARLIAMENTARY REFORMS

It was not until the new Whigs realized that George III's policy was upsetting the balance of the constitution in favour of the crown, for example in using patronage to control Parliament, that they became convinced reform was necessary to restore the balance in favour of Parliament. While the reforms since the 1780s covered much ground, they were insufficient and their provisions were sometimes evaded. The aristocracy and monarchy still profited from abuses such as

210   The Executive and Public Law

patronage, but lost much with the reforms. The prospect of gradual reform to the legislature and the executive, to allow them to adapt to new conditions, needs, and political ideas, was lost due to war with France in 1793. The few reforms in the early nineteenth century were inadequate to meet the needs of a rapidly changing society. Thus, the reforms in 1832 were so drastic that they shattered the eighteenth-century constitution of balanced powers.

Prior to 1832, membership in the Commons was subject to certain qualifications and disqualifications. Property qualifications existed. Disqualifications included having a conviction for treason or felony, being a minor or an alien, being ordained to the clergy (after 1801), and holding an office that derived a pension from the crown. As well, statutes imposed tests of religious orthodoxy and loyalty. As a result, Roman Catholics were disqualified until the law was changed in 1829.[11] So too were Quakers until 1833 because they could not take the oath, and Jews until 1858. These oaths excluded persons who disagreed fundamentally with the doctrines of the established Church, or who were opposed to the Revolution settlement. The property qualifications, established by an Act of 1710, were intended to preserve the ascendancy of the landed gentry in the Commons, and were in force until 1838. However, the rules were systematically evaded because the Industrial Revolution was altering the relative importance of land and other property.

It was, however, the rules respecting the franchise and the manner in which elections were conducted in the eighteenth century that created the most efficient barriers for men owning no property. The franchise was based on property qualifications and on the unreformed anomalous system. Some have argued that notwithstanding the same, it produced a Commons of high intellectual quality and secured a real representation of all classes, and in reality a better result.[12] Elections were financed by the candidates, and were expensive. There were some attempts to suppress bribery and corrupt practices.

The System of Crown Influence   Under the system of crown influence in the unreformed Commons' system of representation, the crown was able to manage Parliament. The crown had many methods to influence elections to the Commons, and used patronage to control its members after election. It was able as well to influence the

Lords, and to use the electoral influence of the peers and great landowners. By this system, the crown and Lords were able to maintain the balance of power in the constitution. On the other hand, patronage could be used by the king to obtain greater power and to destroy the balance of the constitution, as was done by George III.

The 1832 Reforms In 1832, the reconstituted Whig party gained power, winning almost all constituencies with genuine electorates. It obtained the support of the different parliamentary reformers, and carried the reform initiative through. However, the Lords rejected the bill and public violence ensued. The bill was brought back by the Commons, supported by even larger majorities. The Lords realized another rejection was politically unfeasible. Indeed, they decided to use amendments to change the bill's essential character. The king rejected the unanimous advice of Cabinet to create enough peers to pass the bill, and Grey resigned. However, due to the level of political agitation and even violence, Wellington was unable to form a government, leaving William IV with no choice but to recall Grey. The opposition of the Lords was overcome by the crown's threat to create enough peers to pass the bill, and because the only alternative was civil war. These were not radical reformers following the ideas of Rousseau and Paine. Rather, their support came from the middle class, whom their Reform Act enfranchised. Reform was based on utilitarian lines, on individualism, laissez-faire politics, and the economics of reducing government activity to a minimum.

The Reform Act's preamble began by stating that "it is expedient to take effectual Measures for correcting divers Abuses that have long prevailed in the Choice of Members to serve in the Commons."[13] The chief objective was to reduce the number of nomination boroughs and to create new county and borough seats. In so doing, the Act disenfranchised most of the rotten boroughs and reduced the number of nomination boroughs otherwise controlled by peers. The Act also extended the franchise. In addition to 'forty-shilling' freeholders, voting rights were extended to owners of land worth £10, to holders of medium-term leases on land worth £50, and to tenants paying an annual rent of £50.

The Reform Act, 1832, destroyed the balanced English constitution of the eighteenth century as it made the Commons not merely the most influential partner of the state, but the strongest power by far. With the influence of the crown and Lords over elections greatly reduced, the Commons was able to compel the crown to accept the ministers of whom it approved, and by using prerogative for its own purposes reduced the Lords to a secondary chamber. In the Commons, the Act substituted the representation of diverse interests which the unreformed franchise secured, for the representation to those whom a uniform franchise gave predominance. It brought into clear relief the sovereignty of legislature and emphasized the power and duty of legislature to give effect to the wishes of the people by actively using its powers. Although it introduced a moderate measure of democracy which some may have considered inadequate, it created the conditions to increase it. It also introduced the theoretical equality inherent in one person, one vote.

THE EXECUTIVE

Originally prerogative power was the basis of the executive. Royal prerogative became supplemented by legislation. Today, executive government is largely conducted by statute, which can involve administrative, legislative, and judicial powers, and in practice involves the government's use of prerogative.

At the beginning of the eighteenth century, prerogative was a large and indefinite power which could be used with respect to executive power in the modern state. Blackstone's *Commentaries* provide a summary of this power, including the direct and incidental prerogatives. The result of the seventeenth-century events was that all parts of prerogative were subject to the law.

In 1760 a number of fiscal or proprietary privileges were surrendered and made payable to the Aggregate Fund, out of which Parliament granted the crown a fixed civil list,[14] whereas some other obsolete privileges were abolished by legislation in the nineteenth and twentieth centuries.

The Great Rebellion and Revolution decided conclusively that inseparable prerogatives could be taken away by an Act of Parliament. Furthermore, judicial cases determined that prerogative came from and could not override the common law. Only an Act of Parliament could override the common law. Accordingly, prerogative could not be used to prejudice common law rights.

While prerogative was subject to law, it did confer wide powers within which absolute discretion could be exercised. The only safeguards against its oppressive use were, first, the legal remedies of petition of right with respect to certain specific injuries to private persons, and, second, the legal powers held by the Commons, or whatever practical power it could summon for scrutinizing and complaining, including the use of the principle of ministerial responsibility.

However, the constitutional convention was growing that the disapproval of Parliament necessitated resignation, and the criminal prosecution of impeachment was no longer necessary or particularly useful to achieve the Commons' control over the appointment or dismissal of ministers.

The king was first in military command. An illustration of this principle was the Norman kings' successful assertion that all military service which was due from tenant to lord was really service owed to the king. The military power of the crown was settled partly by medieval statutes and partly by seventeenth-century statutes. The position of the standing army was settled on its modern basis at the Revolution. Parliament had to annually sanction and give authority to the crown to enact rules of discipline. These rules depended on the annual Mutiny Acts, on common law, and on the statutory powers of the crown to make articles of war to regulate the army.

Events settled that all exercises of prerogative involving taxation required Parliament's consent. Thus, the crown lost the power to control foreign trade by tariff, which left controlling foreign trade to Parliament.

As the head of the national Church, the king made extensive use of patronage. The overall result on the religious life of the Church was negative, religious enthusiasm was killed, and the Church created a system of humanistic ethics in which the supernatural was left out. The goal was to identify Christian with utilitarian ethics, and Jesus was presented as the first teacher of the greatest happiness principle.[15] The effect of this development was to promote the growth of the idea of toleration, and the close union between Church and State gave popularity and stability to the Church and government at that time, although that Church is currently much in decline today as a result, while tending to remove theological differences from the political arena. It also contributed, in time, to people forgetting the Christian influences on the law and the system of government and the values which help to sustain the British system of government.

The phraseology of toleration would also be used in time to undermine the very concept itself, and would come to mean the required acceptance of a particular political agenda, which leads in fact to intolerance towards the expression of contrary views.

Further details of the use and disuse of prerogative, as well as of statute taking over the areas once regulated by prerogative, can be outlined, but a more detailed examination is not necessary for the purposes of this book. It is sufficient to note at this point that in the eighteenth century, executive power generally resided in the king and depended on prerogative. This power was exercised through councils, ministers, and departments composed of the king's servants. According to the legal theory or fiction of the constitution, they advised the king with respect to the exercise of his prerogatives. In reality, prerogative was often exercised according to the monarch's own discretion. Today, the executive is largely based on statutory powers delegating authority to ministers, departments, and administrative bodies.

This history of the Commons' growing legal control over the executive does not mean that the executive does not continue to play a powerful role in public policy and administration. Specialization, complexity, and bureaucratic knowledge and expertise, as well as the sheer unmanageable size of government bureaucracy today, are important reasons why the bureaucracy exercises significant influence; so is Parliament's general lack of interest in devoting more effort to supervising the work of government, or to drafting more specific legislation to curtail bureaucratic jurisdiction or discretion.

CONSTITUTIONAL CONVENTIONS

The need to establish harmonious relations between the king and Parliament, between the executive and Parliament, and between the two Houses, gave rise to new constitutional practices and understandings. In some of these the seeds of constitutional government can be seen.

The conventions of the eighteenth century centred around the system of influence, and were directed to maintain a system of divided powers and of checks and balances. The conventions of the nineteenth and twentieth centuries centre around Cabinet, and are directed to secure the political predominance of the Commons, and to ensure that the Commons reflects the opinion of the nation.

Public Law in the 18th and 19th Centuries 215

During the eighteenth century, there was separation between legislative and executive authorities, separation between the two Houses within Parliament, and separation of the judiciary from the legislature and executive. However, in order for government to work smoothly, the gap between the legislature and the executive had to be bridged. For most of the eighteenth century, this was mainly done through the use of the system of representation then in place to influence Parliament. The crown had many methods to influence the Commons and the Lords. At this point, Cabinet did not have the solidarity it would have in the nineteenth century. Therefore, it was around the crown, and its influence, that the eighteenth-century constitutional practices chiefly centred.[16]

Bagehot recognized in 1865 that in traditional theory, the goodness of the constitution consisted of the entire separation of the legislative and executive authorities. However, in reality, the efficiency of the constitution lay in the fusion of these authorities through Cabinet.

The king was a constituent part of Parliament. He had the power to reject bills. Blackstone thought this fact, and the fact of the executive forming a part of legislative power, was the most efficacious of the checks and balances, which also helped to preserve the balance of the constitution. It was thought that some link was necessary for the smooth working of a constitution that divided government powers among largely independent and autonomous organs. Royal prerogative was the principal link in the eighteenth century.

By the end of the century, while this legislative-executive link was preserved, events were altering its character and mode of operation by making it less royal. In the following period, the development of cabinet government completed that alteration by giving ministers control over the exercise of crown prerogatives for as long as they retained the confidence of the Commons.[17] Ministerial control of prerogative gave them the power to carry on executive government. The power of the crown to dismiss ministers at pleasure made it possible to get rid of them when they ceased to command a majority in the House. The crown power to dissolve Parliament at its pleasure gave ministers the power to appeal from a hostile majority in the House to the electorate.

The development of cabinet government rendered obsolete the crown prerogative to reject bills. The last instance of a refusal to grant royal assent was exercised in 1707 when Anne rejected the Scotch militia bill.[18] The prerogative to reject bills was not regarded as entirely obsolete in the eighteenth century by all the relevant actors. For example, the Earl of Ilay's 1743 speech in Parliament recognized that "the prerogative of putting a stop to any bill by a negative was grown obsolete, but not given up."[19] In 1788, Lord Loughborough agreed that this was an essential prerogative, but said he could imagine only one possible case in which it would be right to exercise it – if both Houses attacked the rights of the crown in a manner "so repugnant to the sense and feelings of the people at large, that the king's pronouncing his negative on such a bill ... should be considered a popular execution of his prerogative."[20]

THE COMMONS AND LORDS

The Commons' practical authority was increasing at the expense of the Lords' even before the Civil War. One reason is that the Lords were not as active in considering matters of policy. At this time, there was no impetus to eliminate the second chamber because recent events showed a need for some check on tyrannical government. For example, in his 1680 treatise, Neville wrote that "if we had no such peerage now, upon the old constitutions, yet we should be necessitated to make an artificial peerage of senate instead of it."[21] The House of Lords was becoming a second chamber acting as a check on the Commons, and could no longer claim to possess co-ordinate authority, and still less to be an 'Upper House.'[22]

Although the Lords' relation to the Commons was trending towards its modern position of a delaying and revising body, the Lords was still active in this period. In both Houses important legislation originated. The king still played an active part in government, and performed the same sort of function *vis-à-vis* the Commons as did the Lords. The king's authority related to prorogation, dissolution, and the refusal to consent to bills, and he could in substance refer back to one or both Houses. For example, Charles stopped the progress of the Exclusion Bill by dissolution, thus in substance appealing to the country. It was not until the king ceased to play an active part in government that the relations between the Commons and Lords became settled on their modern basis. George II used his influence in the Lords to stop bills he disliked.

Nevertheless, the Lords opposed the change in its constitutional position. As a result, there were more controversies between the two Houses in this period. For a time in the eighteenth century, the disputes ceased, until they arose again in the 1830s and in the later nineteenth century. The defects in the representative system allowed the king and the Lords to exert a large indirect influence over the Commons.

The Lords as a council of the crown became obsolete with the development of Cabinet, and even more so the claim of an individual peer to give advice to the crown. The last time this council was summoned was in 1640. Also, its susceptibility to royal influence weakened its position in the following century, as it tended to emphasize its non-representative character. There were other criticisms of it, such as it being a House of retired ministers. The Lords' rejection of Fox's India Bill in 1783 was the last instance that House took the position of balance in the constitution. Still, until 1832, the influence of the crown and individual peers was substantial.

The Commons' Control over Finance   The Commons obtained complete control over finance. The Commons established the right to originate all bills taxing the people, and successfully resisted the claim of the Lords to amend such bills. A number of precedents establish this constitutional convention. First, in 1661, the Commons rejected a bill to pave streets in the area of Westminster because it imposed a rate. It prepared a bill of its own and attached a proviso. The Lords refused to pass the bill and it died. In 1671, the Commons denied the Lords the ability to amend a money bill. A conference was held, but neither side gave way. In 1678, the Lords again amended a money bill. After several conferences, there was no agreement. However, the substantial victory was with the Commons because, at that time, the two Houses were governed by the rule that "all aids and supplies to His Majesty in Parliament are the sole gift of the Commons; and all bills for granting any such aids and supplies ought to begin with the Commons; and that it is the undoubted and sole right of the Commons to direct, limit, and appoint in such bills, the ends, purposes, and considerations, conditions, limitations, and qualifications, of such grants, which ought not to be changed or altered by the House of Lords."[23]

There may be some controversy as to whether this right is based in law or convention. Holdsworth argues that the claim to originate all taxation bills was not a legal one.[24] He agrees with Stubbs that as a general rule, grants of money from the later fourteenth century originated with the Commons, and had been recognized by Henry IV in 1407. However, they could find no medieval authority that such grants could not originate from the Lords, or that the Lords could not amend such a bill. These authors also raise the question of whether Henry's 1407 dictum was understood to recognize the exclusive right of the Commons to originate the grant. There was a case in 1472 in which the Commons originated a grant to be assessed on the property of the Commons, and the Lords originated another to be assessed on their property. In the Convention Parliament, the Lords amended money bills without objection. In 1661, there were precedents in which the Lords originated similar tax bills. In 1671, they asked for documentary evidence that the claims made by the Commons were ever conceded by the Lords.

There was also merit to the Commons' view. It can be justified by the change in political conditions in that century. The crown needed money to maintain government which must be raised by tax, and the Commons in theory represented all but an insignificant fraction of those on whom the taxes were levied. As the Commons had the power to enforce its claims, it was only fair to its constituents that it should do so.

Legally, if Henry delegated such authority in 1407, or his decision was a legal decision, then the Commons' claim was established in law. Any later precedents, in essence actions contradicting the law, would be legally improper. They could at best establish a convention inconsistent with that law. Furthermore, the Commons also forced the Lords to pass measures by tacking them to money bills.

Accordingly, it can be concluded the rule that money bills must originate in the Commons and cannot be amended by the Lords is a matter of constitutional law, or at least of constitutional convention, and perhaps of mixed convention and law. While this book deals with the issue under the topic of convention, no conclusion is made that it was a matter of convention. In the Canadian case, the matter of originating money bills is dealt with explicitly in the *Constitution Act*, 1867, and is clearly a matter of Constitutional law.

Ministry and Individual Ministerial Responsibility Before the Revolution, the only way to get rid of a minister was by impeachment. After the Revolution, it was clear that in a practical sense the crown could not carry on government with ministers of whom the Commons disapproved. Ministers also realized that they could not carry on in office in face of an adverse vote of the Commons, and that they were responsible to that House. Furthermore, if a ministry loses the confidence of the House of Commons, it must resign. For example, in 1739 Walpole stated that a minister possessed power from the crown, but was answerable to the House of Commons for its exercise. He resigned once it became clear he no longer possessed the House's confidence. In 1746, Bath and Granville were obliged to give up their attempt to form a ministry for the same reason. The Fox-North coalition of 1783 compelled Shelburne to resign. In 1779, North stated that "whenever the majority of the House should disapprove of a minister's conduct, he must give way."[25] North insisted on several occasions that the ministry was jointly and severally responsible for measures taken, and must stand or fall together.

The king could not refuse to give office to a minister if that grant was demanded by the Commons and public opinion, as in the case of the elder Pitt.

Nor could any ministry pursue a policy to which the Commons was definitely opposed. Burke recognized that if the administration did not correspond to the legislature, disorder would result. Walpole gave up his excise scheme when he found that the nation and Commons were definitely opposed to it. In 1782, North told George III that "the Prince on the Throne cannot, with prudence, oppose the deliberate resolutions of the House of Commons."[26]

As soon as the crown influence over Parliament diminished, the logical consequence of the dependence of the ministry or a particular minister on the continued support of the House clearly emerged.[27]

Still, the conventional rules were not as strict as they later became. Resignation of a particular minister did not necessarily mean the resignation of the whole cabinet. For example, at the beginning of George III's reign, Newcastle remained in office after Pitt resigned. Also, a defeat in the Commons, even on an important measure, such as the Peerage Bill of 1719, did not yet necessitate resignation of the

220 The Executive and Public Law

ministry. In 1779, George III told North that ministers must "not mind being now and then in a minority."

CABINET GOVERNMENT

The last stage in the relations of prerogative to government made possible the gradual evolution of cabinet government. This stage settled the controversies of the seventeenth century by placing prerogative powers at the disposal of the majority of the Commons, which led to the growth of constitutional conventions regulating the workings of Cabinet.[28] Accordingly, conventions were developed on top of the law of the constitution or the system of government to ensure its workability.

The executive power of the state was vested in the king and depended on his prerogative. It was exercised through councils, ministers, and departments composed of the king's servants, according to the legal theory of the constitution that they advised the king with respect to the exercise of his prerogatives. In reality, the king often acted according to his own discretion. During the Restoration, the executive was still vested in the king and his privy council. However, Council was becoming too large for executive work. Therefore, there was a tendency to reserve important business for a committee of Council composed of the king's most trusted ministers. From this committee a cabinet developed during the later seventeenth century. Because it gave the king larger control, and made it difficult to render ministers responsible for the policy which they advised or assented, Parliament frequently complained about the cabinet's existence. After the Revolution and Parliament's predominance in the constitution, it was evident that while the king still chose ministers of his cabinet who held their office at his pleasure, the king could not keep in office ministers definitely objected to by Parliament. Ministers were increasingly regarded as responsible to him and to Parliament alike.

The new Whig party in opposition to George III's policy began to introduce changes in the later eighteenth century. Cabinet's responsibility to Parliament increased, and its responsibility to the king decreased. Cabinet became more homogeneous, representing the party commanding a majority in the Commons. Thus, the king's power to choose ministers was curtailed, as those ministers were coming to be nominees of a party rather than of the king.

Parliamentary Acts instituted new developments in the constitution of the executive and its machinery so that government would be according to the wishes of the nation. Still, during the eighteenth century, cabinet government was in its initial stages.

In order for the king to retain an independent sphere of action, he secured developments with respect to ministers and departments similar to the evolution of crown councils. He created new officials and departments of government in more immediate touch with himself. For example, in the thirteenth and fourteenth centuries, the king used the departments of household and wardrobe to give him control over finance independent of the Exchequer. However, the king's capacity to do so was exhausted as the crown and royal household declined, departments of state grew, and parliamentary control strengthened.

Still, there was little progress until the later eighteenth century. For example, Burke's Act of 1782 diminished the indirect control of the king over Parliament by abolishing useless officers who with crown influence secured seats in Parliament, and who supported the king. It became recognized that the king's ministers were dependent on Parliament rather than on the king, that the idea of state service was gradually divorced from the king's household, and that expenses should be removed from the civil list which were solely personal.[29] The distinction arose between the king's personal and royal household expenses, and the expenses of the state. Still, during this time Parliament voted the crown an annual sum out of which the crown paid for household expenses and for civil servants, which perpetuated the idea that central government officials were in form and substance the king's servants. In Victoria's reign, the civil list was restricted to the expenses of the queen and royal household. In William IV's time, the crown surrendered all additional sources of revenue, except from the duchies of Lancaster and Cornwall, in return for a fixed income.[30] This distinction also gave rise to a distinction between the crown's private property and the property of the state. This development was part of the change in the balance of the constitution and in constitutional theory. One effect was that patronage was further withdrawn from the civil list, and thus from the king's control. In reality, members of Cabinet increasingly ceased to be the king's nominees and came to be nominees of the dominant party in the Commons.

This process also contributed to Parliament taking over complete practical control over finance from the king.

Until the Great Rebellion, the privy council was the governing body in the state. It did much work though committees, and sometimes appointed commissions for certain defined judicial and administrative work. The privy council was restored in 1660, but its judicial powers were taken away. However, its actual position had changed because of the limitations put on prerogative by law, and because Parliament could criticize and sometimes control the king's exercise of prerogative. From the later seventeenth century, the privy council was becoming a formal and ceremonial body, doing little more than registering decisions reached by its own committees, or by ministers acting collectively in Cabinet, or acting as department heads.[31] Its one active committee, the Judicial Committee of the Privy Council, heard appeals from the colonies. Real control of central government was by a committee of the privy council, which came to be called 'Cabinet.' Cabinet directed state policy, and the work of government was done by departments over which cabinet ministers presided. The privy council was superseded by Cabinet, and by the development of government departments.

Beginnings of Cabinet Members of Cabinet thought they were entitled to be consulted with respect to important decisions. Charles reformed the privy council in 1679 and promised not to use a single ministry, private advice, or foreign committees. The new privy council was still too large to conduct business efficiently for matters requiring speed and secrecy. Charles again used foreign committees. The transition from government by privy council to government by a few ministers or statesmen in the king's confidence aroused parliamentary opposition, and pejorative terms such as 'private cabinet councils' or 'cabals' were used. One of the criticisms was the difficulty of fixing legal responsibility on the king's ministers for their acts.

Restoring the privy council to its old position could not work, and the Act of Settlement provision was repealed. It was recognized that the executive must be vested in a small body of leading statesmen who could work together. By 1714, Cabinet had superseded the privy council as the governing body, and any member(s) of the committee could not continue to hold office if the Commons definitely objected.

Statute was also at play. Many leading officials heading older departments of state, such as law, revenue, the army, and the navy, were originally officials of the king's court and household, but ceased to be so and became officials of state heading departments of executive government. Those departments were often divided and subdivided, and new departments were created by statute. This machinery gave the chief state officials and their departments much autonomy, subject to the legal control of the king and courts and to the political control of Parliament, and left them able to increase their powers without external interference. There was also much complexity and inefficiency. The system worked to the advantage of officials, and also of the king for patronage. One concern was that the procedures and practices ministers created for individual departments gave rise to or affected substantive rules, with the danger that this process might whittle away liberty. The common law and courts could act against bureaucratic tyranny; however, legislative reform was needed.

Cabinet was gaining new solidarity and the new position arose of the prime minister as its head. The composition of Cabinet was tending to be determined by the strength of rival parties in the Commons.

Subject to the general controls of Parliament and the conventions that were arising, generally the relations of Cabinet to the king and of individual members to the king were closer than their respective relations with Parliament. The king had influence over Cabinet's composition. It was necessary for Cabinet to possess his favour. Second, most state business was transacted by individual ministers with the king. Matters were not brought before Cabinet without the king's permission. The king controlled the exercise of his office and could disregard the counsel given to him. Government was the king's government. He could also obtain advice from other persons besides ministers. Accordingly, the principle of the collective responsibility of Cabinet for national policy was not yet recognized, and cabinets were formed from different groups with different aims. Under these circumstances, a prime minister as understood in modern constitutionalism and politics could not emerge. That is, there was no minister the king could regard as the head and representative of Cabinet, primarily responsible for the conduct of government, and entitled to have the first place in the king's confidence, so long as he could obtain and retain the support of Parliament for his policy. Therefore, the role and position of Cabinet during most of the eighteenth century differed from the modern Cabinet.

By the end of the eighteenth century, Cabinet was strengthened, and crown influence or patronage weakened. Also modifications occurred in the cabinet system with the rise of a 'formed and general opposition' during North's ministry. The hardening of party lines with the rise of an organized opposition made for the growth of Cabinet's collective responsibility for national policy. Also, Cabinet could not consist of other persons besides those holding responsible office. The idea that Cabinet consisted of only those holding responsible office was formally stated in 1801, when Addington was obliged to tell Loughborough, the former Lord Chancellor, after his resignation that he was no longer entitled to attend cabinet meetings, and stated the principle that "the number of cabinet ministers should not exceed persons who are required to be members of it by their responsible office."[32] The greater cabinet solidarity resulting from these changes made it necessary for a prime minister to preside over and represent Cabinet. The principle was first stated by North in 1778, and finally laid down by Pitt in 1803, when he told Dundas that it was "an absolute necessity ... that here should be an avowed and real minister possessing the chief weight in the Council and the principal place in the confidence of the King. The power must rest in the person generally called the First Minister."[33]

The Reform Bill of 1832 swept away crown influence over Parliament. Cabinet could then assume its modern role, and emerge as the only link between the legislature and the executive, and the old theory of separation of powers was gone.

CONSTITUTIONAL CONVENTIONS – RESPONSIBLE GOVERNMENT

Two fundamental aspects of government in Britain are law-making and the executive, which was originally conducted through prerogative. Responsible government is the main convention relevant to the creation and development of countries adopting the parliamentary model of government. Formally, legislation is a bill passed by both the House of Lords and the House of Commons, which is then given royal assent by the monarch. By convention, the king must give royal assent to any bill passed by both Houses. Furthermore, while the Lords possesses co-equal authority to initiate or disapprove of bills, except for money bills, it has by convention lost the power to initiate bills, and the power to veto bills coming from the Commons is restrained. This power of veto is now subject to a Parliamentary Act providing that the Lords may not reject a bill dealing with national finance, and in other areas is limited to a suspensive or delaying veto.

Cabinet is the body of persons holding high office. The law of the constitution and constitutional convention differ in several respects in terms of the relations of Cabinet to king and Parliament, and the manner in which it acts as the executive government.

In law, members of Cabinet are the king's servants. They are appointed by him and dismissible at his pleasure. By convention, cabinet members must be appointed from the leaders of the largest party in the Commons, and continue to hold office as long as that party can keep a majority in the House. They are nominees.

Also, in law, Cabinet advises the king with respect to the exercise of prerogative. If the king decides to act on that advice, he makes his decision on state policy and sets into motion the executive machinery to carry it out. By constitutional convention, Cabinet settles state policy, and its members, acting through prerogative or statutory powers, set in motion the executive machinery to carry out that policy without the king's involvement.

As the change in the balance of power in the constitution occurred gradually and without change in law, it resulted in the growth of conventions. The contrast between the law and the conventions of the constitution with respect to Cabinet is also evident. These conventions began to operate when the formed opposition (arising on the issue of the American War of Independence) gained office in 1782. Until that time, Cabinet was still a body of the king's servants holding office at his pleasure and advising him about state policy. This was so even though Parliament could influence state policy, drive a disliked minister from office, or force the crown to accept a minister of whom Parliament approved.

COURT REFORMS AND INHERENT POWERS

Erskine May observed about the system of justice:

226 The Executive and Public Law

Heart-breaking delays and ruinous costs were the lot of suitors. Justice was dilatory, expensive, uncertain, and remote. To the rich it was a costly lottery: to the poor a denial of right, or certain ruin. The class who profited most by its dark mysteries were the lawyers themselves. A suitor might be reduced to beggary or madness: but his advisers revelled in the chicane and artifices of a lifelong suit and grew rich. Out of a multiplicity of forms and processes arose numberless fees and well-paid offices. Many subordinate functionaries, holding sinecure or superfluous appointments, enjoyed greater emoluments than the judges of the court; and upon the luckless suitors, again, fell the charge of these egregious establishments. If complaints were made, they were repelled as the promptings of ignorance: if amendments of the law were proposed, they were resisted as innovations. To question the perfection of English jurisprudence was to doubt the wisdom of our ancestors – a political heresy which could expect no toleration.[34]

Reforms to the Superior Courts: Judicature Acts

While May's criticism is broad and much of it continues to be a problem today, including the prohibitive costs, delays, and uncertainties surrounding litigation, it is clear that much inconvenience resulted from the ill-defined and clashing jurisdictions of various courts administering separate bodies of law with separate procedures and vocabularies. Litigants might find themselves after much litigation declared to be in the wrong court, concurrent proceedings were possible, and the situation was made more complex as the final appellate courts for each of these courts was different. Another anomaly was the separation between courts of common law and courts of equity. Neither court could administer complete justice within the scope of its jurisdiction. There were rivalry and injunctions to stop proceedings in other courts. Great delays and costs were the result.

Since the early nineteenth century, there were numerous commissions to study the various courts, leading to several reports. The general conclusion was that the powers and machinery of common law courts were insufficient to deal fully with matters falling within the scope of their jurisdiction. One obstacle was that reform would involve clerical staffs and the abolition of some lucrative sinecures or the reduction of emoluments, or offices which constituted valuable patronage for government or judges.

Statute deprived King's Bench of jurisdiction to amend errors of Common Pleas. The 1832 Uniformity of Processes Act[35] abolished the procedures invented by courts (fictions) to gain jurisdiction. The courts were left in possession of the jurisdiction which they exercised, but in future all actions were to be commenced by writ as prescribed by Act, and all subsequent processes according to the rules and forms prescribed. The significance is that the legislation legalized the illegally obtained jurisdiction to that point, but did not empower courts to engage in further illegal activity to expand their power. The Act imposed a single uniform process. The older forms of writ were abolished and a new form of writ was to be used, although the writ had to state the form of action being used.

The Real Property Limitation Act, 1833, abolished most real and mixed actions.[36]

The two courts of Exchequer Chamber were created in 1357–58 and amalgamated in 1585, and a Court of Appeal was made intermediate between the three common law courts and Parliament. One large problem was the complicated system of jurisdiction in error. King's Bench heard errors of the Common Pleas, and the Exchequer Chamber those of the Exchequer. A differently constituted Exchequer Chamber might hear errors from King's Bench, or they might go to Parliament. A third Exchequer Chamber was a court of discussion. One complaint made about the Exchequer Chambers was their delay and expense. In 1830, the system was simplified by abolishing the jurisdiction in error of King's Bench, leaving it a court of first instance. The statutory Exchequer Chambers were amalgamated into one court. The ultimate jurisdiction in error to Parliament was left untouched.[37]

The procedure in error was lengthy, cumbrous, and expensive, leading to statutory reforms in the Common Law Procedure Act, 1852. Finally the Judicature Acts rationalized the system. With the Common Law Procedure Act, 1852, stating a particular form of action in a writ was no longer required.

During the eighteenth century, common law and equity were increasingly working with each other. This connection resulted in procedures and doctrines from Chancery being gradually introduced into common law courts, sometimes by statute and sometimes by bold decision.[38] A statute of 1706 permitted certain equitable defences in common law actions upon bonds under seal.[39] *Read v. Brookman* (1789) was an example of a judicial decision permitting a party in a common law action to plead a deed that had been lost or destroyed without producing it.[40]

The CLPA, 1854, enacted some minor reforms involving a small level of fusion of law and equity.[41] It incorporated some recommendations of the common law procedure commission. Chancery was empowered and bound to decide all questions of common law, take evidence orally in court, and to award in certain cases damages for breach of contract or common law wrongs, and trial by jury was introduced. Courts of common law were authorized to compel discovery (the same power as Chancery possessed), were given a limited power to grant injunctions, were permitted to allow equitable defences, and, in certain cases, were empowered to grant relief from forfeitures. The Act only applied where the court of equity would have granted an absolute and perpetual injunction. In that case, the common law court could give effect to an equitable defence. A remodelling of the whole judicial system was necessary, which was accomplished by the Judicature Acts and the Appellate Jurisdiction Act.

The Judicature Act (1873)[42] removed the last vestiges of the forms of actions. With respect to court structure, the Act consolidated the courts of Chancery, King's Bench, Common Pleas, Exchequer, Admiralty, Probate, Divorce, and London Court of Bankruptcy into one Supreme Court of Judicature in England. The consolidated court was divided into the High Court of Justice and a Court of Appeal. The clause of the Act of Settlement regarding judicial tenure was re-enacted, and judges were incapacitated from sitting in the House of Commons.[43] Rules of law and equity were administered concurrently, and certain rules established in this respect. Where there was a conflict between common law and equity, the rules of equity prevailed.

Especially with respect to matters of industry and commerce, courts were occupied with discussions bearing no relation to the merits of any controversies. With the overhaul of the Judicature Act, a simplified code of procedure was introduced, and judges were given the power to make new rules.[44] The intention was to have the strong points of the various systems of procedure merged in the Supreme Court.

It was not until the end of the eighteenth century that the doctrines of equity became completely fixed.[45] This fact is significant because it preceded the Judicature Act, 1873, therefore the Act limited the court's equity jurisdiction to what had become fixed previously. In fact, it was in Nottingham's time that the decisive step to fix equitable doctrines was taken. He was first to clearly define the sort of conscience by which, in future, the Chancellor must be guided.

An Act of 1907 abolished the writ of error and the Court for Crown Cases Reserved. Appeals involving law or fact were to be made to the newly created Court of Criminal Appeal. In exceptional cases, further appeal was permitted to the House of Lords.

The county court declined. It had inherited obscure technicalities making it inadequate for the new post–Industrial Revolution circumstances. An attempt at reform was made by an Act of 1750. That Act allowed the county clerk of the sheriff (a barrister) of Middlesex and the suitors of the county court to sit for small claims in the various hundreds.[46] A similar procedure was adopted for and applied to all the counties of England by the County Courts Act, 1846.[47] The eighteenth-century courts of requests and courts of conscience were deemed to be branches of the county court. The old court was left untouched with its unlimited jurisdiction if a writ of *justicies* had been brought, and the 1846 Act confined the branches to small business, but as they were popular, their jurisdiction was increased.[48]

Inherent Powers

AN INHERENT SUBSTANTIVE JURISDICTION?

Courts do not possess an inherent substantive jurisdiction, as we saw in chapter 1.

A further illustration of this legal jurisdictional fact is the equitable control over infants, and the issue of guardians. This jurisdiction arises in modern form after the abolition of military tenures and the court of Wards and Liveries. The equitable jurisdiction was not based on any inherent jurisdiction, but on a special delegation by the crown of its prerogative right, as *perens patriae*, of looking after the Ward's interests. As stated in *Falkland v. Bertie* (1696):

230   The Executive and Public Law

> In this court there were several things that belonged to the King as *Pater patriae*, and fell under the care and direction of this court, as charities, infants, ideots, lunatics, etc., afterwards such of them as were of profit and advantage to the King, were removed to the *Court of Wards* by the statute; but upon the dissolution of that court, came back again to Chancery ...[49]

A second point of significance is that statute is of greater legal standing than courts, whose jurisdiction is subject to statute.

This view is generally accepted as the origin of this jurisdiction of the court,[50] and it is true that after the dissolution of the court of Wards, this jurisdiction of Chancery developed. However, Holdsworth notes that it is difficult to maintain that such jurisdiction was ever exercised extensively by Chancery before the court of Wards was created, or to find any evidence of a specific grant of that jurisdiction to Chancery. It might have been possible from the earliest period of history of the court to invoke its jurisdiction to control a guardian in socage; and, this kind of jurisdiction was developing in the preceding period. But, with respect to the guardian of a child holding land by knight service, the primitive notion that guardianship was the profitable right of the lord, lasted till the abolition of military tenures, and effectively prevented the growth of modern ideas with respect to the guardian's duties.[51]

PROCEDURE

It is true of courts and Parliament alike that an adequate procedure is necessary to enable the institution to do its work. For example, it is telling that courts distinguish properly between the law of Parliament and conventions. The reason must be the principle of efficacy. Parliament must have such powers, even if inherently, in order to function. The same is true of courts.

In terms of background, it should be recognized that procedural rules can have an effect on substantive rules, but are still distinguishable. The ability to think of the two as separate requires a civilization reaching a more mature stage. Roman law was able to do it, but the premature attempts in England failed, resulting in obscurity rather than clarity. It is apparent from the rise of the original writs and the forms of action which early English courts initiated that substantive law was discussed in terms of procedure. The rights of parties were expressed in the form of writs and pleas. Gradually, slight modifications were introduced by construction or modification of the forms to address cases involving matters a little outside the ambit of the traditional forms. The result was a change in substantive law, but the machinery of change and its technical expression were the rules concerning writs and pleadings.

Procedural rules or forms may effectively block certain substantive rules from emerging. For example, the lack of an effective trial mechanism that could delve into the intentions of the parties meant that substantive law could not be developed based on the intentions of the parties. This sort of defect was apparent in the old common law, in which trials were held on the basis of compurgation, juries of presentment, and presumptions. The situation was different for the court in Chancery, which could question the parties, and therefore could deal with issues such as accounts, for example in estates administration. Also, procedural rules may affect enforcement of substantive rules. They may even effectively bar the operation of substantive rules. For example, the common law was a highly technical system – any slip in pleadings or in the form of action chosen could be fatal, even if one should win on the merits of the case. Or, a particular writ might have been highly specific, and even though another case was very similar and followed the same legal principle, there might be no right or remedy because of some small and logically inconsequential difference. An action such as *novel disseisin* might only be available to the immediate parties, and so a wrong could be left unremedied because the assize would not apply if one of the original parties died in the meantime, unless there was another writ to address the gap. There are a variety of ways in which the land or chattels of a lawful owner or possessor might come into the possession of another, including circumstances of estrays and title deeds not stolen or bailed. The existing writ might be too narrow to deal with these other circumstances, requiring another writ or different form of writ to exist or be established, as in the case of trover, before ownership or possession could be restored. Another example is that common law might require the personal service of a court document. However, the nobles, or 'over-mighty subjects,' could physically prevent that service through the use of a private army. Thus, law gives action, but a remedy is denied.

These examples illustrate the effect of procedure on substantive law, but procedure and substance are not the same. It is also true that an institution, without an actual procedure established by law, will have to create a procedure to exercise its jurisdiction. And even if it has a procedure established by law, it may have to resolve further ambiguities by creating further informal rules, which can be called conventions. For example, suppose a government department is established in law and its duty is to issue driver's permits for qualified persons as defined by the law. The law might not specify the forms or procedures to obtain the permit. Therefore, the bureaucracy must create forms, as well as procedures such as hours of operation, how and where to apply for the permit, and what documents must be presented. Such actions might be termed 'extra-legal,' but not illegal, in the sense that some procedures or rules are necessary but not covered by the delegating legislation or prerogative. Such rules would not be legal rules, nor would policy statements a bureaucracy might develop in order to assist in guiding its duties or discretion. Other procedural rules may have the force of law, such as writs or some court procedures. This distinction between the legal and non-legal nature of rules can have implications in terms of the supremacy of law, in which actions or decisions can be measured for their legality.

It has been said that from the first, courts of law and equity were free to fashion their own rules of procedure, and to add or vary them to meet the needs of litigants and the development of legal principles.[52] While there is warrant for the general proposition, this statement seems overly broad if it refers to the freedom of courts to fashion laws of procedure directly and intimately connected with substantive law. The statement has more application to the procedure of a particular court. Still, these categories are not mutually exclusive. The procedure and rules of common law courts were technical and narrow, it seems, because courts did not think themselves free, in light of their jurisdictions and powers, to fashion their own rules of procedure and develop legal principles. Such limitations were due to the delegated nature of their jurisdictions after the differentiation within government occurred, and, early on, due to the significant connection with procedure and substantive law. Statutory help was often needed to expand court jurisdiction in substantive law, and to overcome problems of procedure, such as

Public Law in the 18th and 19th Centuries

with respect to criminal appeals, as well as the problems that arose from the common law's development into a rigid and highly technical system.

Courts of law as legal bodies can only exist from the law and are therefore necessarily limited by that law. Their jurisdiction can only come from one of two sources. It can come from the king's prerogative, and only to that extent can actually be delegated. That is, the king cannot delegate any more power by prerogative than he himself possesses. Second, delegations may be made by statute. Generally, there are no limitations to delegation in a parliamentary supremacy.

The only conceivable inherent jurisdiction a court can have is one that is necessarily incidental to the exercise of its jurisdiction as derived from prerogative. If the delegation is by statute, given that statute is higher than prerogative and not controlled by the law unlike prerogative, courts only have such powers as are intended in statute directly or by necessary implication. It is the legislature's intention that is determinative. This is the highest case for inherent jurisdiction. The jurisdiction arises when it is necessary to provide for the efficacy of the exercise of the power delegated to the court to deal with the matter before the court. This principle is not related to enforcement. Courts do not enforce their decisions, except to the extent of contempt jurisdiction. For example, inherent jurisdiction based on this principle means that to deal with issue x, which is in its jurisdiction, the court must necessarily deal with issue y (because x logically and necessarily subsumes y, or x cannot even be dealt with without the existence of y). Therefore, one can make the case that the court has the power to control its own process under this heading of necessity or necessarily incidental to exercising its jurisdiction where the lack of control of its process may undermine the exercising of its jurisdiction.

This principle and application of inherent powers is demonstrable in terms of other governmental institutions as well, which serve to illustrate the point. This same connection is also evident in the early development of jurisdiction and procedure. Quarter Sessions was a court. Like courts of common law, it made rules regulating its own procedure. Procedural rules and rules of substantive law have a habit of shading into one another, and some of these procedural rules made changes of substance. Thus, Quarter Sessions sometimes limited the powers of individual justices or pairs of justices.[53]

234 The Executive and Public Law

Similarly, from the beginning, both branches of the High Court of Parliament, Lords and Commons, developed their own rules of procedure.[54] These rules in the eighteenth century developed into an elaborate code, forming the most considerable part of the *lex et consuetudo Parliamenti*, and are the basis of the modern code of parliamentary procedure.

The autonomy of government organs acting within the law, or within their jurisdiction, can lead to the making and varying of rules with respect to the methods of performing their functions. Thus, the machinery evolved by these organs of central and local government created institutions of government, and rules evolved for the working of this machinery, which created a body of constitutional law defining the rights, duties, and powers of these institutions. As in private law where the working of the forms of action often influenced or created the principles of substantive law, also in government and administration, the machinery and procedural rules of these autonomous organs influenced or created much constitutional law.

Local government, composed of autonomous bodies, assumed large powers to regulate the districts subject to their jurisdiction. In exercising these powers, they sometimes transcended the sphere of administration and took it upon themselves to legislate, to attain the results they saw as expedient. In some cases, these legislative orders were extra-legal (not legally enforceable if one chose to disobey), and even positively illegal (in direct contravention of existing statutes).[55] Here, we see the distinction of legal powers and procedure as opposed to illegal practices. Courts were ready to prevent the encroachment of one organ on another, and were always ready to prevent illegal action. Thus, there was additional security against the tyrannical exercise of powers, and to prevent the organs from overstepping the powers entrusted to them by law.[56]

Finally, as stated earlier, deductions from the fact that the courts were the king's courts gave rise to other incidental prerogatives. However, these were no longer available after the differentiation in government took place and the courts lost their connection with king and Council.

One power that is sometimes thought of as an inherent power is that of courts traversing matters. Royal courts could use writs to transfer matters to and from other courts, such as by pone and certiorari. The jurisdiction and its usage by King's Bench to try ordinary criminal cases was previously discussed. A number of other statutes involved the power to traverse. For example, a statute of Henry VIII permitted judges of King's Bench to remove indictments sent into that court to be tried in the counties where the crime had been committed.[57] In 1576, in order to relieve the common law courts of some of their caseload in term time, a statute of Elizabeth stated that issues joined in Chancery or common law courts should be tried at nisi prius at Westminster in term time, or four days after the end of the term.[58] In 1601, it was provided that writs to remove suits pending before inferior courts must be served before the jury appeared.[59] If a personal action in superior court was worth less than forty shillings, the plaintiff should not be awarded costs in excess of the amount recovered in the action.[60] During the time of James I, statute restricted the removal of cases from inferior courts of record to Westminster if the judge of the inferior court was a barrister of three or more years standing.[61]

The existence of these statutes and writs suggests either no inherent right or no wide powers of courts to move cases between courts, beyond the power delegated to them. It would be reasonable to assume the traversing power was larger when exercised by the king and Curia or Council.

Sometimes courts are thought to have a certain jurisdiction because they exercised it in the past. However, the mere fact of exercising power cannot mean it is within the court's jurisdiction to do so, as we have seen. Furthermore, in discussing the rift between the judiciary and other branches, Hart notes that judges sometimes decided disputed questions of fundamental constitutional law, even regarding uncertainties in the rule of recognition, and their decisions were accepted as authoritative.[62] This acceptance is not because they necessarily had authority to decide such questions. Paradoxically, courts exercise creative powers which settle the ultimate criteria by which the validity of the very laws that confer upon them jurisdiction as judges must itself be tested. Here, success breeds success, and it may appear there was always an 'inherent' power in courts to do what they have done. However, this power cannot be established only on the basis of the success of what has been done.

Conclusion

Our journey through over a millennium of British history, politics, and law has yielded the result that parliamentary sovereignty was established as the most foundational element of the British system of government. The two key elements in understanding the British system of government are Parliament and the courts, together with their respective natures and jurisdictions within that system.

Examining foundational points in its development reveals that the development of legislative and executive government, including courts, overlaps in the first stages, until there was greater definition and separation with respect to these branches or functions of government. The process begins in the twelfth century and is largely complete with respect to all common law courts by the end of the fourteenth century. From this point, the development of legislative and parliamentary sovereignty is separate from that of courts.

The pre- and post-Conquest periods established the importance of divine law and natural law as fundamental pillars within the British system of government and for its laws, either directly or indirectly. Christian and Church influences have been remarkable and enduring, although such influences are not as well known or recognized today.

Pre-Conquest English government had no central court regularly administering a law common to the country. A hodge-podge of customary laws existed, the three main bodies of which corresponded to the main political divisions of the country. While the origin of Parliament is lost, as is much of its progression, the broad lines of that origin and development are evident. Built around the notion and institution of kinship, periodic assemblies of the whole people occurred, which were later based on representation. This body combined the government functions of court of law proceedings and resolutions about the law. Customary law, growing out of social life, was regarded as the inborn right of free man, and not subject to change without his assent, including by the court. If new laws were desired, the people had to be persuaded to adopt and legislate them. Accordingly, there is nothing in pre-Conquest times that gives judges deciding cases the right to change the law or the principles of law, or to invent unwritten constitutional principles or other legal or moral principles to override legislation.

The post-Conquest era establishes the supremacy of legislative power, including over the common law and courts, and the inability of the common law or courts to nullify legislation.

The Conquest established sovereignty over England under the Norman kings. Whether William took sovereignty by conquest or as heir is less important, given that by the time of the Revolution, the issue of sovereignty and the system of government based on parliamentary sovereignty were firmly established. Also, whether William took over as conqueror or heir does not give rise to any court power to nullify legislative power based on the common law or otherwise.

This political and sovereign basis of the supremacy of legislative power, and the inability of the common law or courts to nullify legislation, is supported by the legal basis of the constitution or system of government as established at the Conquest. After the Conquest, the Norman kings were rulers of England, including in law-making. They insisted on being, and effectively laid claim as, undisputed lords over every piece of land. Although they stated that the customary laws of Edward the Confessor would continue, these customary laws were subject to any new laws of the realm, at least in the form of laws of the Curia, Council, and later Parliament. The fact was that legislation not only declared old laws, but changed the common law, even in fundamental ways, and this ability was confirmed by law. Therefore, none of the following can be said: that the judicial portion of common law or custom trumps post-Conquest laws, that legislation may only declare custom, or that judges have any power to declare Acts of Parliament void. Indeed, the immediate consequence of the Norman Conquest was to change the entire basis of land law in England, which was also intimately tied up with the public law of the period. While this change did not wholly supersede the older custom, it did at the very least make fundamental changes.

238   The Executive and Public Law

The Curia exercised undifferentiated jurisdiction, including legislative, administrative, and judicial functions, with a legal power and status above ordinary or customary law, and above other courts. The law of this royal court reflected a species of law superior to all others. From it, the common law, administered by the king's court, was expanded to apply to the whole country and eventually supersede all other laws or courts.

The original writ was not the assertion of the jurisdiction of the court, but was rather a royal commission conferring on the judges the power to try the matters contained in it. The Curia acquired writs that litigants could purchase. Also, the barons, and later Parliament, understanding that the power to make new writs was in substance a power to make new law, limited the king's discretion to invent new remedies. Courts understood that it was not for them to make new law, nor to change it. Thus, the system of common law tended to become rigid and technical, especially when controlled at the end of the thirteenth century by royal courts.

As distinction in government grew, including between Parliament (the legislature) and Council (the executive), discretionary crown powers ceased to be exercised through common law courts. Furthermore, judges ceased to be equal to other members of Council. They were no part of Parliament. They had no voice, but were mere advisers whenever called upon by Parliament, whose advice could be followed or not. Court jurisdiction became substantially limited because courts no longer shared in the power of the Council when they became separate from it. This limitation of court jurisdiction is not only determinative, but is also confirmed through an examination from other perspectives, such as: the source or basis of court power; the *Quo Warranto* episode; the existence of various common law courts; those courts' actual jurisdiction, as well as their substantively and procedurally bounded jurisdiction; and, the simultaneous existence of other courts, which exercised rival and inconsistent jurisdictions. Not only were common law courts, such as King's Bench and Common Pleas, inferior to Parliament, but they were at times inferior to other courts, such as the Court of Exchequer Chamber, Council, and even Star Chamber.

As with all executive power, and all state power for that matter, courts are state institutions created by and which can only operate according to applicable law, with judges as their officers. Courts

Conclusion 239

exercise a legally delegated jurisdiction, primarily by legislation, and historically from royal prerogative. There is a narrow jurisdiction of inherent powers based on necessity. Courts did not automatically or inherently have all such jurisdiction as might be necessary or desirable to enable them to deal with all disputes arising between parties. Furthermore, it is also telling, in terms of the status difference between legislature and courts, that the courts' jurisdiction could be added to or taken away by parliamentary legislation, and that their decisions could be declared incorrect, overridden, or modified.

The legislative supremacy of the Curia and Council developed into the sovereignty of Parliament, marked by omnicompetence in a manner legally omnipotent.

The constitutional issues arising from the Norman Conquest to Magna Carta reveal the prevailing thought that while law was the bridle of state power and law made the king, there was no legal limitation based on fundamental law. Rather, the limitation was based on higher divine or natural law, but was not enforceable by judges, who were inferior officials, to impugn the validity of laws made by the 'king counselled.' Because the constitution was stable as it was based on law, it was possible to distinguish between abstract law and the rulers or judges who were thought to pervert it. Thus, the major question was what would occur if the king refused to obey the law. This question remained unanswered until the Revolution.

Magna Carta attempted to define conditions upon which the king must conduct government. It supported royal justice and the common law. However, even more than that, it marked a period in which law was developed by crown power alone, and began a period establishing Parliament with power to make and develop law.

Chapter 3 made clear the superiority of Parliament's status in lawmaking, as well as the inability of any actor to challenge its laws, except through appeal to higher divine or natural law. At all times, courts have been inferior bodies, although superior to non-royal courts. Courts lack jurisdiction to challenge the validity of statute or to compel Parliament to do anything based on unwritten law, be it natural law or common law, or anything else. Courts do have the authority to use natural law as a basis of statutory interpretation, and also to employ the presumption that Parliament does not intend to derogate from the common law or natural law unless it does so expressly. They cannot go against legislative intention. This

240 The Executive and Public Law

description is accurate even during periods when Parliament was supreme but not sovereign because it lacked the jurisdiction to exercise the fullest extent of sovereign powers.

Parliament gradually became more than an assembly where the king and his council met with the estates of the realm to discuss the state of the nation. It became an essential organ of government, a true legislative assembly, and through control over finance obtained large powers to criticize and control the conduct of the executive.

With the Reformation and annexing supreme authority over the English Church, the king in Parliament became omnicompetent in a manner omnipotent, except with respect to royal succession and to fully controlling prerogative, which authority was later established with the Revolution. The legislation of the period and the understanding of state officials, including courts, demonstrate Parliament's freedom from legal limitations even with regard to the most precious and inviolable rights, notably property rights.

The Civil War and Revolution of 1688 completed the main foundations of the British system of government. The end of this period legally established parliamentary sovereignty and the supremacy of law. In order to understand precisely the meaning and content of those foundations, it is necessary to know what the actors or lawmakers establishing that particular system of government actually established. What was established is determined largely by what they actually intended to establish. A determining factor is that throughout the period it was always maintained that there was a sovereign. All agreed that the king's authority was highest in Parliament and controllable by none, regardless of whether sovereign legislative power belonged to the king alone or to the community as a whole. War conclusively determined legally the location of sovereign power in the constitution. The contest was between two parties: on the one hand, the parliamentary party, common lawyers, and Puritans; on the other, royal prerogative supporters, those supporting rival courts, and those wanting strict compliance with the rites and ceremonies of the state Church. The main question was whether royal prerogative was the sovereign power, or whether parliamentary sovereignty was. Parliamentary sovereignty won out. Many leading persons of the parliamentary party asserted that parliamentary sovereignty came from the ancient common law or ancient constitution. The

Conclusion   241

legislative, executive, and judicial powers assumed the legal position at that time which they now hold in modern law.

The idea of fundamental law limiting parliamentary sovereignty within the domestic legal system is impossible, and wholly contradictory to parliamentary supremacy. This point is determinative legally. It was even more unthinkable that courts as inferior institutions, with judges as their officers, could use the idea of fundamental law to review and strike down legislation made by the superior body, Parliament.

Parliament can and did override the most inviolable of rights and the most fundamental common law principles, including property rights and Magna Carta, which were acknowledged to be lawful even by judges such as Coke, who sometimes wrote as if they believed courts could declare Acts of Parliament void. Such dicta were contrary to the principles of the common law as understood by Coke himself and other lawyers of the parliamentary party. These cases only amount to the proposition that courts will interpret statutes *stricti juris*, that is in such a way as to give meaning in accordance with established principle, and cannot give effect to them if they are meaningless or impossible to apply. The discussion on parliamentary supremacy doubters further reveals that ideas of Parliament's legal power being limited, and even further that such limits can be enforced by courts, stem from the British system of government not being described first and its elements put into their proper place.

Nevertheless, the discourse of fundamental law was an important and enduring one. In view of the fact that divine law and natural law are higher law, there was a real sense in which parliamentary law could not violate these. However, that was no legal limitation on Parliament's power, nor was it a basis for voiding statute under the British system of government, including in its legal system. Nor did the notion or nature of higher law give judges jurisdiction to review and strike down legislation. Violations of such fundamental natural law could release the citizen's obligation to obey, and in cases of oppression give rise to a right of rebellion. The remedy in the end was political; it had no overriding or enforceable effect within the domestic legal system, whether or not one classifies such rights as law or moral rights.

242 The Executive and Public Law

A full detailing of the executive branch of government is generally not necessary to understand the British system of government, which is a legal concept. Executive government initially derived from royal prerogative, but has been overtaken by statute. Further details were provided to explain the actual way in which the system operates in its most fundamental or sovereign aspects, as well as the executive's link with legislature. Also, this information provides important background for studying the former Dominion governments, including the constitutional conventions that were incorporated. Over a very long period of time, the House of Commons was able to put a check on the influences of the king or Council on its activities in legislating, and the Commons obtained ultimate control over the executive. These results were attained through the use of legislation, legal powers, constitutional conventions, and other practices or techniques. Also, the development of parliamentary procedure and privilege were important elements giving Parliament, and especially the Commons, an independent and authoritative position. These developments produced the major workings of government which are commonplace today, including responsible government, cabinet government, the rise of the office of prime minister, organized political parties, and party discipline.

In the course of this institutional development and exposition, the relationship between the courts and Parliament within the British system of government has become evident.

This British system is characterized by parliamentary sovereignty. The king, Lords, and Commons in Parliament together comprise the sovereign power in the state. Blackstone correctly describes Parliament as the sovereign, uncontrollable authority to make, repeal, modify, and expound laws on all possible matters. It can make or unmake any law whatsoever. It follows Whitelocke's view and others of the parliamentary party that Parliament is the place where absolute despotic power resides as entrusted by the constitution. Thus, an Act of Parliament is the highest authority Britain acknowledges on earth. It has the power to bind every subject, even the king. It cannot be altered, amended, dispensed, suspended, or repealed, but by the same form and authority of Parliament.

Accordingly, Parliament may legally legislate anything except that which is impossible, and, aside from debates about the manner and form of legislating, one parliament may not bind a future parliament.

Conclusion 243

There is a territorial limitation to Parliament's power in that it may not legislate for another country, except perhaps with respect to the conduct of British nationals outside its borders. Courts cannot give effect to statute if such statute is meaningless or impossible to apply. For example, a statute may not make murder or stealing lawful, or, as De Lome noted, may not turn a man into a woman, although the law may treat a man as if he were a woman, and *vice versa*. There are no fundamental laws Parliament cannot change, except perhaps parliamentary supremacy.

These limitations to parliamentary power are legal limitations, and none otherwise exist, be they moral rights, unwritten principles, or common law principles. Accordingly, there exist no other legal limitations to legislation recognized in the British system of government, which are actually enforceable. Parliamentary legislation is superior to the common law, and may change it. Perhaps the only exception is that the British Parliament may not undermine its own sovereignty, assuming that is a fundamental law of the common law. This conclusion is determinative of the issue.

As a matter of court jurisdiction, courts have no legal authority to invalidate statutes thought to be contrary to fundamental legal or moral principles. First, courts are legal institutions, with judges as their officers. Courts only exercise a delegated jurisdiction, with a narrow range of inherent jurisdiction. That jurisdiction does not permit them to use unwritten principles, the common law, or common law principles to override legislation. Outside the common law, courts may not even apply unwritten principles as if they have the force of law. At best, such principles can be used as an aid to the interpretation of the common law or legislation. The only exception to overriding legislation is if a subsequent statute repeals or modifies an earlier one. Then courts can be said to have a power to invoke later legislation in order to declare the former one repealed or modified. Second, courts are inferior to Parliament within the British system of government and as such cannot overrule a legally superior institution. Courts do not have the authority, or, at the very least, have thought it is not for them, to consider or question irregularities in the passage of legislation, let alone to rule an Act void on that basis.

The only other question that has arisen more recently is whether the European Convention on Human Rights, a treaty enacted into domestic law, has resulted in that international treaty limiting parliamentary sovereignty for the duration that Parliament continues to accept the treaty. Courts have even held that European Community law takes priority over UK domestic law by virtue of UK legislation, the European Communities Act, 1972, which states such priority is to be given. Also, the creation of elected assemblies for Wales, Scotland, and Northern Ireland by statute might be said by some to move the UK away from a pure model of parliamentary sovereignty; however, the UK Parliament's power to legislate in these places remains unimpaired.

From the system of government, fundamental rules of the system are established. Other readily deducible rules are evident. While the court will interpret statute *stricti juris*, in circumstances in which legislative intent is clear the courts must follow that intention. This principle of interpretation was not only well recognized by Blackstone, but is properly accepted today.

I have shown the utility of this system of government approach to other areas of law, namely judicial review in administrative law. Through the application of fundamental rules and deductions from them, including to cases in which legislative intention of a statutory provision may not be clear, this approach's guidance and benefits become obvious.[1] This book goes beyond that article by providing full legal and theoretical support for the approach.

Understanding accurately the system of government is the proper approach, including the law of the constitution and that system's elements put into their correct place. Understanding the unwritten or conventional aspects of government is also useful in order to avoid confusion. This approach will obtain the best answer in law, and even correct answers in some cases. It can certainly eliminate wrong answers, leaving judges with no legally acceptable alternative but to apply the best or correct answers. Understanding a particular system of government will also reveal the answer to what may otherwise appear as disputed points of law or the constitution. The mapping of this system not only clarifies, but also prevents an appeal to some murky and distant past on the part of state actors and bodies to claim a jurisdiction or power that never existed.

When dealing with a particular legal issue, by specifying with precision the legal concept within the system of government, judges or other legal decision-makers will have real guidance in their decision-making on these issues. With a clear framework in place for decision-making, the task of adjudicating cases will become more straightforward. Accordingly, the framework within which judicial decision-making takes place must be clearly understood. It is rooted in the system of government, which itself is rooted in sovereignty.

Understanding the British system of government is not only valuable for British judges and legal decision-makers, it is also necessary for other countries that have achieved self-government and full independence from Britain. For example, the Supreme Court of Canada's understanding and application of unwritten principles, particularly the "vital unstated assumptions" of the Constitution, are erroneous under the Canadian system of government and outside the framework for judicial review. Canadian judges thereby acted illegally, that is outside their jurisdiction, in the *Judicial Remuneration Reference* by constitutionalizing their own salaries on the basis of unwritten constitutional principles, which were used to override not only legislation but the written Constitution of Canada itself by inventing constitutional imperatives and by imposing the unconstitutional 'constitutional' requirement of judicial compensation committees.[2] In order to come to the result the court did, the judges purported to rely on the British constitution, although they thoroughly and utterly misunderstood that constitution. Courts in Britain dating from pre-Conquest times, or those in Canada, have never had the legal authority to employ unwritten principles to override the Constitution or legislation, including to compel parliaments to do anything in legislating. Nor is such an asserted power legally possible under a parliamentary model of government. It can be said with justification that judges misappropriated multi-millions of dollars from Canadians. They were already the highest paid profession in 1998 in Canada at the time of the decision. As a result of the decision, the judges obtained salary increases of sixty percent or more, despite the global recession, and, of course, have continuously remained the highest paid profession.

Historical and factual inquiry provides other benefits in terms of lessons in respect of governmental institutions and actors. This inquiry confirms that at times various state actors have generally acted beneficially, but have also misbehaved and even acted illegally. These facts assist in providing a realistic appraisal of the institution in question as opposed to a romanticized vision, and provide an

246 The Executive and Public Law

informed basis to deal with improprieties occurring within the system. As history demonstrates, Parliament has been the traditional upholder of the rule of law, and a main guardian of democracy, the constitution, law, and the liberties of citizens. On the other hand, during certain periods, abuse of parliamentary privilege has occurred. The beneficial lessons of the past should serve to temper or balance the more recent decline in public esteem for parliamentarians and even for Parliament itself. Perhaps, the reasons for this decline include the benefits of Parliament being so prevalent that they are taken for granted, as well as other factors such as traditional bonds of unity dissolving, and declining deference toward such institutions on the part of the public generally for any of a number of reasons, including cultural ones.[3]

History has shown the utility of judges and judicial independence in upholding the rule of law and in defending individual liberty. Those benefits were obtained from judges applying the law of the land, and not from judges inventing their own policies or applying the results of their own philosophizing, which is the arbitrary and personal rule of judges and not the rule of law. However, the history of courts and the judiciary also show that, at times, judges have acted unscrupulously and illegally, for example, as they did in usurping jurisdiction, including through the invention of 'fictions' known to be untrue, and even much to the detriment of the development of the law. Whereas judges today may be held in general confidence by citizens, this was not always the case. During certain periods of time there was widespread judicial corruption. During the Civil War many judges acted as an obstacle to democracy and Parliament, instead siding with the king and royal prerogative. Other examples include times when judicial decisions refused to recognize the property rights acquired by tenants by lease or through tacit agreement or concession by lords. Also, the common law courts and manorial courts played an important role in inventing the dogma that the freehold in a villein's lands was in the lord, which depressed the inhabitants of the manor who were originally free to the position of serfs.

Today, some degree of public confidence in judges is due to the mysticism surrounding judges and the work they do. The public does not scrutinize judges, an exercise which should be done, mainly because they generally have difficulty in following judicial decisions,

Conclusion 247

and by and large are not active participants in the legal system. These are facts of which judges are well aware.

While these organs of government have performed valuable work throughout history, their officers can also act improperly, including judges substituting their own preferred policy for the law. Perhaps worse, a not altogether rare practice or trend exists today of some judges deciding who they want to win first and then finding law or making findings of fact to support their position. Anyone suing a judge or someone closely related to a judge will soon find out how quickly the rule of law vanishes, and just how easily this most cherished principle of law can be undermined. The usefulness of applying the basic rules of the system of government not only reveals that some British judges have, at times, acted improperly, but shows that judges in other countries with a rule of law tradition have also done so. In these countries, such instances of judicial corruption are covered with hypocrisy. Nevertheless, these countries should be clearly and sharply distinguished from ideologically or some religiously based countries today, or countries suffering from widespread corruption, in which the rule of law does not exist and sham trials occur regularly.

The important point is that all state institutions and actors must be scrutinized in order to ensure that the law, the rule of law, the benefits these institutions are expected to deliver, and the rights and liberties of individuals are protected and carried out. This book has attempted to provide the first main step to aid citizens in developing the necessary ability to conduct this needed scrutiny.

At the same time, this inquiry reminds us of history and facts that should not be forgotten. This collective memory is necessary to uphold and sustain the principles, ideas, and institutions which have brought us to establishing parliamentary democracy, development, prosperity, and the freedom that we now enjoy. It also prompts us to remember that changes to these founding principles, ideas, values, and institutions may in fact undermine them, and we should be wary and cognizant that the changes advocated for, particularly since the last half century, may not produce beneficial effects. It is no surprise that typical attacks on our values involve a dislike of parliamentary government (as not being democratic), of the rule of law, and of reason and truth, and that such attacks often include the attempt to bully or silence those with whom these partisans disagree, including culturally as well as through the use of law. These challengers also display a preference for arbitrary executive government, as well as a high degree of government interventionism and regulation according to their political ideology. Many such activist groups use sympathetic judges in the courts to obtain their policy preference, particularly in countries with an entrenched bill of rights, when the legislature declines to act on their agenda. As in previous eras, people immersed in current events have difficulty perceiving the great changes afoot in their times.

The history that has been examined also reminds us of what efforts it took over a long period of time to actually establish parliamentary sovereignty, the rule of law, and other important protections such as judicial independence. This knowledge should also give readers pause to consider that if we change the values underlying our traditions and our system of government, it may not be so easy to re-establish or to regain the benefits arising from these values or system of government. Without such tradition and values, parliamentary sovereignty can be a dangerous form of government when in the wrong hands.

APPENDIX

Table of Kings and Queens

Egbert	800–836
Alfred	871–901
Edward the Elder	901–924
Edward the Confessor	1042–1066
William I	1066–1087
William II	1087–1100
Henry I	1100–1135
Stephen	1135–1154
Henry II	1154–1189
Richard I	1189–1199
John	1199–1216
Henry III	1216–1272
Edward I	1272–1307
Edward II	1307–1322
Edward III	1322–1377
Richard II	1377–1399
Henry IV	1399–1413
Henry V	1413–1422
Henry VI	1422–1461
Edward IV	1461–1483
Edward V	1483
Richard III	1483–1485
Henry VII	1485–1509
Henry VIII	1509–1547
Edward VI	1547–1553
Mary	1553–1558
Elizabeth	1558–1603

James I	1603–1625
Charles I	1625–1649
The Commonwealth	1649–1660
Charles II	1660–1685
James II	1685–1688
William and Mary	1689–1695
William III	1695–1702
Anne	1702–1714
George I	1714–1727
George II	1727–1760
George III	1760–1820

Notes

INTRODUCTION

1 William Holdsworth, *A History of English Law* (London: Methuen & Co. Ltd. and Sweet & Maxwell Ltd., 1996), 2:131–2. Indeed, Hitler was a disciple of Nietzsche who called for the replacement of religious values, particularly Christian ones, in order to achieve his 'superman.' Holdsworth argues that if the European nations had not been trained by medieval thinkers to acknowledge the supremacy of the idea of right, the struggle of succeeding centuries between modern European nations would have been far more bitter, even fatal, to the continued development of Western civilization. Further evidence of the effect of the neglect of such values can be seen in marxist/communist and radical atheist countries, such as the Soviet Union, and the mass murder and oppression that occurred there on a scale never before known in the world.

2 It is possible that over a particular territory occupied by persons there is no state government or sovereignty. This condition might describe the first immigrants to North America, the natives or aboriginals, who had not yet developed a state and institutions that held political authority over a given territory and exercised government functions, including and especially law-making. This condition describes the most primitive societies. It might describe societies regulated by custom, where such custom only involves regulating relationships among people based on consent, and has not developed into a custom or contract formally establishing government together with its main institutions and functions, including legislating and the authoritative deciding of disputes. This absence of a sovereign state may also exist where sovereignty has not been established over a given territory, for example due to different warring factions, none of which have yet been able to lay effective claim to it, or when there has been a coup

252

Notes to page 7

d'etat or revolution and it is uncertain who or what is the sovereign at the time.

To determine when a primitive society first becomes a sovereign state can be difficult, particularly in terms of when it first developed, including when it displayed and exercised sufficient characteristics of sovereignty. Fortunately, we need not concern ourselves over such fine matters of theoretical and practical details, as for the most part the answer is clear today, and is certainly obvious for the geographical area under study.

3 Bodin is often thought to be the father of sovereignty theory. Jean Bodin, *Les six livres de la republique* (Paris: Chez lacques du Pays, 1579). For an overview of sovereignty theory, see Hymen Ezra Cohen, *Recent Theories of Sovereignty* (Chicago: University of Chicago Press, 1937).

4 There are a large number of influential writers on divine or natural law, or whose works were influenced by those ideas. St Augustine of Hippo is a pre-eminent Doctor of the Church. His thoughts profoundly influenced the medieval view. His books include *De Doctrina Christiana, The City of God, Confessions*, and *On the Trinity*. St Thomas Aquinas was another Doctor of the Church whose writings on natural law, such as *Summa Theologica* and *Summa Contra Gentiles*, have been very influential in the Western world. Influential persons or writers in England who were influenced by natural law are too numerous to mention here, but include Henry de Bracton, John Fortescue, Christopher St. Germain, Edward Coke, John Locke, and William Blackstone. C.S. Lewis is a later writer whose books *Mere Christianity* and *Abolition of Man* reflect natural law. As for modern writers, John Finnis is one of the most prominent contemporary legal philosophers. Particularly important is his book *Natural Law and Natural Rights*. Other modern natural law scholars include Augusto Zimmermann and Bradley Miller.

5 There is reason and justice to Locke's position that a social contract of limited government exists as the basis of English state sovereignty. It is true, as is sometimes maintained in criticism of such a theory, that today it can hardly be said that any person has formally assented to such a contract, or even tacitly consented to it. Nevertheless, this position can still be defended and is quite accurate if we examine the history. For example, feudalism was a contractual relationship, based largely on property, which also entailed government powers and functions (such as a lord's ability to make decisions pertaining to tenants, as well as the relation of the king and lord in law-making).

Also, contract underlies the customary development of the state and state institutions. For example, in Anglo-Saxon times there was the

Notes to pages 8–17 253

development of institutions based on the consent and practice of the people, including the legislative for the people.

Under such circumstances, it would not be odd to say that custom limited the scope of the power exercised by the sovereign state. In the Middle Ages, people would not have imagined that state institutions could legislate contrary to the laws of God, or to natural law. The only question is what the nature of the *legal* limitation on government is – that is, whether it is a legal, political, or moral one.

6   In this book 'Constitution' is used to refer to a written Constitution, whereas 'constitution' refers to its unwritten aspects.

CHAPTER ONE

1   Holdsworth, *English Law*, 2:5.

2   Ibid., 2:4.

3   Harold J. Berman, *Law and Revolution: The Formation of the Western Legal Tradition* (Cambridge, MA: Harvard University Press, 1983); Harold J. Berman, *Law and Revolution II: The Impact of the Protestant Reformations on the Western Legal Tradition* (Cambridge, MA: The Belknap Press of Harvard University Press, 2003); Theodore F.T. Plucknett, *A Concise History of the Common Law*, 5th ed. (Boston: Little, Brown and Company, 1956), 8, 301. For valuable accounts of the general influence of both the Roman and Christian Churches, see Meynial, "Roman Law," and Le Bras, "Canon Law," both in *Legacy of the Middle Ages*, edited by C.G. Crump and E.F. Jacob (Oxford, UK: The Clarendon Press, 1943).

For the broader influence of Christianity on Western civilization, and also on India, written from the perspective of an Indian writer, see Vishal Mangalwadi, *The Book that Made Your World: How the Bible Created the Soul of Western Civilization* (Nashville, TN: Thomas Nelson, 2011). While in a couple of places the book repeats some misconceptions spread at the time of the Reformation, it is generally a good and interesting read. For example, one misconception is that Roman Catholics were not the first to translate the Bible into the vernacular. In fact, not only did the Church first translate the Bible into the main languages of the world at the time, Greek and Latin, but as European nations emerged, vernacular versions of the Bible appeared with them. There were approximately six hundred Catholic Bible editions, two hundred of which were in the vernacular, before the first Protestant version appeared. Another misleading comment is that Catholic ecclesiastics chained the Bible in the churches. True. However, the reason was to allow more people access to it. Before the invention

254 Notes to pages 18–24

of the printing press, each Bible had to be transcribed by hand on parchment, which was made from the skins of sheep. These Bibles were often beautifully illustrated. There could be no errors in the transcription, and the Church had to vouch for the accuracy and integrity of each volume. The cost of the parchment alone to produce one Bible was the equivalent of ten years' wages of the time. Accordingly, precautions had to be taken for its security.

4 Le Bras, *Legacy of the Middle Ages*, 361; cited in Theodore F.T. Plucknett, *A Concise History of the Common Law*, 305–6.

5 Plucknett, *Common Law*, 5.

6 Holdsworth, *English Law*, 2:5–7.

7 Maitland, *Prologue to a History of English Law*, L.Q.R. xiv 15; also cited in Holdsworth, *English Law*, 2:7.

8 See for example Holdsworth, *English Law*, 2:6–7.

9 Plucknett, *Common Law*, 8.

10 See for example ibid., 297.

11 Vinogradoff, cited in ibid., 255. See also ibid., 297, 518–19.

12 Seebohm, *Tribal Custom*, cited in Holdsworth, *English Law*, 2:53. See also Plucknett, *Common Law*, 9.

13 Pollock, cited in Holdsworth, *English* Law, 2:65. See also Plucknett, *Common Law*, 304.

14 Plucknett, *Common Law*, 298.

15 Ibid., 305. For a comprehensive view of the Reformation influences, see Berman, *Law and Revolution II*.

16 McIlwain, Powicke, cited in Plucknett, *Common Law*, 21.

17 Jeffrey Goldsworthy, *The Sovereignty of Parliament: History and Philosophy* (New York: Oxford University Press, 1999), 16.

18 *Summa Theologica*, cited in Goldsworthy, *Parliament*, 21.

19 Edward Coke, *Part Four of the Reports*, in *The Selected Writings of Sir Edward Coke*, edited by Steve Sheppard (Indianapolis, IN: Liberty Fund, Inc., 2003), 104–5.

20 Coke, *Part Three of the Reports*, in Sheppard, ed., 59–60.

21 See for example Holdsworth, *English Law*, 2:9–11.

22 Ibid., 1:4.

23 See Rudolf Gneist, *The English Parliament: In Its Transformations through a Thousand Years*, translated by Jenery Shee (London: H. Grevel & Co., 1886), 9–11; Holdsworth, *English Law*, 2:17.

24 Vinogradoff, cited in Plucknett, *Common Law*, 261–2. Bracton dealt with questions concerning obligation and contract, fraud and negligence, for which the common law had no rules. He necessarily used Roman terms

Notes to pages 24–6

and rules. Bracton's influence was high in his day, and again during the Romanizing movement of Elizabethan times when there were several eminent civilians in the public service. Coke also seized upon him. Bracton influenced private law in the eighteenth century when the speculative questions he raised became practical reality, and the answers were based on Roman law. For example, in the celebrated case of *Coggs v. Bernard* (1703), 2 Ld. Raym. 909, Holt uses the Roman passages in Bracton to bring the law of bailment into line with Roman law. Also, during the seventeenth and eighteenth centuries, passages from Bracton were used in settling the law of easements. See, generally, Henry de Bracton, *On the Laws and Customs of England*, translated with revisions and notes by Samuel E. Thorne (Cambridge: The Belknap Press of Harvard University Press in association with the Selden Society, 1983), and *Bracton's Note Book: A Collection of Cases Decided in the King's Courts during the Reign of Henry the Third*, annotated by a lawyer of the time, seemingly by Henry of Bracton, and edited by F.W. Maitland (Littleton, CO: F.B. Rothman, 1983).

25 Plucknett, *Common Law*, 261, 297–98. The *Treatise on the Laws and Customs of the Realm of England: Commonly Called Glanvill*, edited and translated by G.D.G. Hall, dealt with the new common law exclusively. The new common law was royal, flowing from the king's court, and the treatise was strongly procedural. Hazeltine suggests that the treatise imitates some of the books of canonical procedure. Vinogradoff argues that Longchamp, justiciar to Richard I, wrote a treatise on canonical procedure in which he urged establishing a definite formula of actions, which had some influence on Glanvill. Canon law rules on the competence of witnesses were borrowed by Glanvill, who used them as challenges to jurors, for example on the ground of relationship, interest, etc. He gives the different forms of contract known to Roman law, but the king's court took no notice of them.

26 William Blackstone, *Commentaries on the Law of England: In Four Books*, with the last corrections of the author and notes and additions by Edward Christian (New York: E. Duycknick, 1822), 1:147.

27 Gneist, *English Parliament*, 7.

28 Plucknett, *Common Law*, 318.

29 Gneist, *English Parliament*, 13–15.

30 Plucknett, *Common Law*, 317.

31 Ibid.

32 Gniest, *English Parliament*, 16.

33 Plucknett, *Common Law*, 308–9.

256 Notes to pages 26–33

34 Stubbs, Anson, cited in Holdsworth, *English Law*, 10:429.

35 Gneist, *English Parliament*, 16–17.

36 Ibid., 19.

37 Ibid., 23.

38 S.B. Chrimes, "Introductory Essay," in Holdsworth, *English Law*, 1:2.

39 Plucknett, *Common Law*, 92. The one exception is with respect to the post-Conquest royal viscontrial writ to render to a plaintiff the debt owed.

40 Holdsworth, *English Law*, 10:158; 2:441–3; 4:357–8; 2:253–5, 435–6, 441; 4:187–9. For a general discussion on prerogative, see Blackstone's *Commentaries*, Vol. I, especially ch. 7.

41 For a more detailed examination of this controversy, see for example J.G.A. Pocock, *The Ancient Constitution and the Feudal Law: A Study of English Historical Thought in the Seventeenth Century – A Reissue with a Retrospect* (Cambridge: Cambridge University Press, 1987).

42 Coke, *Part Three of the Reports*, in Sheppard, ed., 64–7.

43 William Petyt, *The Antient Right of the Commons Asserted* (1680), 39–41.

44 *Historical Manuscripts Commission, XIIth Report*, Appendix VI, 14 et. seq.; cited in Pocock, *Ancient Constitution*, 230. The idea of Gothic origins did not appear to be significant in Petyt's *Antient Right of the Commons*, in which Parliament was presented as immemorial within Britain.

45 Pocock, *Ancient Constitution*, 210.

46 Humanists focus less on studying the past and more on defining the present's relation to it by distinguishing the two periods more sharply and pointing out in what respects the life of the past differed from that of the present. They then raise the question of the relation between past and present, but tend to emphasize the differences between societies at different points in time. Sometimes, humanist historians have attempted to discover the fundamental principles of various systems of law (often seeing none of them as more than relatively important), which suggest law's universal quality and which may be applied in future. The search for universal principles is indeed a valuable approach, and one which even leads to identifying universal principles and statements of truth and validity. The approach means that each system must be studied critically. However, for these humanists, it implies a readiness to reduce the system to the context of the society from which it has sprung, which holds the threat of parochialism or context artificially submerging the universal. The approach is not so relevant legally, and the attempt to categorize the past as a concrete instance and no longer relevant today may even be misleading.

This latter tendency of the approach to parochialize can also sometimes lead to fallacious, politically minded thinking, such as the idea that

Notes to page 34 — 257

because society has changed (which is a claim made more incessantly and frequently particularly more recently and in respect of more doubt-- ful assertions), therefore the laws of the past are no longer relevant. Often the approach is used by activist groups who assert the idea of a changed society – even if society has not changed in the manner they claim or is highly divided on a particular issue – to attempt to undermine laws which may have functioned well for the society and continue to do so, but with which they ideologically disagree and which they wish to alter to conform to their ideology. It is evident that laws in respect of feudal society may not be adequate for those of a post–Industrial Revolution commercial society, but the activist claims made within the last half-century are not of this kind, and are both politically and rationally suspect.

47 Thomas Hobbes, *The English Works of Thomas Hobbes of Malmesbury*, collected and edited by William Molesworth (London: John Bohn, 1839–45; Aalen, Germany: Scientia, 1966), 4:147.

48 Historical evidence exists of William taking title to the crown as legitimate heir, such as Edward the Confessor's negative relations with and enmity for the Godwins; his relations with the Norman allies; the fact of Harold Godwinson's capture and knighthood in Normandy with Harold swearing some oath to Duke William, which is supported by the seventy-meter-long Bia Tapestry illustrating Harold swearing an oath to help William take the English crown; and, William's immediate and later reactions to the news of Harold's coronation.

49 We have already mentioned how the view that all lands were incorporated into the new Norman feudal order is contradicted by evidence, and by the *Domesday Book*. The lack of complete incorporation is also supported by the fact that large sections of land were not held as tenant in chief of the king, such as in the palantine jurisdictions.

Many feudal and private courts did not employ new Norman law. The laws of the Confessor continued, for example, in the county and hundred. Later, the king would encroach on many of these jurisdictions by writ, by judicial decision, and by statute.

If the fully developed feudal Norman system meant that only tenants in chief had a duty to attend the king, it says nothing about the king's prerogative to summon anyone whose advice he wished or thought desirable. Whether or not the king used that prerogative at a particular time, does not mean that he did not have the power.

This is also the safest conclusion to maintain given that the parliamentary forces and view won out in the end, including the idea of an immemorial unwritten law, particularly in relation to Parliament, and this 'non-

258 Notes to pages 35–7

Conquest' view is most consistent with theirs. Furthermore, the military victory of Parliament leads to the conclusion that there was no Conquest, or perhaps stronger yet, that the supremacy of Parliament was either established conclusively legally or re-established as vindicating immemorial custom. In such circumstances, as we will see, the intentions of the framers or actors in the circumstances are crucial.

There is also a paradox in emphasizing the purely feudal nature of the king's authority as recipient of every freeholder's homage for the land that he held, and claiming that somehow the king obtained from it sovereign authority (virtually?!), therefore the king consented to rights and liberties but could withhold them and was not bound by his coronation oath. If that is so, then why were not the people below him able to revoke their homage to the king? If the assertion was based on oath and the king broke his, then the people should or ought to have been released from theirs. The fact that the king had more actual power than an individual is irrelevant. Even the king's power to take away one's land at his pleasure became limited by law for certain offences (felonies). The power of the individual was that they could rebel, and could appeal to divine or natural law in order to do so.

Also, the fact that most feudal lands were held of the king made him powerful. However, it is a different question to determine where primary law-making powers resided. The king's exercises of prerogative were bounded, but not law-making by Parliament.

50 Matthew Hale, "*Reflections by the Lrd. Cheife Justice Hale on Mr. Hobbes His Dialogue of the Lawe*," reproduced in Appendix III – "Sir Matthew Hale's Criticisms on Hobbes's Dialogue of the Common Laws" – of Holdsworth, *English Law*, 5:508.

51 Ibid., 28.

52 Hale cites the statutes: 25 Ed. I Cap. 6 (Confirmatio cartarum, c. 6); 34 Ed. I Cap. I (Holdsworth states that Hale probably refers to the apocryphal statute *De tallagio non concedendo*, which was then generally believed to be authentic. Hale cites it again in this tract); I Ed. III St. 2, c. 6. The Petition of Right 3 Car. I. Cap. I.

53 See also Holdsworth, *English Law*, 6:206–7.

54 Hale, cited in Goldsworthy, *Parliament*, 157, 121.

55 Plucknett, *Common Law*, 13.

56 This was the basis of the law administered in the communal courts. Holdsworth, *English Law*, 2:151–4. See also Plucknett, *Common Law*, 13.

57 Holdsworth, *English Law*, 2:150.

58 Plucknett, *Common Law*, 318.

59 Ibid., 14.

60 Ibid., 318.

61 Pollock and Maitland, cited in Plucknett, *Common Law*, 319.

62 Plucknett, *Common Law*, 319.

63 Ibid., 17.

64 Coke, *Part Three of the Reports*, in Sheppard, ed., 76.

65 Holdsworth, *English Law*, 1:4.

66 For a more detailed description, see ibid., 2:166–71.

67 Ibid., 446.

68 Ibid., 447.

69 For a more detailed examination of the technical development of the common law, see for example F.W. Maitland, *The Forms of Action at Common Law, 1909* (Lectures), http//:www.fordham.edu/halsall/basis/maitland-formsofaction.asp, accessed October 2011.

70 For an overview of the process, see Holdsworth, *English Law*, vol. I., chs. 1–3, 5–7; 2:154, 290, 401–5; 5:66–7, 116–17, 120–6, 140–6, 149–54; H.W. Arthurs, *'Without the Law': Administrative Justice and Legal Pluralism in Nineteenth-Century England* (Toronto: University of Toronto Press, 1985).

71 Holdsworth, *English Law*, 1:16.

72 Ibid.

73 Brown, cited in Goldsworthy, *Parliament*, 25.

74 For further statements see Goldsworthy, *Parliament*, 26. Also, the legal treatise *Fleta* sets down the maxim that the Prince's pleasure has the force of law to be justified because it is not the king's wish, but is determined by due deliberation by the king and his magnates.

75 Adams cited in Holdsworth, *English Law*, 1:16. G.R. Elton, *Studies in Tudor and Stuart Politics and Government: Papers and Reviews 1946–1972* (Cambridge: Cambridge University Press, 1974), 2:21.

76 Holdsworth, *English Law*, 2:10, 15–16, 23.

77 Ibid., 125. See also Plucknett, *Common Law*, 517.

78 Holdsworth, *English Law*, 1:39.

79 Vinogradoff, cited in Holdsworth, *English Law*, 1:39.

80 Wells, cited in Plucknett, *Common Law*, 119.

81 Followers or witnesses brought to support the case.

82 Holdsworth, *English Law*, 2:123.

83 Woolf, *Bartolus of Sasso-Ferrato*, 45–7, 160–1, cited in Holdsworth, *English Law*, 2:131.

84 Bracton; Holmes, *Common Law*; cited in Holdsworth, *English Law*, 2:282–6, 288. See also Plucknett, *Common Law*, 118–19. England was

260 Notes to pages 46–53

later in acting on Church influence to abolish ordeals. Innocent III in the Fourth Lateran Council (1215) forbade clergy from performing any religious ceremonies in connection with ordeals. With the religious sanction of ordeal lost, it was practically abolished as a regular means of trial. Henry III's Council immediately recognised the decree, which was reflected in a writ to the justices in Eyre issued in 1219.

85 Holdsworth, *English Law*, 2:143–4.
86 Blackstone's *Commentaries*, 1:63, 64, 70.
87 A.V. Dicey, *Introduction to the Study of the Law of the Constitution*, 10th ed. (London: Macmillan & Co. Ltd., 1965), 40.
88 See for example *Reference re Amendment of the Constitution of Canada* (1982), 125 D.L.R. (3d) 1 (S.C.C.).
89 Hale, *History of the Common Law*, 9, cited in Holdsworth, *English Law*, 2:220. Plucknett, *Common Law*, 327.
90 Plucknett, *Common Law*, 327, 340.
91 Holdsworth, *English Law*, 2:427.
92 Plucknett, *Common Law*, 327.
93 Plucknett, *Statutes and their Interpretation*, 70, cited in Plucknett, *Common Law*, 332.
94 Holdsworth, *English Law*, 1:47, 447; 2:194.
95 Glanvill cited in Holdsworth, *English Law*, 2:194. See also Plucknett, *Common Law*, 157–8.
96 Bracton, cited in Holdsworth, *English Law*, 2:245.
97 Holdsworth, *English Law*, 2:309–10.
98 Y.B. 16 Edward III (Roll Series), i. 90 (1342); Y.B. 17 Edward III (Roll Series), 142 (1343); Y.B. 17, 18 Edward III (Rolls Series), 446; Y.B. 18 Edward III (Rolls Series), 131; Y.B. 17 Edward III (Rolls Series), 370 (1343); cited in Plucknett, *Common Law*, 332–3.
99 Such as Walker, Detmold, Allan, Edwards, Allot, McIlwain, Baumer, Kern, cited in Goldsworthy, *Parliament*, 7, 38.
100 See for example Hanson, cited in Goldsworthy, *Parliament*, 41.
101 Stephenson and Marcham, cited in Goldsworthy, *Parliament*, 41.
102 Coke, *Fourth Part of the Reports*, in Sheppard, ed., 94–5; Tierney, cited in Goldsworthy, *Parliament*, 41.
103 See for example Plucknett, *Common Law*, 124–5.
104 Powicke, quoting the Norwich chronicler's report at Westminster, cited in Goldsworthy, *Parliament*, 21. Plucknett, *Common Law*, 28.
105 Plucknett, Allen, Gough, cited in Goldsworthy, *Parliament*, 41.
106 Chrimes, cited in Goldsworthy, *Parliament*, 41.
107 Holdsworth, *English Law*, 2:196.

Notes to pages 53–9   261

108 Hale, *History of the Common Law*, 9, cited in Holdsworth, *English Law*, 2:220.

109 Holdsworth, *English Law*, 2:301–3.

110 Coke, *Second Institute*, 525; *The Prince's Case* (1605), 8 Co. Rep. 19 cites many instances, such as Magna Carta, statute of Leap Year, and *Articuli cleri*.

111 Holdsworth, *English Law*, 2:427.

112 Pocock, *Ancient Constitution*, 174–5.

113 Plucknett, *Common Law*, 320–2.

114 *Bracton's Note Book*, cited in Holdsworth, *English Law*, 2:253.

115 See Eccleshall, Corwin, Richardson and Sayless, Lewis, Teirney, Post, Wilkinson, cited in Goldsworthy, *Parliament*, 22.

116 Bracton, Hanson, Brown, cited in Goldsworthy, *Parliament*, 26.

117 Goldsworthy, *Parliament*, 28.

118 Other judges also held this view. For example, in a letter from certain justices to the Bishop of Winchester, the Earl Marshal, and Hubert de Burgh with respect to a request made on behalf of the Earl of Albermarle (Royal Letters (R.S.) I. No. 16), they declined to suspend the execution of a judgment in an assize of *novel disseisin* as everything was done regularly, and they were sworn to do justice to all without respect to persons.

    In cases in which the king's interests were concerned, the judges would not proceed *rege inconsulto*, but when they did proceed, the king's rights were treated like those of any other person; see R.P. I 186, p. 187 – land given to the queen by the king was recovered, and the king gave compensation as any other donor might have done – Y.B. 21, 22 Ed. I (R.S.) 54, 56 Gillingham J. stating that it is against the common law and statutes to make such a taking unless he be the king's bailiff, *notwithstanding any franchise which the king may have granted*. See also Holdsworth, *English Law*, 2:254.

119 Blackstone's *Commentaries*, 1:243.

120 Turner, cited by Goldsworthy, *Parliament*, 24.

121 John Nevil Figgis, *Divine Right of Kings*, 2nd ed. (Cambridge: Cambridge University Press, 1922), 32–3.

CHAPTER TWO

1 Holdsworth, *English Law*, 1:41.

2 Ibid., 1:52.

3 Plucknett, *Common Law*, 25–6.

4 Vinogradoff, cited in Holdsworth, *English Law*, 2:210.

262 Notes to pages 59–66

5 See for example Coke, *Second Institute*, 1–4, in Sheppard, ed., 754–62; Pocock, *Ancient Constitution*, 207.

6 Coke, *Second Institute*, 45–51, in Sheppard, ed., 848–60; Holdsworth, *English Law*, 1:59.

7 Holdsworth, *English Law*, 1:59.

8 *Bracton's Note Book* 1:56; Holdsworth, *English Law*, 1:196.

9 *Bracton's Note Book* 1:56, case 1166; case 1189 (1236–37) Y.B. 12, 14 Ed. III (R.S.) xli; Holdsworth, *English Law*, 1:196.

10 Blackstone's *Commentaries*, 1:266–7.

11 See Holdsworth, *English Law*, 1:91–2.

12 Ibid., 1:15.

13 For example, in the Assizes of Clarendon and Northampton, exclusive jurisdiction over all serious crimes was established. The ordinance of the Grand Assize and legislation establishing petty assizes asserted its jurisdiction over most disputes with respect to land held by free tenure, even if the dispute in respect of such land or services was taken to the lord's court, and the lord could not exercise jurisdiction without the king's writ. The Exchequer exercised tight financial control over sheriffs and accountants. Also, itinerant justices exercised constant supervision over all local government.

14 Bracton, cited in Holdsworth, *English Law*, 1:87. See also *Fleta*, cited in Plucknett, *Common Law*, 80–1.

15 Holdsworth, *English Law*, 1:87–8.

16 Plucknett, *Common Law*, 80.

17 Holdsworth, *English Law*, 1:88.

18 The medieval view on this point is summed up by Coke in *Abbot of Strata Marcella* 10 Co. Rep. 24a, see ff. 28 a, b. See also Holdsworth, *English Law*, 1:89.

19 Y.B. 21, 22 Ed. I (R.S.) 55–6, per Gislingham J., cited in Holdsworth, *English Law*, 1:89.

20 Y.B. 20 Ed. III ii (R.S.) 562, per Sharshulle J., cited in Holdsworth, *English Law*, 1:198.

21 Holdsworth, *English Law*, 1:198–9.

22 Ibid., 1:205–6.

23 Ibid., 1:206.

24 For example, Y.B. 8 Hy. IV Hil. pl. 3, 19, which Holdsworth does not find very conclusive. Y.B. 8 Hy. VI Hil. pl. 6 is a case involving the franchises of the University of Oxford, in which the rule is discussed that one cannot be a judge in his own case.

25 Holdsworth, *English Law*, 1:207.

Notes to pages 66–71

26 In (1608) 12 Co. Rep. 65, Coke disagrees with the king's statement that the law was founded on reason and he and others had reason as well as the judges. Coke replied that the king was not learned in the laws, and causes relevant to the life or inheritance or goods or fortunes of his subjects were not to be decided by natural reason, but by the artificial reason and judgment of the law, which the king had offended.

27 Holdsworth, *English Law*, 1:210.

28 Coke, *Fourth Institute*, cited in Holdsworth, *English Law*, 1:212.

29 Ibid., 1:219.

30 Holdsworth, *English Law*, 1:219. Plucknett, *Common Law*, 386–7.

31 Christopher Edward Taucar, *Canadian Federalism and Quebec Sovereignty* (New York: Peter Lang Publishing, Inc., 2004), 14.

32 31 Eliz. c. 1, ss. 2, 3.

33 Holdsworth, *English Law*, 1:285.

34 Y.BB. I, 2 Ed. II (S.S.) 110–11; 12, 13 Ed. III (R.S.) 364, 366; 21 Ed. IV Pasch. pl. 23, p. 10; Select Cases before the Council (S.S.) XXVIII, and cases therein cited. Holdsworth, *English Law*, 1:526, 530; 2:309–10; 4:117–19, 140–2. See also William Prynne, *Animadversion on the Fourth Part of Coke's Institutes* (London: Printed for T. Ratcliffe and T. Daniel, for A. Crooke, W. Leake, A. Roper, [etc.], 1669), 90–5; and Perkins, cited in Holdsworth, *English Law*, 5:116.

35 Y.B. 48 Ed. III. Hil. pl. 6, per Finchden; and, especially Y.B. 32 Hy. VII Mich. pl. 32, per Fineux that "Release oultre mer est void; mes si contract soit tirable parcel deins ce Realm, et parcel oultre la mer, il sera trie icy en tout." (Roughly, this means that a contract made overseas is not triable in England, but if any part of the contract is made in England it is triable there.) See Holdsworth, *English Law*, 5:140.

36 Blackstone's *Commentaries*, 3:107; Plucknett, *Common Law*, 663; Holdsworth, *English Law*, 1:554, 5:140–2. The fiction was that the plaintiff alleged an act taking place outside the realm, then asserted that the foreign place was in England (Y.B. 48 Ed. III Hil. pl 6). It was stated in *Dowsdale's Case* (1606) Co. Rep. 47b: "Where as well the contract as the performance of it is wholly made or be done beyond sea, *and so it appears*, then it is not triable in our law." By the aid of this fiction, it never "so appeared."

The old common law rule was that parties were required to designate with specificity the place where events happened, as the sheriff could not otherwise summon a jury who would know the real facts. However, this rule was inconvenient in cases involving events occurring in different jurisdictions.

264   Notes to pages 71–5

37 Complaint by Spanish Ambassador concerning delays in Admiralty caused by Prohibitions, cited in Holdsworth, *English Law*, 1:555. See also Plucknett, *Common Law*, 663–4.
38 Holdsworth, *English Law*, 1:558, also citing Prynne, Zouch, and Jenkins.
39 See *Leges Henrici Primi*, vii 3 (Stubbs, *Select Charters*), cited in Plucknett, *Common Law*, 12.
40 Holdsworth, *English Law*, 1:194.
41 The Eyre was a form of itinerant court with important commissions empowering justices to hear all pleas. In the thirteenth and early fourteenth centuries the Eyre held an important place in the government of the country with respect to both administration and judicial matters.
42 Holdsworth, *English Law*, 1:399. Cf. Plucknett, *Common Law*, 333.
43 Lambard, cited in Holdsworth, *English Law*, 1:399. See also St. Germain, *Doctor and Student. Two Dialogues in English between a Doctor of Divinity, and a Student of the Laws of England: of the Roads of the Said Laws and of Conscience* (London: Printed by the assigns of R. and E. Atkins, 1709), vol. I c. 16: "Since the deeds and acts of men, for which laws have been ordained, happen in divers matters indefinitely, it is not possible to make any general rule of law, but it shall fail in some case." Smith states that common law rules are rigid, therefore there is the need of a Praetor who might give actions where none existed, mitigate the rigour of the law, give exceptions, and maintain laws. Thomas Smith, *De Republica Anglorum: A Discourse on the Commonwealth of England*, edited by L. Alston (Cambridge: Cambridge University Press, 1906), 71.
44 See, for example, Holdsworth, *English Law*, 1:405–6.
45 Bracton practically admits there is no such thing as a consensual contract in English law. In order to respond to rivalry and to extend jurisdiction, common law courts developed the action of assumpsit (actionable as a deceit) which became common at the beginning of the fifteenth century and was an adequate enough remedy for the breach of simple contracts. The common law courts developed later the common law theory that contract was an agreement based on consideration. This development and view was later accepted by Chancery.

Sometimes it is mistakenly or simplistically thought, perhaps reflecting nationalism, that this fact and the development of contract law along domestic lines and according to the procedural forms of the past mean that the development of a systematic contract law in England was not much influenced by canon or Roman law. However, this view does not give due consideration to a number of facts. For example, the common law had no overall theory of contract, nor could it enforce executory contracts, while such contracts and theory were established under canon law and even applied in England through the Chancellor. Due to competition with other courts, common law courts began to involve themselves in the area of contract. Because the common law was at war with Chancery, it had to find another formalistic ground to do exactly the same thing in substance. Canon law familiarized the English with the idea that executory contracts were enforceable and that there was a theory of contract.

Confusion should be dispelled between the forms applied or the formal reasons given by judges, and what was really being done. Sometimes it is said that canon law had little influence because the rigidity of procedure was overcome with *Slade's Case*. See for example Plucknett, *Common Law*, 652–3. However, as in many other cases, the reality is that reasons judges use in their decisions involve unarticulated premises. For example, there was the self-interested desirability of common law courts entering upon the field of contract, which was in a backward state in England, but was demonstrated to be enforceable under other systems, such as canon law. Canon law, natural law, and mercantile practices were indeed at least latent in English thinking.

There was even more to this. *Slade's Case* (1602), 4 Co. Rep. 92b, 94a–94b, changed the express assumpsit into a legal obligation imposed by the law itself on the parties to executory contracts; that is, from the fact that promises were made, the court imposed the new rule or *fiction* that the common law assumed deceit (and actual deceit needed not be proven). Later, contract and covenant developed along the lines of consideration. The decision suffers from the logical fallacy of circularity in which it asserts the very thing that must be proven, and the premises do not lead to the conclusion but simply assert:

it was resolved that contract executory imports in itself an *assumpsit*, for when one agrees to pay money or to deliver any thing, thereby he assumes or promises to pay, or deliver it, and therefore when one sells any goods to another, and agrees to deliver them at a day to come, and the other in consideration thereof agrees to pay so much money on such a day, in that case both parties have an action of debt, or an action of the case on *assumpsit*, for the mutual executory agreement of both parties imports in itself reciprocal actions upon the case, as well as actions of debt.

There are two other problems which undermine such a bare acceptance of the words used. The first is that the court created a fiction, a falsity. One who promises to do something may not perform it at a future date for

266   Notes to pages 76–81

any of a number of reasons, but this does not mean there was deceit at the time of making the promise if the person intended to fulfill it at the time.

Second, it was obvious that *Slade's Case* was plainly wrong in principle. It obliterated the distinction between debt and deceit, which had been so tenaciously and sharply distinguished previously for such a great period of time, and erased the distinction between contract and tort. It introduced much confusion into the scheme of forms of action. In fact decades later, in *Edgcomb v. Dee* (1670), Vaughan, 101, Vaughan J. perceived this case to be a "false gloss" designed to substitute assumpsit for debt.

46   Ceaser; Vinogradoff; Gerson (*Doctor and Student*); Holdsworth, *English Law*, 4:276–8. Plucknett, *Common Law*, 685–6.

47   *Cook v. Fountain* (1672), 3 Swanst. 585, p. 600.

48   13 Ed. I St. I c. 24. Chapter 24 states that "whenever from henceforth it shall happen in the Chancery that there is to be found a writ in one case, but not in another case although involving the same law and requiring the same remedy, the clerks of the Chancery shall agree in framing a writ, or else they shall adjourn the plaintiffs to the next Parliament, or else they shall write down the points upon which they cannot agree and refer them to the next Parliament, and so a writ shall be framed by the consent of the learned in the law; to the end that the court from henceforth shall no longer fail those who seek justice."

49   The Statute of Westminster I contains 51 chapters dealing with such matters as maintenance, champerty, *peine forte et dur, scandalum magnatum*, wardship, distress, limitation of actions, and essoins.

50   The Statute of Westminster II contains 50 chapters creating an estate tail, and dealing with such matters as distraint, dower, advowsons, mortmain, approvement of common, the writ of account, appeals for crime, remedies available to executors, assize of novel disseisin, *nisi prius*, bills of exceptions, process of execution for debt, and the issuing of writs in *consimili casu*.

51   For example, see the Statutes (R.C.) I. 26, 71; Reeves, cited in Holdsworth, *English Law*, 2:300.

52   R.P. I. 133.

53   Y.B. (Selden Society), vol. ii, p. 52 with respect to 5 Ed. II, article xxix.

54   25 Ed. III, Stat. 5, cap. ii.

55   Plucknett, *Common Law*, 29. See *Bridgman v. Holt* (1693) Sower P.C. 111 as a late example of this attitude.

56   Gneist, *English Parliament*, 107; Holdsworth, *English Law*, 2:405.

57   Even during the reign of Henry II, criminal reforms, confirmed by Magna Carta, removed pleas of the crown from the sheriff and county. Later a

Notes to pages 81–4 267

new jurisdiction was set up in the justices of the peace. It was increasingly unnecessary for one to answer an action for land unless it was brought by the king's writ. The Statute of Marlborough, 1257, 52 Hen. III, c. 20, reserved all writs of false judgment for the king's court, which prevented the county from becoming a court of review over lesser local jurisdictions. Other civil jurisdiction was limited by legislation; for example, from the Statute of Gloucester (1278), c. 8, that royal courts should not entertain claims for less than 40 shillings, it was implied that county courts could not hear cases involving more than 40 shillings.

58 Plucknett, *Common Law*, 81.

59 See for example *Jentlemean's Case* (1583) 6 Co. Rep. 11. The stages have been described by Thorne, "Courts of Record in England," *West Virginia Law Quarterly* xl: 355; cited in Plucknett, *Common Law*, 92.

60 Holdsworth, *English Law*, 1:414.

61 Ibid., 1:395–7.

62 Ibid., 1:402.

63 For example, (1394) 17 Rich. II c. 6 empowered the Chancellor to give damages if the suggestions in the bill were found untrue. (1436) 15 Hy. VI c. 4 confirmed this power, and added the power to take security for costs. Later, the court considered that it had inherent power to give costs. See *Corporation of Burford v. Lenthall* (1743) 2 Atk. 551, per L. Hardwick, Chancellor; cp. *Andrews v. Barnes* (1888) 39 C.D. at 138–41.

64 For example, Huse and Fairfax; Y.B. 22 Ed. IV Mich. pl. 21.

65 See for example *Heath v. Rydley* (1614) Cro. Jac. 335.

66 Holdsworth, *Common Law*, 1:421–6.

67 Ibid., 4:84.

68 Ibid., 1:513.

69 16 Car. I c. 10.

70 Coke makes much out of this in *Beecher's Case* (1609) 8 Co. Rep., at 60b; and *Godfrey's Case* (1615) 11 Co. Rep., at 43b. With respect to the power to fine, Coke had some support in authority in some dicta in Y.BB. 7 Hy. VI. Mich. pl. 17 and 10 Hy. VI Mich. pl. 22, per Candish; and F.N.B. 73 D. However, the dicta was not very explicit and the court was thinking primarily of the distinction between an amercement which is affected by the suitors, and a fine assessed by the judge, and not a distinction between a court of record and one not of record. Coke used these cases to give, if not a wholly new meaning to the later distinction (see Y.B. 10 Hy. VI Mich. pl. 22, per Newton), at least a new emphasis.

With respect to the power to imprison, Coke's conclusion is contradicted by Y.B. 37 Hy. VI Hil. pl. 3, p. 14, in which Prisot states that the court of

268   Notes to pages 85–93

Chancery, though not a court of record when acting as a court of equity, has this power. See also Holdsworth, *English Law*, 1:159, and for other misstatements by Coke to magnify the powers of common law courts, see 1:431–2, 476–8.

71 See for example Holdsworth, *English Law*, 1:215–16, 317; 5:161.

72 Plucknett, *Common Law*, 57.

73 Holdsworth, *English Law*, 2:253; 3:465.

74 Hanson cited in Goldsworthy, *Parliament*, 27.

75 R.P. v. 376 (39 Hy. VI no. 2), cited in Holdsworth, *English Law*, 2:445.

76 Hist. MSS. Com. 12th Rep. App. Pt. VI 15–17, cited in Holdsworth, *English Law*, 1:230.

CHAPTER THREE

1 Holt, cited in Goldsworthy, *Parliament*, 28. See also Spelman, cited in Pocock, *Ancient Constitution*, 182–3, and Dugdale, cited in Pocock, *Ancient Constitution*, 182, 185.

2 For example, during Henry I's reign, Vergil and Selden accepted that 'all the people' had assembled at the king's coronation and made laws. The regular summons by writ under Henry III alludes to the first extant summons of knights of the shire or burgesses by writ to the sheriff. See for example Pocock, *Ancient Constitution*, 153.

3 Edwards, Sommerville, cited in Goldsworthy, *Parliament*, 30.

4 See *Fleta* ii 2, I, cited in Holdsworth, *English Law*, 1:352; this proposition is also reflected in the Parliamentary Roll of 1305.

5 Coke, *Fourth Institute*, 27–8; Maitland, *Parliamentary Roll*, lxxxii, cited in Charles Howard McIlwain, *The High Court of Parliament and its Supremacy: An Historical Essay on the Boundaries Between Legislation and Adjudication in England* (New Haven, CT: Yale University Press, 1919), 20–1.

6 See Joseph Redlich, *Procedure of the House of Commons, a Study of Its History and Present Form*, translated by A. Ernest Steinthal (London: Constable, 1908); for earlier authority for the principle than Articuli Baronum of 1215, see for example *Leges Henrici Primi* 5, 6. It is not until 1367 that it was settled that a jury verdict must be unanimous. From the Year Books of the fifteenth century, it was clearly accepted as an ordinary and obvious principle by then; see Y.B. 19 Hy. VI Pasch. pl., 63; 15 Ed. IV Mich. pl. 2, 2, per Littlejohn. All cited in Holdsworth, *English Law*, 2:431.

7 See William Stubbs, *The Constitutional History of England in Its Origin and Development*, 5th ed. (Oxford, UK: Clarendon Press, 1891), 2:268–9.

Stubbs believes the Statute of Quia Emptores was probably the last case in which the assent of the Commons was taken for granted. Holdsworth is more doubtful given that the statute Migamis (4 Ed. I St. 3) was made by bishops and others of the council, and accepted as statute because Council "as well justices and others" assented: Reeves H.E.L. ii 53; and cp. Pollard, *Evolution of Parliament*, 241–2, cited in Holdsworth, *English Law*, 2:308. See also Plucknett, *Common Law*, 321–2; McIlwain, *High Court of Parliament*, 22.

8 (1305) Y.B. 33–5 Ed. I (R.S.) 83 turned on the Statute of Westminster. Barbazon J. said that he would confer with his companions about the meaning of 34 Ed. I St. I as they were there at its making; cp. the Chief Justice stated "Do no gloss the Statute; we understand it better than you do, for we made it!" cp. also Y.B. 32, 33 Ed. I (R.S.) 429.

9 Holdsworth, *English Law*, 2:308. Plucknett, *Common Law*, 328–9.

10 Y.B. 30, 31 Ed. I (Rolls Series), 441; Y.B. 40 Ed. III, f. 34 b. Plucknett, *Common Law*, 329.

11 See Plucknett, *Common Law*, 330–1.

12 See *Statutes of the Realm*, vol. II, 104; cf. McIlwain, *High Court of Parliament*, 39–40.

13 Smith, *De Republica Anglorum*, 51.

14 Hariss, Chrimes, cited in Goldsworthy, *Parliament*, 34.

15 See Belknap and Candish JJ. in 49 Ass. pl. 8, cited in Holdsworth, *English Law*, 2:311.

16 Goldsworthy, *Parliament*, 29.

17 Y.B. 22 Ed. III Hil. pl. 25.

18 R.P. 1 416 no. 2 in reply to a petition, cited in Holdsworth, *English Law*, 2:437.

19 Pollard, *Evolution of Parliament*, 118 and later, cited in Holdsworth, *English Law*, 2:437.

20 Richardson and Sayles, cited in Plucknett, *Common Law*, 323.

21 Holdsworth, *English Law*, 2:429.

22 In *Trewynard's Case*, 36–37 Hy. VIII, *Dyer* fol 60a, involving the question of the privilege of a member of the Commons, it was stated that the "court of parliament is the most high court, and hath more privileges than any other court in the Kingdom." In *Earl of Leicester v. Heydon*, during 13 Eliz., *Plowden* 384 and later, Parliament is spoken of as "a Court of the greatest Honour and Justice, of which none can imagine a dishonourable thing."

   See also Coke, *Fourth Part of the Reports*, in Sheppard, ed., 94, and *Eighth Part of the Reports*, in Sheppard, ed., 301.

270 Notes to pages 97–9

23 Smith, *De Republica Anglorum*, 48, 57.

24 Cited in William Lambard, *Archeoin: Or A Discourse upon the High Courts of Justice in England*, edited by Charles H. McIlwain and Paul L. Ward (Cambridge, MA: Harvard University Press, 1957); also cited in Plucknett, *Common Law*.

25 Henry Finch, *Law, or, a Discourse Thereof: In Foure Bookes* (London: Printed [by Adam Islip] for the Societe of Stationers, 1627), 233.

26 (1653) 5 S.T. 386.

27 Holdsworth, *English Law*, 4:183; see also Sayless, Edward, Chrimes, all cited in Goldsworthy, *Parliament*, 39.

28 Holdsworth, *English Law*, 2:183–7.

29 For example, Coke stated in his address to the Commons in 1592–93 that this court was not a court alone. In it were representatives of the king and the three estates – the great corporation or body politic of the kingdom (*Fourth Institute*). This view was founded on earlier authorities, such as Y.B. 14 Hy. VIII Mich. pl. 3. This view of Parliament forming one body politic was accepted by writers such as St. Germain and Smith, and endorsed by Henry VIII; see G.R. Elton, *The Parliament of England 1559– 1581* (Cambridge: Cambridge University Press, 1986), 17–18.

30 See also Plucknett, Arnold, cited in Goldsworthy, *Parliament*, 40.

31 See Stubbs, Hallam, cited in Holdsworth, *English Law*, 2:439.

32 *R. v. Bishop of Chichester* (1365) Y.B. 39 Ed. III Pasch., pl. 7, per Thorpe C.J. In that case, the crown was prosecuting a bishop under a statute of premunire. One defence rejected was that the statute was very recent and had not been proclaimed in the counties. Thorpe C.J. stated:

> Although proclamation was not made in the county, everyone is now bound to know that is done in Parliament, for as soon as Parliament has concluded a matter, the law holds that every person has knowledge of it, for the Parliament represents the body of all the realm, and so proclamation is unnecessary for the statute has already become effective.

In the fifteenth century, this view was widely believed. In the sixteenth century, it became commonplace and is seen in statements in Parliament. See G.R. Elton, *The Tudor Constitution: Documents and Commentary*, 2nd ed. (Cambridge: Cambridge University Press, 1982), 236; Goldsworthy, *Parliament*, 68.

In *Chudleigh's Case* (1595), 1 Coke's *Reports* 120a, 76 E.R. 270, Popham C.J. argued that for this reason, Parliament's authority was superior to any judge as it was the judgment of all the judges and all the realm which ought to bind all.

Notes to pages 99–107 271

33 Redlich, *Procedure of the House of Commons*, 1:19–20, cited in Holdsworth, *English Law*, 2:440.

34 Smith, *De Republica Anglorum*, 48–9, 57; Elton, *Tudor Constitution*, 235–6.

35 Holdsworth, *English Law*, 1:360; Plucknett, *Common Law*, 32.

36 Plucknett, *Common Law*, 32.

37 Smith, *De Republica Anglorum*, Bk. II., c. 1, 49; Elton, *Tudor Constitution*, 235–6.

38 Holdsworth, *English Law*, 1:360–1; 2:430, 433–4; Elton, *Parliament of England*, 16.

39 Holdsworth, *English Law*, 4:3–4.

40 See for example Berman, *Law and Revolution II*.

41 Holdsworth, *English Law*, 4:251–3, 274–5; 5:167.

42 Smith, *De Republica Anglorum*, Bk II c. 3.

43 Plucknett, *Common Law*, 15.

44 Elton, *Parliament of England*, 34–5.

45 Fabian Philipps, *Investigatio Jurim Antiquorum*, 299, cited in Pocock, *Ancient Constitution*, 220.

46 Goldsworthy, *Parliament*, 51.

47 See Elton, *Tudor Constitution*, 238; Goldsworthy, *Parliament*, 56.

48 See letter of Gardiner to Protector Somerset in 1 S.T. at p. 588, cited in Holdsworth, *English Law*, 4:283. All English writers on political theory in this period recognized the constitutional character of the English monarchy. Ibid., 283, 209–15.

49 Elton, *Parliament of England*, 22, 39; *Tudor Constitution*, 240.

50 Y.B. 3, 4 Ed. II (S.S.) 38, 39, per Herle and Toudeby arg., cited in Holdsworth, *English Law*, 1:208.

51 Pike, *History of the House of Lords*, 44–5; cp *R. v. Rouceby* (1354) Select Cases before the Council (S.S.) 38. Y.B. 12, 13 Ed. III (R.S.) xciv; Y.B. 12, 13 Ed. III (R.S.) xciv–c (1336–1341); (1346) Y.B. 20 Ed. III ii (R.S.) 126, cited in Holdsworth, *English Law*, 1:208.

52 Y.B. 13, 14 Ed. III (R.S.) xxxvi–xlii (1340–45), cited in Holdsworth, *English Law*, 1:209.

53 Holdsworth, *English Law*, 1:478.

54 Y.B. 29 Ed. III, Pasch., 14.

55 Baldwin, *The King's Council*, 336, cited in Holdsworth, *English Law*, 1:361.

56 Jurisdiction of the House of Lords, ch. xxii; cp. Pike, *House of Lords*, 290–4.

57 Coke, *Fourth Institute*, 23. Coke notes erroneous judgments in Parliament in the House of Lords MSS in 1624, Hist. MSS Comm. Third Rep. App. Pt.

272 Notes to pages 107–17

I, 34–5, I, in which the idea of the need for consent of the House of Commons appears.

58 In *R. v. Knollys* (1694) 1 Ld. Raym. at p. 15, Holt C.J. states: "the judicial power is only in the Lords, but legally and virtually it is the judgement of the King as well as of the Lords, and perhaps of the Commons too."

59 Cited in Holdsworth, *English Law*, 1:362.

60 Ibid., 1:363.

61 Ibid., 1:478.

62 Ibid., 2:477.

CHAPTER FOUR

1 Holdsworth, *English Law*, 4:190.

2 See for example Bodin and Figgis.

3 Bodin, *Six livres*, Book VI, ch. iv, 713.

4 Ibid., Book I, ch. viii, 90, 93, 96–100.

5 Ibid., Book I, ch. viii, 91, 97; Holdsworth, *English Law*, 4:195.

6 Bodin, *Six livres*, Book I, ch. x, 163: "Et par ainse toute las force des loix et coutumes gist au pouvoir du prince souverain." (This roughly means "In this manner, all the force of the laws and customs comes from the power of the sovereign prince.") This view was also accepted by Hobbes.

7 See *Catechism of the Catholic Church*, 2nd ed., revised in accordance with the official Latin text promulgated by Pope John Paul II (Citta del Vaticano: Libreria Editrice Vaticana, 1994, 1997, 2000); *The Holy Bible*, New Revised Standard Version (Scarborough, ON: Thomas Nelson Publishers, 1993), Revelation 11:15, Mark 12:17, Acts 5:29; *Gaudium et Spes* 10 § 3; cf. 45 § 2.

8 Manegold of Lautenbach, *Liber ad Gebehardum*, 1085 A.D.

9 Holdsworth, *English Law*, 4:291–2; Plucknett, *Common Law*, 40–1.

10 See for example *Case of Proclamations* (1611) 12 Co. Rep. at 76; Coke, *Part Four of the Reports*, in Sheppard, ed., 102, Coke, *Second Institute*, 36, *Third Institute*, 84.

11 Holdsworth, *English Law*, 4:206–8.

12 Smith, *De Republica Anglorum*, 49.

13 Holdsworth, *English Law*, 4:201–9, 6:87–107.

14 See *Bates's Case* (1606) 2 S.T. at 389, per Fleming C.B.

15 See James I's Speech in the Star Chamber, *Works* 557; *Letters and Life of Bacon* ii 371, both cited in Holdsworth, *English Law*, 6:21–2. See also Burgess, Henshall, Zagorin, cited in Goldsworthy, *Parliament*, 82.

16 (1637) 3 S.T. 825.

Notes to pages 117–25

17 (1637) 3 S.T. 825, 1235, per Finch C.J.

18 (1637) 3 S.T. 825, 1089–99, per Berkeley J.

19 *Darnel's Case* (1627) 3 S.T. 1.

20 *Bates's Case* (1606) 2 S.T. 371.

21 *Hampden's Case* (1637) 3 S.T. 825.

22 Figgis, *Divine Right of Kings*, 231; Holdsworth, *English Law*, 6:83, 67–8.

23 The theory was stated in debate on impositions in 1610. See 2 S.T. 482; Parliamentary Debates in 1610 (C.S.) 103–9; Holdsworth, *English Law*, 6:84.

24 Elton, *Studies in Tudor and Stuart Politics and Government*, 2:228–9; Elton, Stout, cited in Goldsworthy, *Parliament*, 68.

25 Elton, *Studies in Tudor and Stuart Politics and Government*, 2:229.

26 Goldsworthy, *Parliament*, 73–4.

27 Cited in Goldsworthy, *Parliament*, 129.

28 Parker, Mendle, cited in Goldsworthy, *Parliament*, 130.

29 Allen, cited in Goldsworthy, *Parliament*, 130.

30 Greenberg, cited in Goldsworthy, *Parliament*, 131.

31 Goldsworthy, *Parliament*, 131–4.

32 Ibid., 97.

33 See for example Marsh, Godwin, *Apology of the Commons of 1604*, cited in Goldsworthy, *Parliament*, 100.

34 Goldsworthy, *Parliament*, 101.

35 Supporters of such views would include Petyt, Prynne, Parker, and Pym, and their opinion is reflected in *Streater's Case* (1653).

36 See Foster, Whitelocke, Fuller, Kenyon, Prynne, Rushworth, J. Milton, all cited in Goldsworthy, *Parliament*, 106.

37 See Sommerville, Christian, cited in Goldsworthy, *Parliament*, 78; Pocock, *Ancient Constitution*, 46–9.

38 Hedley's speech in Elizabeth Reed Foster, ed., *Proceedings in Parliament 1610*, vol. 2, *House of Commons* (New Haven, CT: Yale University Press, 1966), 172–4; Pocock, *Ancient Constitution*, 270–1.

39 See for example Herle, Pocock, Nenner, Hill, Parker, Pym, cited in Goldsworthy, *Parliament*, 109; Pocock, *Ancient Constitution*, 49, 234.

40 J.W. Gough, *Fundamental Law in English Constitutional History* (London: Oxford University Press, 1961), 58–9.

41 Pocock, *Ancient Constitution*, 302–3.

42 Ibid., 325–31.

43 16 Car. I c. 8.

44 16 Car. II c. 10.

45 16 Car. I c. 1.

274   Notes to pages 126–34

46   Holdsworth, *English Law*, 6:148–9.

47   Weston and Greenberg cited in Pocock, *Ancient Constitution*, 357.

48   12 Car. II c. 1.

49   13 Car. II. St. 1 cc. 7 and 11.

50   Holdsworth, *English Law*, 6:165–73.

51   See *Calendar of Treasury Books ii 1667–1668*, xxxv–vi, cited in Holdsworth, *English Law*, 6:174.

52   For example, the 1667 commission to enquire into public accounts produced no adequate remedies. The Commons found it easier to attack individuals than to conduct a fiscal investigation.

53   Lacey, Harris, cited in Goldsworthy, *Parliament*, 149.

54   Goldsworthy, *Parliament*, 149–50.

55   Ibid., 153–4.

56   Nenner, cited in Goldsworthy, *Parliament*, 158.

57   1 Wm. and M. c. 1.

58   1 Wm. and M. sess. 2 c. 2.

59   1 Wm. and M. c. 5.

60   1 Wm. and M. c. 18.

61   2 Wm. and M. c. 1.

62   See for example Dicey, *Law of the Constitution*, 197, 199, 207.

63   1 Wm. and M. sess. 2, c. 2.

64   12, 13 Wm. III. c. 2.

65   12, 13 Wm. III c. 2.

66   Holdsworth, *English Law*, 6:242–3.

67   Coke, *Part Three of the Reports*, in Sheppard, ed., 59–60; Plucknett, *Common Law*, 49.

68   See Preface to Prynne's *Animadversions*, cited in Holdsworth, *English Law*, 5:469–70. See also Sheppard, ed., xxiii, xxviii, xxxi.

69   For example, Henry VIII's various marriages were followed by statutes which resettled succession, and made certain acts done in contravention treason. By statute of 1533, Henry's marriage with Catherine was declared void, and his marriage with Anne declared valid. Anyone slandering the king's marriage or persons upon whom the crown was settled by the Act was guilty of treason. If the king died leaving infants, they were to be kept in the guardianship of their mother and a council, and it was treason to oppose the mother and council. The statute of 1536 annulled the marriage with Anne and settled the crown on the issue of the king and Jane Seymour. It contained similar but more stringent provisions. It was treason to do anything to prejudice the king's present marriage or any future marriage, or to adjudge his former marriages valid, or to refuse to answer

Notes to pages 134–5 275

interrogatories or make the oath required by the Act. It was treason for the king's heirs or children to claim the crown contrary to the line of descent limited in the Act. The 1540 statute annulled his marriage with Anne of Cleves, and made it treasonable to assert its validity. The 1543 statute finally settled the crown and gave the king power to limit succession by his will on the failure of his issue, and again made it treasonable to attempt anything contrary to the settlement made. The statute (1547) 1 Ed. VI c 12, s. 8, contained a provision similar to that contained in the statute of 1536, making it treason for the king's heirs or successors to attempt to alter the line of succession as provided for in the statute of 1543.

70 For example, Petyt stated that William I was chosen in Parliament. He was crowned in England. At the time, the archbishop asked of the English, "will you be pleased to have this king?" They said yes. Rufus, Henry I, Stephen, Henry II, and Henry III all claimed no right but by Parliament. See Petyt's address in January 1689 to the House of Lords in respect of the Commons' resolution asking them to agree that James had broken the original contract between king and people. *Historical Manuscripts Commission, XIIth Report*, Appendix VI, 14 ff.

71 Holdsworth, *English Law*, 2:7, 23.

72 In Saxon times, there were several instances in which kings were deposed. The strength of the Norman and Angevin kings, and the growth of the hereditary principle, tended to make both the elective principle and the right of the nation to depose an unworthy king fall into the background. The rise of Parliament revived the elective principle and the right of deposition in another form. Edward II and Richard II were deposed. After Richard II was deposed, Parliament recognized Henry IV as king, thus departing from strict hereditary succession, and subsequently settled the crown on him and his four sons. Parliament reverted to hereditary rule when it recognized Edward II as king in 1461, and resettled the crown when Henry VII prevailed over the Yorkists in 1485. The *immediate* occasion for these parliamentary resettlements was the fortune of war. But the fact that Parliament was called on to legalize the results emphasized in new form the elective character of the monarchy. The power of the crown was reestablished by the Tudors. They made the crown the predominant partner in the constitution. Henry VIII thought it necessary to get parliamentary sanction for his various settlements of the crown, which kept alive Parliament's power and the elective principle. Acts of Parliament recognized the hereditary right of Mary and Elizabeth, and in 1571 it was declared that Acts of Parliament could limit the descent of the crown. James I succeeded in defiance of the settlement that Henry VIII made by statutory powers

276 Notes to pages 135–7

conferred on him. Parliament was called to recognize and acknowledge his right. The exclusion controversy during Charles II proved that the crown was hereditary and indefeasible unless reassigned by Parliament, and Parliament had the power to defeat the inheritance. These propositions were made clear by the Bill of Rights and the Act of Settlement. Parliament in both cases made resettlements of the crown, and departed from the strict line of hereditary succession. Due to widespread controversy, the Acts of 1707 and 1571 made it a criminal offence to maintain that the king in Parliament could not make laws to bind the crown and its descent. With the Revolution, the crown settled on William and Mary, eldest daughter of James II, for their joint lives, then on the survivor, then on the issue of Mary, and on failure of her issue on Anne, James II's second daughter, and her issue, and lastly on the issue of William II, the grandson of Charles I and the nephew and son-in-law of James II. Thus, William, Mary, and Anne took the crown, not by hereditary right, but by purchase. The Act of Settlement settled the crown on Sophia of Brunswick, granddaughter of James I, and her issue. Both these resettlements of the crown went further than previous parliamentary settlements or resettlements. Both placed restrictions on crown prerogative, and barred a Catholic or a person married to a Catholic. The Act of Settlement required the king to make a declaration against transubstantiation, take the coronation oath in the form settled by (1689) 1 Wm. and M. St. 1 c. 6, and join in communion with the Church of England. The Acts of Union with Scotland and Ireland made the same provisions for the devolution of the crown of Britain and Ireland; and, the Act of Union with Scotland stated that the king must take oaths for the preservation of the Church of England and the Presbyterian Church in Scotland.

　　See also Holdsworth, *English Law*, 10:430–2.

73　Blackstone's *Commentaries*, 1:194, 209.

74　(1760) 1 Geo. III c. s. 23.

75　See Maine, *Early Law and Custom*, 164, cited in Holdsworth, *English Law*, 6:218; 2:443 and n. 5.

76　Holdsworth, *English Law*, 6:218; 2:442, n. 2; 443–4.

77　Holdsworth, *English Law*, 6:220; 2:444; 4:198–9, 216.

78　11 Co. Rep. 84b.

79　7 Co. Rep. 36.

80　12 Co. Rep. 18.

81　Glanvill's speech before a committee of both Houses recognized the king's power to dispense statutes *mala prohibita*, but not *mala in se*, 3 S.T. 206, cited in Holdsworth, *English Law*, 6:221.

Notes to pages 137–46

82 Vaughan at 334, 341–4.
83 11 S.T. 116, 1261–67.
84 Holdsworth, *English Law*, 6:225.
85 Elton, cited in Goldsworthy, *Parliament*, 57.
86 Cited in Goldsworthy, *Parliament*, 57.
87 Ibid.

CHAPTER FIVE

1   Holdsworth, *English Law*, 6:258.
2   Dicey, *Law of the Constitution*, 73.
3   Holdsworth, *English Law*, 6:262.
4   Holdsworth, *English Law*, 10:31. This view was so generally recognized that it was the essence of the defence on Sacheverell's impeachment. That is, the inability to resist does not apply to the Revolution because the supreme power was not resisted. 15 S.T. at 196, 366.
5   Edmond Burke, *Thoughts on the Cause of the Present Discontents*, edited with introduction and notes by F.G. Selby (London: Macmillan, 1902), 350.
6   Holdsworth, *English Law*, 10:527.
7   Ibid., 10:527–8; 2:443–4; 6:218–19.
8   *Doctor and Student*, caption 10 of the additions to the second Dialogue, cited in Holdsworth, *English Law*, 10:527–8.
9   Holdsworth, *English Law*, 10:528.
10 Ibid., 10:528; 6:284–6.
11 J. Locke, *Second Treatise on Government* [1699] (New York: Library of Liberal Arts, 1962), 51c.
12 Blackstone's *Commentaries*, 1:161–2, 244–5.
13 Ibid., 1:124.
14 See Lewis, cited in Goldsworthy, *Parliament*, 18.
15 Blackstone's *Commentaries*, 1:245.
16 Austin, cited in Goldsworthy, *Parliament*, 19.
17 Dicey, *Law of the Constitution*, 78.
18 Goldsworthy, *Parliament*, 173.
19 Ibid., 178.
20 Ibid., 179.
21 Ibid., 186.
22 See for example Perry, Langford, Pallister, Bailyn, Toohey, Thomson, Clark, all cited in Goldsworthy, *Parliament*, 196.
23 For example, in the debate over the Septennial Act of 1716, many members of the Commons thought the legislature had no power to repeal the

278 Notes to pages 146–9

existing Triennial Act and prolong its own existence. They denied the proposition that there were no legal restrictions on the legislature's powers. In the debate over the Regency Bill, 1751, Beckford denied that Parliament could prolong its own existence without the consent of the electors. In 1753, one objection to Hardwicke's Marriage Act was that its provisions were contrary to the law of God and nature, and of such a nature that no Christian legislature had power to enact them. Beckford argued that a contract could not be declared void, which was good and valid by the laws of Christianity. Such objections were seriously urged and considered. See Holdsworth, *English Law*, 10:530.

24 Ibid., 10:530.
25 Ibid., 6:287; Plucknett, *Common Law*, 62–3.
26 In Locke, cited in Goldsworthy, *Parliament*, 151.
27 Locke, *Two Treatises of Government*, Book II, s. 6.
28 Ibid., s. 96.
29 Ibid., s. 131.
30 Locke, cited in Goldsworthy, *Parliament*, 151.
31 Ibid.
32 Locke, *Two Treatises of Government*, Book II, s. 221.
33 Locke, cited in Goldsworthy, *Parliament*, 151.
34 Holdsworth, *English Law*, 6:294.
35 Ibid., 2:442.
36 McIlwain, *High Court of Parliament*; see for example 321–2, 324–8.
37 Ibid., chapter 5, esp. 343, 350, 354, 356–7, 375–6. For example, at p. 350, while he states that neither theory of royal or parliamentary legislative supremacy could find precedent in common law, he admits that "[t]he changes by which the principle was finally grafted upon the English constitution are rightly called 'The Revolution.'" And at 354: "From that time up to the present the practice as well as the theory of parliamentary sovereignty may be said to have been definitely settled." In his view, legislative sovereignty cannot be safely dated much before the Reformation. He states that during and after the civil wars, the 'new' theory made rapid progress; that its general acceptance cannot be denied; and that it gives a satisfactory explanation of the working and of the accepted theory of the English constitution following the Revolution. In what appears to be a contradiction to his main argument, he states that "[i]t could hardly be otherwise, for it was in reality a deduction from that constitution itself." Later, he states that due credit must not be denied to the English theory of parliamentary omnipotence: it accomplished its purpose, and the result was omnipotent parliament.

Notes to pages 149–53

38 Ibid., 133.

39 Ibid., 203–4.

40 Goldsworthy, *Parliament*, vii.

41 See McIlwain, *High Court of Parliament*, 143–4, 156; see also Burgess, cited in Goldsworthy, *Parliament*, 17.

42 Goldsworthy, *Parliament*, 17.

43 Holdsworth, *English Law*, 2:442.

44 Gough, *Fundamental Law*, 2–3, 212.

45 Azo, cited in Plucknett, *Common Law*, 308.

46 Plucknett, *Common Law*, 308.

47 Jenks, cited in Plucknett, *Common Law*, 316.

48 McIlwain, *High Court of Parliament*, vii, viii.

49 Goldsworthy, *Parliament*, 42.

50 See also *Quia Emptores*. See also Arnold, Milson, cited in Goldsworthy, *Parliament*, 43; Plucknett, *Common Law*, 28.

51 The Statute of Westminster (1275) 3 Ed. 1, CAP XII provided:
    > that notorious Felons, and which openly be of evil Name, and will not put themselves in Enquests of Felonies, that men shall charge them with before the Justices at the King's Suit shall have strong and hard Imprisonment, as they which refuse to stand to the *Common Law of the Land*. But this is not to be understood of such Prisoners as be taken of light Suspicion. (emphasis added) (trans.)

    Accordingly, by this time the crown felt itself strong enough to impose jury trial by force. Trial by jury was declared the law of the land, although imposed only for "notorious felons."

    The words *"prison forte et dure"* became transformed into *"peine forte et dure,"* and finally into torture by the sixteenth century, in order to compel the accused to accept trial by jury or die. See Plucknett, *Common Law*, 126.

52 Elton, *Tudor Constitution*, 234.

53 See also Hanson, cited in Goldsworthy, *Parliament*, 43.

54 *R. v. Hampden* (1637) 3 S.T. at 1235; *Godden v. Hales* (1685) II S.T. 1165.

55 Holdsworth, *English Law*, 2:443, 445–56.

56 Coke, *Fourth Institute*, 37–8. One illustration is the episode in which Henry VIII commanded a King's Bench judge to attend the Chief Justices to answer whether a certain man might be attainted of high treason by Parliament and never called to his answer. The judges replied it was a dangerous question, and the High Court of Parliament ought to give good example to inferior courts for proceeding according to Justice. However, as it was by the express commandment of the king and pressed by Cromwell

280 Notes to pages 153–5

to give a direct answer, they stated that if a person had been attainted by Parliament, it could not be questioned whether he was called to answer or not. The Act of Attainder being passed by Parliament therefore binds. Cited in Holdsworth, *English Law*, 4:185.

57 See letter of Gardiner to Protector Somerset in 1 S.T. at 588, cited in Holdsworth, *English Law*, 4:283. All English writers on political theory in this period recognized the constitutional character of the English monarchy. Holdsworth, *English Law*, 4:283, 209–15.

58 Spedding, ed., *Works* VII at 625, cited in Holdsworth, *English Law*, 4:186.

59 Holdsworth, *English Law*, 4:185.

60 See for example Sommerville, Weston, Pocock, cited in Goldsworthy, *Parliament*, 110.

61 (1609) 8 Co. Rep. 107, p. 118; 77 E.R. 638, p. 652.

62 (1609) 7 Co. Rep., p. 13a, 25a.

63 Holdsworth, *English Law*, 4:186–8.

64 Bacon: Argument in *Chudleigh's Case*, in *The Works of Francis Bacon*, collected and edited by James Spedding et al. (Boston: Brown and Taggard, 1860–64), 7:625. The argument is that the law carries authority in itself. Also, the same view was repeated, for example at 623: the judges' authority over laws is "to expound them faithfully and apply them properly"; also, at 633 in response to the argument that the limitations in that case should be allowed because they would be a refuge in time of trouble to great houses, he says: "[i]f force prevail above lawful regiment, how easy will it be to procure an Act of Parliament to pass according to the humour and bent of the state to sweep away all their perpetuities."

Bacon stated that an Act of Parliament cannot bind a future Parliament, "for a supreme and absolute power cannot conclude itself," in *Works*, 6:160.

In Discourse on the Commission of Bridewell, in *Works* 7:509–16, at 513 Bacon talks as if he thought an Act of Parliament which contravened Magna Carta would be void, but such a view is opposed to the latter part of the Discourse, where he expressly admits that departures from the clause of Magna Carta he is considering are valid because they were made by Parliament. See Holdsworth, *English Law*, 4:186.

65 Holdsworth, *English Law*, 5:474, 4:186. Pocock, *Ancient Constitution*, 67–8. Sheppard, ed., xxxi.

66 Coke, *Part Three of the Reports*, in Sheppard, ed., 62–3.

67 Plucknett, *Common Law*, 284.

68 For example, in the *Fourth Institute*, 14, Coke states that the Commons may say they cannot answer without conference with their constituents. See Holdsworth, *English Law*, 4:186–7; Plucknett, *Common Law*, 282–4.

Notes to pages 156–9   281

69 Blackstone's *Commentaries*, 1:160–1; Dicey, *Law of the Constitution*, 46; Holdsworth, *English Law*, 4:187; Goldsworthy, *Parliament*, 114–16.

70 Coke, *Fourth Institute*, 36–8.

71 Coke, *Eighth Part of the Reports*, in Sheppard, ed., 302.

72 Coke, *Fourth Institute*, 37–8, 41; Proeme, *Second Institute*, 50–1, 74.

73 Coke, *Second Institute*, in Sheppard, ed., 751–2; Goldsworthy, *Parliament*, 113.

74 Judson, MacKay, cited in Goldsworthy, *Parliament*, 114.

75 Coke, *Part Nine of the Reports*, in Sheppard, ed., 300.

76 Coke, *Eighth Part of the Reports*, in Sheppard, ed., 306; *Fourth Part of the Reports*, in Sheppard, ed., 94–6.

77 See for example Campbell, Plucknett, Gray, Mackay, Boudin, Stoner, Allen, Gough, all cited in Goldsworthy, *Parliament*, 44.

78 Plucknett, *Common Law*, 336.

79 Blackstone's *Commentaries*, 1:40–1; see also Dicey, *Law of the Constitution*, 59–60.

80 Theodore F. Plucknett, "Bonham's Case and Judicial Review," *Harvard Law Review* vol. 40, no. 1 (Nov. 1926): 30; also cited in Plucknett, *Common Law*, 51.

81 Elton, *Parliament of England*, 39, 32.

82 Sommerville, cited in Goldsworthy, *Parliament*, 122.

83 R.P. v. 377 (39 Hy. VI no. 16).

84 Holdsworth, *English Law*, 2:442.

85 Y.B. 33 Hy. VI, Pasch. pl. 8.

86 Cited in Goldsworthy, *Parliament*, 44.

87 Plucknett's study of statute law in the first half of the fourteenth century found only a few decisions in the Year Books in which pertinent statutes were not applied, and those decisions were not based on any jurisprudential principle subordinating parliamentary authority to fundamental principles of natural or common law. The judges simply applied what they regarded as the best law for the circumstances. Thorne states that statutory provisions were given as merely policy suggestions and were treated with unconcern as to the precise content. Judges freely extended and restricted them as part of the duty to administer justice between litigants. The approach reflected the different relationship between legislation and adjudication that prevailed. The powers of the Council, courts, and Parliament were not clearly differentiated; all wielded the authority of the king, and all participated in legislation and adjudication not clearly distinguished from one another. Council and Parliament engaged in statutory interpretation and adjudication. Judges helped draft legislation, and

282   Notes to pages 159–63

judicial interpretation was acknowledged to be virtually legislation. Therefore, judges did not think of statutes as the commands of an external
authority requiring strict construction. As royal servants administering the
king's justice, they exercised the fusion of judicial and legislative powers
rather than opposing the underlying policies of the king and Parliament.

88 Holdsworth, *English Law*, 2:442; see also Goldsworthy, *Parliament*, 111.

89 Blackstone's *Commentaries*, 1:91.

90 Holdsworth, *English Law*, 2:443.

91 The *Case of the City of London* (1610), 8 Co. Rep. 121b, p. 126a; 77 E.R.
    658, p. 664. See also Burgess, cited in Goldsworthy, *Parliament*, 111.

92 Thorne, Plucknett, Holdsworth, cited in Goldsworthy, *Parliament*, 111.
    Gough, *Fundamental Law*, 45–6.

93 Goldsworthy, *Parliament*, 111.

94 Boudin suggests that Coke later dropped the idea, while Thorne concluded
    that he never held it; see Plucknett, *Common Law*, 51 n. 2.

95 Coke, *Fourth Institute*, 41; *Second Institute*, Proeme, 50–1, 74; *Part Four
    of the Reports*, in Sheppard, ed., 95–6.

96 Gray, cited in Goldsworthy, *Parliament*, 123.

97 (1614) Hobart 85, 87; 80 E.R. 235, 237. Gough cited in Goldsworthy, *Par-
    liament*, 123.

98 Gough, *Fundamental Law*, 103–4.

99 Dallison, Smith, cited in Goldsworthy, *Parliament*, 123–4.

100 Cited in Goldsworthy, *Parliament*, 45.

101 Ibid.

102 Ibid.

103 *Observacions upon Coke's Reportes* (1615), in Knafka, cited in Golds-
    worthy, *Parliament*, 97.

104 Coke, *Part Nine of the Reports*, in Sheppard, ed., 301; *Fourth Institute*, 36.

105 (1695) Skin, at 526.

106 Holdsworth, *English Law*, 2:442–3.

107 Philip A. Hamburger, "Revolution and Judicial Review: Chief Justice
    Holt's Opinion in *City of London v. Wood*," *Columbia Law Review*
    (1994): 2091, 2093, 2096, 2119–21, 2137–9, 2141.

108 For example, in *Triquet v. Bath* (1764) 3 Burr. at p. 1480, Mansfield J.'s
    conclusion was based on the wide premise that the law of nations was part
    of the law of England, citing dicta of Holt, Talbot, and Hardwicke.

109 (1767) 4 Burr. at p. 2106.

110 Holdsworth, *English Law*, 10:372–6.

111 (1677) Vaughan Reports 330, p. 336; 124 E.R. 1098, p. 1102.

112 Goldsworthy, *Parliament*, 158.

Notes to pages 163–72

113 (1701), 12 Mod. 669, p. 687; 88 E.R. 1592, p. 1602; Allen, Plucknett, Gough, all cited in Goldsworthy, *Parliament*, 197.

114 Hamburger, "Revolution and Judicial Review," 2142, and n. 162.

115 *City of London v. Wood* (unpublished analysis) quoted in Hamburger, "Revolution and Judicial Review," 2139; Goldsworthy, *Parliament*, 198–9.

116 *The Judgments Delivered by the Lord Chief Justice Holt in the Case of Ashby v. White and Others, and in the Case of John Paty and Others,* quoted in Hamburger, cited in Goldsworthy, *Parliament*, 198.

117 Hamburger, "Revolution and Judicial Review," 2142; Holdsworthy, *English Law*, 198.

118 (1742) 2 Strange 1173, 93 E.R. 1107, p. 1108 (K.B.); (1849) 23 Beav. 63, p. 77, 50 E.R. 984, p. 989 (Chancery) respectively.

119 Cited in Goldsworthy, *Parliament*, 198, and see also 198–201.

120 This idea is illustrated in R.P. ii 41 (4 Ed. III no. 52) involving a petition of persons who thought the lands of the Templars should have escheated, and not gone to the Hospitallers, saying it was contrary to law (and reason).

121 Gough, *Fundamental Law*, 45, 143.

122 Ibid., 141.

123 13 Car. II St. I c. 1.

124 13 Car. II St. I c. 2.

125 Blackstone's *Commentaries*, 1:185, 160.

126 See for example ibid., 1:185–6.

127 Dicey, *Law of the Constitution*, 39–40.

128 Goldsworthy, *Parliament*, 10.

129 Ibid., 12–16.

130 *Bribery Commissioner v. Ranasinghe*, [1965] A.C. 172, 200.

131 Hale, "Reflections by the Lrd. Cheife Justice Hale on Mr. Hobbes His Dialogue of the Law," the Harleaian MS 711ff, 37–8; also reproduced in Holdsworth, *English Law*, vol. V, app. III.

132 See Figgis, *Divine Right of Kings*, 27–9.

133 See for example Goldsworthy, *Parliament*, 4–5, citing the arguments of those such as Allan, Detmold, Edwards, and Walker. See also McIlwain, *High Court of Parliament*, with respect to pre-Revolution times.

134 Blackstone's *Commentaries*, 1:70.

135 See also Dicey, *Law of the Constitution*, 68.

136 Brazier, Rishworth, Kirby, cited in Goldsworthy, *Parliament*, 238.

137 Goldsworthy, *Parliament*, 239.

138 Cited in Goldsworthy, *Parliament*, 242.

139 *Reference re Remuneration of Judges of the Provincial Court of Prince Edward Island; Reference re Independence and Impartiality of Judges of*

284 Notes to pages 174–83

the Provincial Court of Prince Edward Island; and *R. v. Campbell; R. v. Ekmecic; R. v. Wickman* and *Manitoba Provincial Judges Association v. Manitoba (Minister of Justice),* [1997] 3 S.C.R. 3.

140 Winterton, cited in Goldsworthy, *Parliament,* 243.

CHAPTER SIX

1 Holdsworth, *English Law,* 2:220.

2 For example through the use of the first clause of Magna Carta that no man shall be condemned save by lawful judgment of his peers or by the law of the land. The statute (1328) 2 Ed. III c. 8 stated that the great or little seal shall not be used to disturb or delay common rights, and if it is done, the judges shall ignore it. (1331) 5 Ed. III c. 9 opposes proceedings contrary to Magna Carta and the law of the land. (1350) 25 Ed. III St. 5, c. 4 states that none shall be taken by petition or suggestion to the king or his Council except by indictment or presentment of good and lawful people from the same neighbourhood where the deed was done in due manner or process by original writ at common law. Also, no forfeiture of property was to occur unless there was a hearing by the course of the law. Other statutes to the same effect include (1354) 28 Ed. III c. 3 and (1368) 42 Ed. III c. 3. These measures prevented Council from dealing with questions of freehold property determined by common law courts in real actions, and questions of treason or felony involving the death penalty and forfeiture of freehold. Thus, it could only give minor corporal punishments and fines. As a result, the most serious crimes were tried by common law courts and the prisoner received a fairer trial than under the inquisitorial system in which torture played an important part. See also Holdsworth, *English Law,* 1:487–90.

3 See for example Holdsworth, *English Law,* 1:490.

4 Ehrilch, Vinogradoff, cited in Holdsworth, *English Law,* 2:449.

5 8 Rich. II c. 4; R.P. iii 164 (7 Rich. II no. 57); Holdsworth, *English Law,* 2:457–8.

6 Bacon, *History of Henry VII*; Hudson, *Star Chamber*; Lambard; Hawarde, cited in Holdsworth, *English Law,* 4:85–7.

7 For example, Bacon held such fears.

8 Holdsworth, *English Law,* 4:70.

9 In his *Fourth Institutes,* 20–1, Coke speaks of the episode in which on the king's direction an Information was preferred against thirty-nine of the members of the Commons for departing without licence. Six submitted themselves to fines, but whether any paid or how small the amount

Notes to pages 184–92

was not known. The greater constitutional issue related to privileges of the Commons to discipline its members. The episode shows that the MPs had no great joy in continuing in Parliament and departed.

10 Holdsworth, *English Law*, 1:380–1.

11 31 Hy. VIII c. 8, amended by 34 and 35 Hy. VIII c. 23.

12 Hale, cited in Holdsworth, *English Law*, 4:33–8, 368.

13 *The Case of Monopolies* (1602) 11 Co. Rep. 84b–88b; also cited in *Darcy v. Allen*, Moore K.B. 671–5; *Darcy v. Allin*, Noy 173–85.

14 (1637) 3 S.T. 825, 1235–7, 1230–1, per Finch C.J.

15 Parliamentary Debates (1610) (CS) 23–5; Gardiner, *History of England* ii, 67; cited in Holdsworth, *English Law*, 4:23.

16 (1627) 3 S.T. 1.

17 (1615) 2 S.T. 899.

18 1 Rich. III c. 2.

19 See Stubbs, Dowell, cited in Holdsworth, *English Law*, 6:43.

20 *Antiqua Custuma* – export duties on wools, wool-fells, and leather, the rates of which were fixed in 1275. *Nova Custuma* – a further tax on goods exported by aliens, the rates of which were fixed by *Cara Meratoria* of 1303. See Hall, Prisage, and Butlerage, cited in Holdsworth, *English Law*, 6:43. For a detailed description of aids and subsidies, see Coke, *Fourth Institute*, 28 et seq.

21 (1606) 2 S.T. 371. While Bates was English, the imposition was on the currents while in the hands of Venetians, and Bates importing them became liable to pay.

22 16 Car. I, c. 8; 1 Wm. and M., sess. 2 c. 2, s. 1.

23 See R.P. 51 Ed. III, no. 25; Hy. IV no. 22; 8 Hy. V no. 6.

24 (1607) 12 Co. Rep. 12.

25 Holdsworth, 6:251–5.

26 Smith, *De Republica Anglorum*, Bk II, c. 2.

27 Coke, *Fourth Institute*, cited in Holdsworth, *English Law*, 6:88.

28 Redlich, *Procedure of the House of Commons* 2:4, cited in Holdsworth, *English Law*, 6:89.

29 For example, the Short Parliament insisted on the privilege to control its business and refused to vote supplies before peace was made with Scotland and grievances redressed. That was a main cause of the dissolution of the Short Parliament in 1640.

30 "Apology of the House of Commons," 1604, in Prothero, *Select Documents*, 278–9, cited in Holdsworth, *English Law*, 6:94.

31 For example, in 1621 James I told the Commons that these privileges were not their ancient and undoubted right, but derived "from the grace

286   Notes to pages 192–5

and permission of himself and his ancestors for most of them grow from precedents, which shows rather a toleration than inheritance." He also warned that if they persisted in trenching upon his prerogative, he would trench upon their privileges. Letter of the king, Dec. 1621, Prothero, *Select Documents*, 313, cited in Holdsworth, *English Law*, 6:94.

32   For example, Bacon argued (debate on Impositions 1610, 2 S.T. 398) that it is conjecture that the more ancient customs were by Act of Parliament, as Acts of Parliament were infrequent before Magna Carta (9 Hy. III). Therefore, the ancient custom was by common law. The only way for it to arise is by the king.

  The contrary view was stated by Pym in 1628 (3 S.T. 341) that the law of England whereby the subject is exempted from taxes or laws was not granted by common consent of Parliament, was not introduced by statute, or any charter or sanction of the princes, but was the ancient and fundamental law issuing from the first time and constitution of the kingdom.

33   Y.B. 33 Hy. VI Pasch. pl. 8, p. 18.

34   May, *Law and Practice of Parliament* (11th ed), 46, cited in Holdsworth, *English Law*, 6:256.

35   31, 32 Vict. c. 125.

36   Redlich, *Procedure of the House of Commons*, 1:55, n. 1, cited in Holdsworth, *English Law*, 10:533.

37   Even prior to the Revolution, members of the Lords and Commons, and their servants, had large immunities from being sued while Parliament was sitting and for forty days after a session, which was particularly a denial of justice when Parliament was in perpetual session. See for example Coke, *Fourth Institute*, 9 and 25, who states that by statute of 4 Hy. VIII all litigation or execution on any member of Parliament was void, which clause is declaratory of the ancient law and custom of Parliament. The MP has privilege and neither he nor his servants, nor his goods are subject to execution. There was also an immunity from sub poena. See also Holdsworth, *English Law*, 1:382; 6:256–7. Thus, the Act of 1700 was passed to allow personal actions against these members and their servants after dissolution or prorogation, or adjournment for more than fourteen days until Parliament assembled.

38   R.P. v. 339 (32 Hy. VI no. 26).

39   (1694) 1 Ld. Raym. 10.

40   (1704) 2 Ld. Raym. 938.

41   (1705) 2 Ld. Raym 1105.

42   (1705) 2 Ld. Raym 1105, 1112.

Notes to pages 195–210   287

43   Erskine May, *Treatise on the Law, Privileges, Proceedings and Usage of Parliament*, (London: Butterworth, 1971), 126.

44   (1839) 9 A. and E. 1.

45   (1840) 11 A. and E. 273.

46   (1884) 12 Q.B.D. 271.

47   Gardiner, *Documents*, cited in Holdsworth, *English Law*, 6:100.

48   Edmund Burke, *Reflections on the French Revolution*, 28; Holdsworth, *English Law*, 6:4.

49   See for example Dicey, *Law of the Constitution*; Geoffrey Marshall, *Constitutional Conventions: The Rules and Forms of Political Accountability* (Oxford: Oxford University Press, 1986); Ivor Jennings, *The Law and the Constitution*, 5th ed. (London: University of London Press Ltd, 1959); Andrew Heard, *Canadian Constitutional Conventions* (Toronto: Oxford University Press, 1991).

50   Dicey, *Law of the Constitution*, chs. 14, 15.

51   Andrew Heard, *Canadian Constitutional Conventions* (Toronto: Oxford University Press, 1991), 2–3.

52   Ivor Jennings, *The Law and the Constitution*, 5th ed. (London: University of London Press, Ltd, 1959), 73, 81, 86–91, 102, 127, 135.

53   Geoffrey Marshall, *Constitutional Conventions: The Rules and Forms of Political Accountability* (Oxford: Oxford University Press, 1986), 2–4.

54   See for example Heard, *Canadian Conventions*, vii, 14, 143–5.

55   Holdsworth, *English Law*, 10:631.

CHAPTER SEVEN

1   Blackstone's *Commentaries*, 1:269.

2   Charles de Secondat Montesquieu, *De L'Esprit des Lois*, text established and presented by Jean Brèthe de la Gressaye (Paris: Les Belle Lettres, 1950–61), Bk. XI, chap. VI.

3   Plucknett, *Common Law*, 63.

4   Holdsworth, *English Law*, 4:152.

5   Ibid., 6:58–60.

6   Edmund Burke, *Present Discontents, Works* (Bohn's ed.) I, 313, 350; cited in Holdsworth, *English Law*, 10:100–1.

7   See for example Holdsworth, *English Law*, 10:419.

8   Ibid., 10:102.

9   22 Geo. III c. 45.

10   22 Geo. III c. 41.

11   10 Geo. IV c. 7.

288   Notes to pages 210–27

12   See for example Holdsworth, *English Law*, 10:565, 602.

13   *An Act to Amend the Representation of the People in England and Wales* 1832 2, 3 Wm. IV c. 45.

14   1 Geo. III c. 1.

15   Holdsworth, *English Law*, 10:423.

16   Ibid., 10:630.

17   Ibid., 10:412.

18   Anson, *Parliament* (2nd ed.), 287; cited in Holdsworth, *English Law*, 10:412.

19   Cited in Holdsworth, *English Law*, 10:412.

20   Ibid.

21   Neville's 1680 treatise, cited in Firth, *The House of Lords during the Civil War*, 296; Holdsworth, *English Law*, 6:247–8.

22   For example, Holdsworth provides two illustrations. First, the Lords rejecting the Exclusion Bill in 1680 was the action expected of a second chamber that was not convinced the country had made up its mind on the matter. Second, its conduct in giving way to the Commons in 1688 and accepting its resolution with respect to the vacancy of the throne was the action expected of a second chamber that had reason to think the Commons has the nation behind it and that knew a decision was a matter of great urgency.

23   *Commons Journal* ix, 509, cited in Porritt, *The Unreformed Parliament I*, 550–54; cited in Holdsworth, *English Law*, 6:250.

24   Holdsworth, *English Law*, 6:250–1.

25   Cited in Holdsworth, *English Law*, 10:591.

26   Fortescue, *Papers of George III*, cited in Holdsworth, *English Law*, 10:636.

27   Holdsworth, *English Law*, 10:592.

28   Ibid., 6:262.

29   Ibid., 10:460–1.

30   Ibid., 10:484–5.

31   Ibid., 10:466.

32   Anson, *The Crown*, cited in Holdsworth, *English Law*, 10:642–3.

33   Ibid., 10:643.

34   Thomas Erskine May, *The Constitutional History of England since the Accession of George the Third, 1760–1860* (Littleton, CO: F.B. Rothman, 1986), 2:384; Plucknett, *Common Law*, 73.

35   2 Wm. IV. c. 39.

36   3, 4 Wm. IV c. 27, s. 36.

37   Plucknett, *Common Law*, 210.

Notes to pages 228–33 289

38 Ibid., 210–11.

39 4, 5 A., c. 3.

40 (1789) 3 Term Rep. 151.

41 *An Act for the Further Amendment of the Process, Practice, and Mode of Pleading in and Enlarging the Jurisdiction of the Superior Courts of Common Law at Westminster, and of the Superior Courts of Common Law of the Counties Palantine of Lancaster and Durham* (1854), 17, 18 Vict. c. 125, s. 22 – how far a party may discredit his own witness (Adverse), s. 68 – Action for Mandamus to enforce the performance of duties, s. 79 – claim of Writ of Injunction, s. 83 – equitable defence may be pleaded.

42 *An Act for the Constitution of a Supreme Court, and for Other Purposes Relating to the Better Administration of Justice in England; and to Authorize the Transfer to the Appellate Division of Such Supreme Court of the Jurisdiction of the Judicial Committee of Her Majesty's Privy Council* 36, 37 Vict. c. 66, ss. 3, 4, 16 – jurisdiction of High Court of Justice as a Superior Court of Record and s. 18 – jurisdiction transferred to Court of Appeal; by 38, 39 Vict. c. 77, s. 9 the London Court of Bankruptcy was not merged into the Supreme Court, but again merged by 46, 47 Vict. c. 52, s. 93.

43 36, 37 Vict. c. 66, s. 9; and 38, 39 Vict. c. 77, s. 5 – concerning Master of the Rolls.

44 36, 37 Vict. c. 65, s. 23 – rules as to the exercise of jurisdiction, and Sched. of Rules of Procedure; *An Act for Amending the Law in Respect of the Appellate Jurisdiction of the House of Lords; and for Other Purposes* (1876), 39, 40 Vict. c. 59, s. 17 – regulations as to the business of the High Court; *An Act to Amend the Supreme Court of Judicature Acts* (1881), 44, 45 Vict. c. 68, s. 19 – power to make rules under 39, 40 Vict. c. 59; 56, 57 Vict. c. 66; 57, 58 Vict. c. 59, s. 17.

45 Holdsworth, *English Law*, 1:468–9, 6:547.

46 23 Geo. III, c. 33.

47 9, 10 Vict., c. 95.

48 Plucknett, *Common Law*, 208–9.

49 (1696) 2 Vern., at p. 342. For a general discussion on the topic see Holdsworth, *English Law*, 1:475, 5:315.

50 *In re Spence* (1848) 2 Ph. 247, at 251, per Cottenham, L.C.; cp *The Queen v. Gyngall*, [1893] 2 Q.B., at 240, per Esher, M.R., and at 246–47 per Kay, L.J.

51 Holdsworth, *English Law*, 6:648.

52 Ibid., 2:512, 3:623–4, 627–33.

53 Ibid., 10:151.

54   Ibid., 2:431–4; 4:174–8; 6:88–92, 255–6.
55   Sidney Webb and Beatrice Webb, *The Parish and the County* (Hamden, CT: Archon Books, 1963), 534; Holdsworth, *English Law*, 10:234.
56   Holdsworth, *English Law*, 10:256.
57   (1514–15) 6 Hy. VIII. c. 6.
58   (1575) 18 Eliz. c. 12.
59   43 Eliz. c. 5.
60   43 Eliz. c. 6.
61   21 James I c. 23.
62   Hart, cited in Goldsworthy, *Parliament*, 241.

CONCLUSION

1   Christopher Edward Taucar, "Standards of Judicial Review of Administrative Bodies: The Consideration of Citizen Participation," *Canadian Public Administration* 53, no. 1 (March 2010): 67.
2   *Reference re Remuneration of Judges of the Provincial Court of Prince Edward Island; Reference re Independence and Impartiality of Judges of the Provincial Court of Prince Edward Island;* and *R. v. Campbell; R. v. Ekmecic; R. v. Wickman* and *Manitoba Provincial Judges Association v. Manitoba (Minister of Justice)*, [1997] 3 S.C.R. 3.
3   Berman, *Law and Revolution*, vi. This sort of process has been seen in other countries as well. See, for example, Niel Nevette, *The Decline of Deference: Canadian Value Changes in Cross-National Perspective* (Peterborough, ON: Broadview Press, 1996).

Bibliography

CASES

Abbot of Strata Marcella, 10 Co. Rep. 24a.
A.-G. v. Jonathan Cape Ltd., [1976] Q.B. 752.
Ashby v. White (1704), 2 Ld. Raym. 938.
Bates's Case (1606), 2 S.T. 371.
Beecher's Case (1609), 8 Co. Rep., 60b.
Bradlaugh v. Gosset (1884), 12 Q.B.D. 271.
Bribery Commissioner v. Ranasinghe, [1965] A.C. 172.
Bridgman v. Holt (1693), Sower P.C. 111.
British Coal Corp. v. The King, [1935] A.C. 500.
Calvin's Case (1609), 7 Co. Rep. 13a, 25a.
Case of Captain John Streater (1653), 5 *St. Tr.* 386.
Case of Monopolies (1602), 11 Co. Rep. 84b.
Case of Non Obstante (1611), 12 Co. Rep. 18.
Case of Penal Statutes (1605), 7 Co. Rep. 36.
Case of Proclamations (1611), 12 Co. Rep. at p. 76.
Case of Ship Money (1637), 3 S.T. 825, pp. 1235–7, 1230–1.
Chudleigh's Case (1595), 1 Coke's Reports 120a; 76 E.R. 270.
Coggs v. Bernard (1703), 2 Ld. Raym. 909.
Cook v. Fountain (1672), 3 Swanst. 585.
Corporation of Burford v. Lenthall (1743), 2 Atk. 551.
Darcy v. Allen, Moore K.B. 671–5.
Darcy v. Allin, Noy 173–85.
Darnel's Case (1627), 3 S.T. 1.
Day v. Savadge (1614), Hobart 85, 80 E.R. 235.
Dowsdale's Case (1606), Co. Rep. 47b.

292 Bibliography

Dr. Bonham (1609), 8 Co. Rep. 107a 77 E.R. 638.

Dr. Bonham (1609), 8 Co. Rep. 113b 77 E.R. 646

Earl of Leicester v. Heydon, during 13 Eliz., *Plowden* 384.

Edgcomb v. Dee (1670), Vaughan, 101.

Falkland v. Bertie (1696), 2 Vern., at p. 342.

Godden v. Hales (1686), 11 S.T. 116, 1261–7.

Godfrey's Case (1615), 11 Co. Rep., at 43b.

Grand Junction Canal Co. v. Dimes (1849), 23 Beav. 63, 50 E.R. 984 (Chancery).

Hampden's Case (1637), 3 S.T. 825.

Heath v. Rydley (1614), Cro. Jac. 335.

Heathfield v. Chilton (1767), 4 Burr. at p. 2106.

Hodge v. R. (1883), 9 A.C. 117.

In re Spence (1848), 2 Ph. 247.

Jentlemean's Case (1583), 6 Co. Rep. 11.

Liquidators of the Maritime Band of Canada v. Receiver-General of New Brunswick, [1892] A.C. 437.

Madzimbamuto v. Lardner-Burke, [1969] 1 A.C. 645 (P.C.).

Manuel v. Attorney-General, [1893] Ch. 77 (C.A.).

Oliver St. John (1615), 2 S.T. 899.

Parish of Great Charter v. Parish of Kennington (1742), 2 Strange 1173, 93 E.R. 1107 (K.B.).

Paty's Case (1705), 2 Ld. Raym 1105.

Provincial Court Judges' Assn. of New Brunswick v. New Brunswick (Minister of Justice); Ontario Judges' Assn. v. Ontario (Management Board); Bodner v. Alberta; Conférence des juges du Québec v. Quebec (Attorney General); Minc v. Quebec (Attorney General), [2005] 2 S.C.R. 285, 2005 S.C.C. 44.

R. v. Bishop of Chichester (1365), Y.B. 39 Ed. III Pasch., pl. 7.

R. v. Knollys (1694), 1 Ld. Raym. at p. 15; *Rex v. Knollys* (1695), (1695) Skin, at p. 526.

Read v. Brookman (1789), 3 Term Rep. 151.

Reference re Amendment of the Constitution of Canada (1982), 125 D.L.R. (3rd) 1 (S.C.C.).

Reference re Remuneration of Judges of the Provincial Court of Prince Edward Island; Reference re Independence and Impartiality of Judges of the Provincial Court of Prince Edward Island; and R. v. Campbell; R. v. Ekmecic; R. v. Wickman and Manitoba Provincial Judges Association v. Manitoba (Minister of Justice), [1997] 3 S.C.R. 3. (*Remuneration Reference*).

Sheriff of Middlesex (1840), 11 A. and E.273.

Slade's Case (1602), 4 Rep. 92b.

Stockdale v. Hansard (1839), 9 A. and E. 1 (K.B.), 112 E.R. 1112.

The Case of the City of London (1610), 8 Co. Rep. 121b; 77 E.R. 658.

The City of London v. Wood (1701), 12 Mod. 669, 88 E.R. 1592.

The Prince's Case (1605), 8 Co. Rep. 19.

The Queen v. Gyngall, [1893] 2 Q.B., at pp. 240, 246–7.

Thomas v. Sorrell (1677), Vaughan Reports 330, 124 E.R. 1098.

Thorpe's Case R.P. v 339 (32 Hy. VI no. 26).

Trewynard's Case 36–7 Hy. VIII, *Dyer* fol 60a.

Triquet v. Bath (1764), 3 Burr. at p. 1480.

Valin v. Langois (1879), 3 S.C.R. 1.

Year Books of the reign of King Edward the First (Roll Series). Originally published 1866 by Her Majesty's Stationary Office, London. Kraus Reprint Ltd., 1964.

Year Books of Edward II (Selden Society). London: B Quaritch, 1917.

Year Books of the reign of King Edward the Third (Roll Series). Originally published 1866 by Her Majesty's Stationary Office, London. Kraus Reprint Ltd., 1964.

Year Books of the reign of Edward the Fourth, Pasch. pl. 23; Mich. pl. 21.

Year Books of Henry III. London: Selden Society, 2002.

PRINTED SOURCES

Alexander, Larry. "Of Living Trees and Dead Hands: The Interpretation of Constitutional Rights." London, ON: the Oxford Lecture at the University of Western Ontario Law School, 26 November 2008.

Anson, William R. *The Law and Custom of the Constitution.* 2 vols. Oxford, UK: The Clarendon Press, 1922–35.

Aquinas, Thomas. *Summa Theologica.* Literally translated by Fathers of Dominican province. London: Burns Oats and Washbourne, 1912–25.

– *Summa Contra Gentiles.* Notre Dame, IN: University of Notre Dame Press, 1975.

Apology of the House of Commons, 1604.

Augustine of Hippo. *De Doctrina Christiana.* Translated with an introduction by D.W. Robertson Jr. New York: Liberal Arts Press, 1958.

- *The City of God*. Translated by John Healey. Vols. I and II. [1610] Edinburgh: J. Grant, 1909.
- *The Confessions of St. Augustine*. Translated by E.B. Pusey, with a foreword by A.H. Armstrong. London: J.M. Dent; New York: E.P. Dutton, 1907.
Arthurs, H.W. *'Without the Law': Administrative Justice and Legal Pluralism in Nineteenth-Century England*. Toronto: University of Toronto Press, 1985.
Baar, Carl. "The Emergence of the Judiciary as an Institution." *Journal of Judicial Administration* 8 (1999): 216.
Bacon, Francis. (Debate on Impositions). 1610, 2 S.T. 398.
- *The Works of Francis Bacon*. Collected and edited by James Spedding et al. Vols. I, II, III. Boston: Brown and Taggard, 1860–64.
- *Bacon's History of the Reign of King Henry VII*. With notes by the Rev. J. Rawson Lamby. London: Cambridge University Press, 1902.
Bagehot, Walter. *The English Constitution*. London: Oxford University Press, H. Milford, 1933.
Berman, Howard J. *Law and Revolution: The Formation of the Western Legal Tradition*. Cambridge, MA: Harvard University Press, 1983.
- *Law and Revolution II: The Impact of the Protestant Reformations on the Western Legal Tradition*. Cambridge, MA: The Belknap Press of Harvard University Press, 2003.
William Blackstone. *Commentaries on the Law of England: In Four Books*. With the last corrections of the author and notes and additions by Edward Christian. New York: E. Duycknick, 1822.
Bodin, Jean. *Les six livres de la republique*. Paris: Chez lacques du Puys, 1579.
Bracton, Henry de. *Bracton's Note Book: A Collection of Cases Decided in the King's Courts during the Reign of Henry the Third*. Annotated by a lawyer of the time, seemingly by Henry of Bracton, and edited by F.W. Maitland. Littleton, CO: F.B. Rothman, 1983.
- *On the Laws and Customs of England*. Translated with revisions and notes by Samuel E. Thorne. Cambridge, MA: The Belknap Press of Harvard University Press in association with the Selden Society, 1983.
"Brutus." Essay XV, from the *Anti-Federalist Papers*.
Burke, Edmund. *Reflections on the Revolution in France*. Edited with an introduction and notes by L.G. Mitchell. Oxford and New York: Oxford University Press, 1999.

Bibliography

– *Thoughts on the cause of the present discontents.* Edited with introduction and notes by F.G. Selby. London: Macmillan, 1902.

Catechism of the Catholic Church, 2nd ed. Revised in accordance with the official Latin text promulgated by Pope John Paul II. Vatican City: Libreria Editrice Vaticana, 1994, 1997, 2000.

Chrimes, S.B. "Introductory Essay." In *A History of English Law*, vol. I, edited by William Holdsworth. London: Methuen & Co. and Sweet & Maxwell Ltd., 1996.

Coke, Edward. *Part One of the Reports.* In *The Selected Writings of Sir Edward Coke*, edited by Steve Sheppard. Indianapolis, IN: Liberty Fund, Inc., 2003.

– *Part Two of the Reports.*

– *Part Three of the Reports.*

– *Part Four of the Reports.*

– *Part Five of the Reports.*

– *Part Six of the Reports.*

– *Part Seven of the Reports.*

– *Part Eight of the Reports.*

– *Part Nine of the Reports.*

– *Part Ten of the Reports.*

– *Part Eleven of the Reports.*

– *Institutes of the Laws of England, First Part of the Institutes.*

– *Second Part of the Institutes.*

– *Third Part of the Institutes.*

– *Fourth Part of the Institutes.*

– (1608) 12 Co. Rep. 65.

– (1607) 12 Co. Rep. 12.

Cohen, Hymen Ezra. *Recent Theories of Sovereignty.* Chicago: University of Chicago Press, 1937.

Crump, C.G., and E.F. Jacob, eds. *Legacy of the Middle Ages.* Oxford, UK: The Clarendon Press, 1943.

Dicey, A.V. *Introduction to the Study of the Law of the Constitution*, 10th ed. Contains the last edition written in 1914. London: MacMillan & Co. Ltd., 1965.

Earl of Albermarle. Royal Letters (RS) I. No. 16.

Elton, G.R. *The Parliament of England 1559–1581.* Cambridge, UK: Cambridge University Press, 1986.

296   Bibliography

- *Studies in Tudor and Stuart Politics and Government: Papers and Reviews 1946–1972*, Vol. II. Cambridge, UK: Cambridge University Press, 1974.
- *The Tudor Constitution: Documents and Commentary*, 2nd ed. Cambridge, UK: Cambridge University Press, 1982.

Figgis, John Nevill. *Divine Right of Kings*, 2nd ed. Cambridge, UK: Cambridge University Press, 1922.

Finch's Law, or, a Discourse Thereof: In Foure Bookes. London: Printed [by Adam Islip] for the Societie of Stationers, 1627.

Finnis, John. *Natural Law and Natural Rights*, 2nd ed. Oxford and New York: Oxford University Press, 2011.

Fleta. Edited with a translation by H.G. Richardson and G.O. Sayless. London: B Quartich, 1955–72.

Foster, Elizabeth Reed, ed. *Proceedings in Parliament 1610*: Vol. 2, *House of Commons*. New Haven, CT: Yale University Press, 1966.

Friedland, M.L. *A Place Apart: Judicial Independence and Accountability in Canada* (A Report Prepared for the Canadian Judicial Council). Ottawa: Canadian Judicial Council, 1995.

Glanvill, Ranulf de. *Treatise on the Laws and Customs of the Realm of England: Commonly called Glanvill*. Edited with introduction, notes, and translation by G.D.G. Hall. London: Nelson, 1965.

Gneist, Rudolf. *The English Parliament: In Its Transformations through a Thousand Years*. Translated by Jenery Shee. London: H. Grevel & Co., 1886.

Goldsworthy, Jeffrey. *The Sovereignty of Parliament: History and Philosophy*. New York: Oxford University Press, 1999.

Gough, J.W. *Fundamental Law in English Constitutional History*. London: Oxford University Press, 1961.

Greene, Ian. *The Courts*. Vancouver: University of British Columbia Press [Canadian Democratic Audit Project], 2006.

Greene, Ian, et al. *Final Appeal: Decision-Making in Canadian Courts of Appeal*. Toronto: James Lorimer and Co., 1997.

Hale, Matthew. "Reflections by the Lrd. Cheife Justice Hale on Mr. Hobbes His Dialogue of the Lawe." Also reproduced in Appendix III – William Holdsworth, *A History of English Law,* Vol. V. London: Methuen & Co. and Sweet & Maxwell Ltd., 1996.

Hallam, Henry. *The Constitutional History of England: From the Accession of Henry VII to the Death of George II*, in two volumes, 6th ed. London: John Murray, Albemarle Street, 1850.

Bibliography 297

Hamburger, Philip A. "Revolution and Judicial Review: Chief Justice Holt's Opinion in *City of London v. Wood.*" *Columbia Law Review* (1994): 2091.

Hamilton, Alexander, *The Federalist Papers,* number 78.

Hart, H.L.A. *The Concept of the Law.* Oxford, UK: Oxford University Press, 1961.

Heard, Andrew. *Canadian Constitutional Conventions.* Toronto: Oxford University Press, 1991.

Hedley's Speech. In *Proceedings in Parliament 1610,* edited by Elizabeth Reed Foster, 172–4.

Historical Manuscripts Commission. *XIIth Report*, Appendix VI.

Hobbes, Thomas. *The English Works of Thomas Hobbes of Malmesbury,* Vol. VI. Collected and edited by William Molesworth. London: John Bohn, 1839–45; Aalen, Germany: Scientia, 1966.

– *Leviathan.* London: J.M. Dent, [1924?].

Hogg, Peter W. *Constitutional Law of Canada,* 2009. Toronto: Thomson Reuters Canada Limited, 2009.

Holdsworth, William. *A History of English Law.* Vols. I–VI, IX, X. London: Methuen & Co. and Sweet & Maxwell Ltd., 1996.

The Holy Bible. The New Revised Standard Version. Scarborough, ON: Thomas Nelson Publishers, 1993.

Holmes, Oliver Wendel. *Common Law.* Boston: Little Brown, 1923.

Jennings, Ivor. *The Law of the Constitution,* 4th ed. London: University of London Press, 1952.

– *The Law and the Constitution,* 5th ed. London: University of London Press Ltd., 1959.

Lambard, William. *Archeion, or a Discourse upon the High Courts of Justice in England.* Edited by Charles H. McIlwain and Paul L. Ward. Cambridge, MA: Harvard University Press, 1957.

Lederman, W.R. "The Independence of the Judiciary." *Canadian Bar Review* 34 (1956): 769–809; 1139–79.

Lewis, C.S. *Mere Christianity.* London: Collins, 1955.

– *Abolition of Man: or, Reflections on Education with Special Reference to the Teaching of English in the Upper Forms of Schools.* New York: Macmillan, 1955.

Locke, John. *Second Treatise on Government.* New York: Library of Liberal Arts, 1962. 51c. 1699.

– *Two Treatises of Government,* Book II. Introduction by W.S. Carpenter. London: Dent, 1924.

Maitland, F.W. *The Forms of Action at Common Law, 1909* (Lectures). Accessed October 2011. http//:www.fordham.edu/halsall/basis/maitland-formsofaction.asp.

– *The Constitutional History of England*. Cambridge: University Press, 1919.

Manegold of Lautenbach. *Liber ad Gebehardum*. 1085 AD.

Mangalwadi, Vishal. *The Book that Made Your World: How the Bible Created the Soul of Western Civilization*. Nashville, TN: Thomas Nelson, 2011.

Marshall, Geoffrey. *Constitutional Conventions: The Rules and Forms of Political Accountability*. Oxford, UK: Oxford University Press, 1986.

Marshall, Geoffrey, and Graeme Moodie. *Some Problems of the Canadian Constitution*. London: Hutchinson, 1959.

May, Erskine. *Treatise on the Law, Privileges, Proceedings and Usage of Parliament*. London: Butterworth, 1971.

– *A Treatise on the Law, Privileges, Proceedings and Usage of Parliament*, 11th ed. London: W. Clowes and Sons, 1906.

– *The Constitutional History of England since the Accession of George the Third, 1760–1860*, Vol. II. Littleton, CO: F.B. Rothman, 1986.

McIlwain, Charles Howard. *The High Court of Parliament and Its Supremacy: An Historical Essay on the Boundaries Between Legislation and Adjudication in England*. New Haven, CT: Yale University Press, 1919.

Montesquieu, Charles de Secondat. *De L'Esprit des Lois*. Text established and presented by Jean Brèthe de la Gressaye. Paris: Les Belles Lettres, 1950–61.

Nevette, Niel. *The Decline of Deference: Canadian Value Changes in Cross-National Perspective*. Peterborough, ON: Broadview Press, 1996.

Parliamentary Debates (1610) (CS) 23–5.

Petyt, William. *The Antient Right of the Commons Asserted*. 1680.

– Petyt's address in January 1689 to the House of Lords in respect of the Commons resolution asking them to agree that James had broken the original contract between king and people. *Historical Manuscripts Commission, XIIth Report*, Appendix VI, pp. 14 ff.

Plucknett, Theodore F.T. *A Concise History of the Common Law*, 5th ed. Boston: Little, Brown and Company, 1956.

– *A Concise History of the Common Law,* 3rd ed. London: Butterworth and Co., 1940.

- "Bonham's Case and Judicial Review." *Harvard Law Review* 40, no. 1 (November 1926): 30.
- *Statutes and Their Interpretation in the First Half of the Fourteenth Century*. Buffalo, NY: W.S. Hein, 1980.

Pocock, J.G.A. *The Ancient Constitution and the Feudal Law: A Study of English Historical Thought in the Seventeenth Century – A Reissue with a Retrospect*. Cambridge, UK: Cambridge University Press, 1987.

Prynne, William. *Animadversion on the Fourth Part of Coke's Institutes*. London: Printed for T. Ratcliffe and T. Daniel, for A. Crooke, W. Leake, A. Roper, [etc.], 1669.
- *Soveraigne Power of Parliaments and Kingdomes: Divided into Fovre Parts*, together with an Appendix. New York: Garland Pub., 1979.

Pym, John. As reported in 1628, 3 S.T. 341.

Redlich, Josef. *Procedure of the House of Commons, a study of its history and present form*, Volumes I–III. Translated by A. Ernest Steinthal, with an introduction and supplementary chapter by Sir Courtenay Ilbert. London: Constable, 1908.

Sheppard, Steve, ed. *The Selected Writings of Sir Edward Coke*. Indianapolis, IN: Liberty Fund, Inc., 2003.

Shetreet, Shimon, and Jules Deschênes, eds. *Judicial Independence: The Contemporary Debate*. Dordrecht, Netherlands: Martinus Nihhoff Publishers, 1985.

Shetreet, Shimon. *Judges on Trial: A Study of the Accountability of the English Judiciary*. Ansterdam: North Holland Pub. Co., 1976.

Smith, Thomas. *De Republica Anglorum: A Discourse on the Commonwealth of England*. Edited by L. Alston. Cambridge, UK: Cambridge University Press, 1906.

St. Germain. *Doctor and Student. Two Dialogues in English between a Doctor of Divinity, and a Student of the Laws of England: of the Roads of the Said Laws and of Conscience*. London: Printed by the assigns of R. and E. Atkins, 1709.

Stubbs, William. *The Constitutional History of England in its origin and development*, 5th ed. Vols. I and II. Oxford, UK: Clarenden Press, 1891.

Taucar, Christopher Edward. *Canadian Federalism and Quebec Sovereignty*. New York: Peter Lang Publishing, Inc., 2004.
- "Standards of Judicial Review of Administrative Bodies: The Consideration of Citizen Participation." *Canadian Political Administration*, vol. 53, no. 1 (March 2010): 67.

Todd, Alpheus. *Parliamentary Government in England*. London: Longmans, Green and Co., 1867.

Vipond, Robert C. "1787 and 1867: The Federal Principle and Canadian Confederation Reconsidered." *Canadian Journal of Political Science 3*, vol. 22, no. 1 (March 1989).

Walters, Mark. "The Common Law Constitution in Canada: Return of *Lex Non Scripta* as Fundamental Law." *University of Toronto Law Journal* 91 (2001).

Webb, Sidney, and Beatrice Webb. *The Parish and the County*. Introduction by B. Keith-Lucas. Hamden, CT: Archon Books, 1963.

Wheare, K.C. *Federal Government*, 3rd ed. London: Oxford University Press, 1953.

Index

Act of Settlement, 131–3, 141, 142, 204, 208, 222, 228, 276n72

Aquinas, St Thomas, 22, 252n4

Bacon, Francis, 153–4, 189, 280n64, 286n32

Becket, Archbishop, 38, 157

Bill of Rights, 130–3, 189, 276n72

Blackstone, William, 24, 46, 57, 61, 86, 135, 143, 144, 157, 159, 162, 165–6, 170, 203, 209, 252n4, 260n86

Bracton, Henry de, 24, 49, 53, 56–7, 62, 63, 93, 252n4, 254n24, 260n96, 264n45

Burke, Edmond, 141, 196, 202, 208, 209

cabinet government, 141, 204, 207, 208, 214, 215, 217, 220–5

Chancery or Chancellor. *See* equity

Christianity and the Church, influences of, 6, 17–23, 24, 25, 38, 41, 44, 45–6, 60, 71, 72, 75–7, 93, 101–2, 111–12, 124, 133, 135, 146, 157, 252n4, 253n3, 264–5n45

Church as independent of the State, 103–4. *See also* Magna Carta

Coke, Edward, 23, 31, 39, 54, 60, 66, 67, 72, 82–3, 84–5, 133–4, 255n24, 267–8n70; general discussion and legal criticism concerning, 154–7, 159

common law: contracts, 18, 21, 22, 254–5n24; criminal law, 20, 21; development, post-Conquest, 37–40, 42, 45–6, 48–9, 59, 61, 65, 95, 99–100, 102, 125, 133; intention, concept of, 20, 21; meaning of, 46–8, 51–2, 61; narrowing scope of, 50–1, 64, 70–2; pre-Conquest early development and influences, 18, 20–1, 24; trial, jury, or proof, 20, 21, 24, 28, 38, 44, 51–2, 60–1, 62, 81, 153, 279n51; writs and the writ system, 40–2, 49, 55, 62, 68, 72–4, 77, 82, 259n69

common law theories of the state or 'fundamental law,' 122–3, 129–30. *See also* Hale

Commons. *See* House of Commons

Conquest of 1066, debates about and their significance, 30–6, 257n48–9

Constitution, 7, 8, 253n6

constitutional conventions, 12–13, 141, 175, 196–201, 214–15; responsible government, 193, 198, 200–1, 208–9, 213, 215–16, 219–20, 224–5. *See also* cabinet government

Council, 11, 12, 81, 83–4, 85, 93, 102–3, 106–7, 131, 180–3, 284n2

courts: Canadian, 118, 172, 245; Common Pleas, 64–5, 67; communal, local, franchise, 23, 80–1 (see also *Quo Warranto*); development of common law courts, 43–4, 58–9, 69–70, 107; inherent powers, 149, 229–30, 233–5, 267n63; jurisdiction, 4–5, 9, 10, 14, 26, 29, 41, 42, 47–8, 50–2, 55–6, 64–7, 69–77, 77–8, 83–4, 86–7, 91, 95, 105, 120–1, 148–9, 151, 159, 164, 166, 169, 174, 175, 230, 239, 243, 260n98; King's Bench, 64–8, 69; myths and fallacies, 168–71, 171–2, 173, 175; nature of, 10, 11, 35, 50, 52–3, 61–4, 69, 74–5, 91, 166, 169, 171, 173, 232–3, 238–9; pre-Conquest, 23, 27–8; reforms, 226–9

Curia Regis, 37, 40, 42–4, 58–9, 62, 63, 66, 74, 151, 179–81

custom or customary law, 19, 23, 24, 25–6, 37, 38, 39, 48–9, 63, 104, 145, 146, 151, 169–70, 174–5

Declaration of 27 May 1642, 124

Dicey, A.V., 46, 140, 143–4, 150, 166, 197–8

differentiation within government, 10, 50, 58–61, 65–6, 93, 182

divine law and its influences, 7, 8, 10, 11, 19, 22, 55–6, 76–7, 104, 110, 112, 119, 130–1, 133, 136, 142–3, 144, 146–7, 150, 157–8, 239, 252n4, 252–3n5. *See also* natural law

divine right of kings. *See* royalists and their theories

Dr. Bonham, 154, 156–7, 160, 161, 162

Edward the Confessor, 31, 34, 37–9, 48, 257n48–9, 258n56

equity, 74–7, 264n43; Chancery 81–3

Exchequer Court, 68–9

feudalism, 23, 24, 25, 31–2, 39–40, 42, 45, 63, 92, 145–6, 252n5, 257–8n49

feudum. *See* feudalism

framer intention, 93–4, 109, 114–15, 239, 258n49, 269n8

fundamental law, 150–4, 157, 158–9, 165, 170, 175, 239, 241

Glanvill, Ranulf de, 24, 49, 255n25, 276n81

Glorious Revolution. *See* Revolution of 1688

Great Rebellion and Restoration, 126–9

Hale, Matthew, 35–6, 53, 142, 168

Hobbes, Thomas, 33–4, 36, 123, 141, 142, 143, 147–8, 173

House of Commons: control over finance, 186, 217–18; eliminating controls of the executive on, 207–12; growing autonomy and influence, 183–6, 190–1, 204–5, 209–11, 216–17; powers and privileges (*see under* Parliament); qualifications for, 210

House of Lords, 161–2, 184, 204, 210–11, 216–17, 288n22; powers and privileges (*see under* Parliament)

humanism, 32–3, 256–7n46; humanistic ethics' influence on the English Church, 213–14

impeachment, 132, 183–5

judges, 10, 13, 29, 56–7, 93–4; actions different from law or reasons, 86, 122, 170, 265n45; corruption, illegal behaviour, or unscrupulousness, 53, 67–8, 69, 71–2, 79, 81, 82–5, 86, 108, 121, 125, 129, 134, 159, 170, 172, 181, 182, 203, 227, 239, 245, 246–7, 263n35–6, 266n55, 284n5; jurisdiction, 9, 14; parliamentary committees examining, 106

Judicature Acts. *See* courts: reforms

king. *See* monarchy

law of nature. *See* natural law

Locke, John, 7, 130, 142–3, 146–7, 163, 203–4, 252n4–5

legislation, 37–40, 42–3, 44, 51–2, 73, 93, 95–6, 98, 99, 100, 106, 121, 259n74; early uncertainties about statute, 46–7, 53–5; interpretation, 154, 159, 161, 169, 203, 239, 241, 280n64; relationship to courts (*see* Parliament: relation to courts)

Lords. *See* House of Lords

Magna Carta, 22, 38–9, 59–61, 92–3, 145, 150

ministerial responsibility, 181, 182–5, 200, 209, 212, 215, 219–20

monarch or monarchy, 12, 19, 20, 22, 25, 28, 43, 55–7, 73, 87, 96, 110–13, 116–18, 120, 123–4, 126, 128, 135; succession, 134–5, 274–5n69–70, 275–6n72. *See also* royal prerogative

Montesquieu, Charles de Secondat, 203–4

natural law and its influences, 7, 8, 10, 11, 18–19, 22, 55–6, 76–7, 91, 104, 110–12, 121, 136, 142–3, 144–5, 146–7, 157–8, 161, 162, 163, 164–5, 167–8, 239, 252n4, 252–3n5, 277–8n23. *See also* divine law

Parliament, 5, ch. 3; as highest court, 51, 68, 79, 85, 92–5, 96–100, 107, 121, 140, 145, 149, 192, 269–70n22, 271–2n57, 272n58; as principal guardian of liberty, 121–2, 129, 163, 246; committee system, 195–6; early development, 24–7, 30, 31, 33–4, 42, 92–101; parliamentary sovereignty or supremacy, meaning of, 9, 10, 55–6, 97–100, 102, 103, 104, 105–6, 113–14, 118, 119–21, 131, 135, 144, 145, 147, 153, 154, 158, 159, 162–3, 164, 165–6, 242–3, 279–80n56; parliamentary sovereignty, development of, 34, 42, 59, 141; parliamentary sovereignty, hesitations about, 142–3; 146, 148; parliamentary supremacy doubters, 148–54; parliamentary supremacy, fallacy of coming from court recognition, 139, 170,

171–2, 173, 174, 175; powers and privileges, 96–7, 179, 191–5, 285–6n31, 286n37; relation to courts or common law, 9, 10, 11, 35, 37–40, 42, 47–9, 50–2, 56, 69–70, 77–80, 84, 91–5, 97–8, 100, 105, 106–8, 121, 125, 144, 147, 149, 151, 153, 154, 158, 159, 160–1, 164, 166, 169, 170, 171, 174, 195–6, 227–9, 235; relation to executive, 12, 54, 66, 74, 94, 97, 101, 107, 125–6, 128–9, 204–5, 207–14, 214–22, 225; relation to king, 42, 94, 104, 123–5, 133, 141, 204–5, 206–14, 221–2; taxation, 35, 97, 100, 102, 116, 119, 125, 128, 148, 158, 187–9, 213, 217–18, 190–1, 220–1

parliamentarians and their theories, 30, 109, 118–22
Petition of Right, 117, 125, 127, 137, 156, 188, 189
Petyt, William, 31, 92, 126, 130
prerogative. *See* royal prerogative
proclamation. *See* royal prerogative
property, fundamental right of, 60, 105, 123, 127, 147, 163, 186, 195, 240, 241

queen. *See* monarchy
Quo Warranto episode, 11, 62–4

Reform Act of 1832, 211–12
Reformation, 91, 101–2, 103–6
Revolution of 1688, 57, 91, 92, 129–37
royalists and their theories, 30, 109–10, 115–18, 143, 188, 190
royal prerogative, 29–30, 35–6, 55, 99–100, 106, 109–10, 112–13,

116–18, 131, 133, 137, 141, 164, 186–90, 212–14; dispensing and suspending powers, 136–7
rule of law, 5, 13, 19, 29, 60, 80, 81, 85–6, 109, 112, 122, 133–4, 148, 164, 167–8, 182, 184–5, 200, 247, 248, 251n1; connection with liberty, 5, 6, 21, 60, 118, 131, 132, 182, 184, 187, 206; and courts, 170–1, 246–7

separation of Church and State, 19
separation of powers, and checks and balances, 202–4, 205–6, 209–11, 234; limiting judicial power, 203
Smith, Thomas, 94, 97, 100, 103, 113, 264n43
sovereignty, 6–8, 30, 35, 36, 102, 113–14, 115, 119, 123, 134, 138–41, 143, 174–5, 251–2n2, 252n3; new theory of, 109–12, 272n3, 272n7; 'political' or popular sovereign, 140, 144, 147, 197
Star Chamber, 11, 83–4, 85, 103, 117, 125, 127, 131, 182–3
statute. *See* legislation
supremacy of law. *See* rule of law
system of government theory and its uses, 4–9, 13, 14, 32, 34, 35, 36, 47–8, 62, 80, 86, 113–15, 128, 138, 140–1, 149–50, 152, 167, 169, 171, 172–4, 179, 241, 244–5, 247

Triennial Act, 125, 132, 277–8n23

Whitelocke. *See* parliamentarians and their theories
Witan, 25, 26–7, 28